PRAISE FO

WHAT MY LEFT HAND
CONFESSIONS OF A GRASSROOTS ACTIVIST

"When Joann Castle chose to devote her life to the community, rather than a convent, she stepped into the epicenter of political struggle in Detroit. Her unique perspective as a white woman offers a searing, unflinching account of black and white political activism in the '60s and '70s. The social justice in the marrow of her bones inspires a memoir that lacks neither truth nor passion. It's another Detroit story we all need to know."

—HERB BOYD,
AUTHOR OF BLACK DETROIT: A PEOPLE'S
HISTORY OF SELF- DETERMINATION

"If one wants to understand how a white Catholic working-class girl, who grew up in a relatively conservative, racially insensitive environment, became a political activist, a crusader for social and racial justice, and later a committed revolutionary—this poignantly written, sensitive memoir is a must-read. This is a story about America, slated to be a classic of American literature."

—MICHAEL GOLDFIELD,
AUTHOR OF THE COLOR OF POLITICS:
RACE AND THE MAINSPRINGS OF AMERICAN
POLITICS AND THE DECLINE OF ORGANIZED
LABOR IN THE UNITED STATES

"*Joann's life story, which unfolds during one of the most intense times in Detroit history, will resonate with social justice mothers struggling with racial injustices today as well as inspire the activists of tomorrow.*"

—RASHIDA TLAIB,
COMMUNITY AND ENVIRONMENTAL ACTIVIST,
FORMER STATE REPRESENTATIVE, AND RECIPIENT
OF THE 2017 PRESIDENT'S AWARD FROM
THE AUDUBON SOCIETY

"What My Left Hand Was Doing *is powerful proof that while we do not choose the times we live in, we do choose how to respond to them. Joann captures rarely documented responses to the black revolution of the 1960s. She shares the courageous choices she made and the spiritual, personal, familial, religious, and political challenges these choices created . . . Joann's life gives substance and grit to the words of Grace Lee Boggs: "These are the times to grow our souls.*"

—RICH FELDMAN,
JAMES AND GRACE LEE BOGGS CENTER

WHAT MY LEFT HAND WAS DOING

WHAT MY LEFT HAND WAS DOING

*Lessons from a
Grassroots Activist*

JOANN CASTLE

AGAINST
THE TIDE
BOOKS

Published in the United States by Against the Tide Books, P.O. Box 44793, Detroit, Michigan 48244

www.againstthetidebooks.com
joanncastle@againstthetidebooks.com

This book flows from my all-too-human memory, which is, at best, imperfect. To protect anonymity, in some instances I have changed the names and identifying characteristics of people and places. Events and conversations have been reconstructed to the best of my recollection.

Page 319 constitutes an extension of this copyright page.

Cover design: Kristine Mills / bklyndesigner.com
Interior design: Cindy Shaw / CreativeDetails.net

Grateful acknowledgment is made to the Walter P. Reuther Library, Archives of Labor and Urban Affairs, Wayne State University for their generous support and assistance. And to Dennie Maloney, who shared with me his diary entries from the period surrounding the Detroit Rebellion.

Front cover: Mike Hamlin still, courtesy of *Finally Got the News*, a Blackstar Production; Anti-STRESS contingent, courtesy of Ken Castle; Joann Castle, courtesy of Ken Castle. Spine: 12th Street rebellion, from Detroit News Collection, courtesy of the Walter P. Reuther Library, Archives of Labor and Urban Affairs, Wayne State University. Back cover: Frank Ditto, courtesy of Ken Castle; cops on 12th Street, public domain; Father William Cunningham, from Detroit News Collection, courtesy of the Walter P. Reuther Library, Archives of Labor and Urban Affairs, Wayne State University; Castle-Hamlin children at West Boston Boulevard house, from the author's collection

Library of Congress Control Number: 2017959583
Trade paperback ISBN: 978-0-9886714-0-9

10 9 8 7 6 5 4 3 2 1
1st edition, February 2018
Printed in the United States of America

This work is dedicated to Viola Liuzzo,
whose story compelled me to begin the journey of a lifetime.
And to my children, grandchildren, and great-grandchildren,
who hold our future in their hands.

*These are days when no one
should rely unduly on his "competence."*

*Strength lies in improvisation. All the
decisive blows are struck left-handed.*

–WALTER BENJAMIN
GERMAN PHILOSOPHER, 1882-1940

*What resemblance more perfect than that between our two
hands! And yet what a striking inequality there is!*

*To the right hand go honours, flattering designations,
prerogatives: it acts, orders, and takes. The left hand,
on the contrary, is despised and reduced to the role
of a humble auxiliary: by itself it can do nothing;
it helps, it supports, it holds.*

*The right hand is the symbol and model of all
aristocracy, the left hand of all common people.*

*What are the titles of nobility of the right hand? And
whence comes the servitude of the left?*

–ROBERT HERTZ
ANTHROPOLOGIST AND SOCIOLOGIST, 1913, FRANCE

CONTENTS

WHAT MY LEFT HAND
WAS DOING

FOOT SOLDIERS

It has always been the many faceless men, those foot soldiers,
who have suffered most, who have died. It is they who make a nation.
—F. SIONIL JOSÉ

THE UNFAMILIAR KEYSTROKES on the page give it away: these are old documents, made when people still used typewriters to create official records. Emblazoned across the top of each report are the words, in all capitals, **DETROIT POLICE DEPARTMENT**. Each one is directed to the commanding officer, Intelligence Division. They are all photocopied versions of the originals. Black masks the names of the people conducting the surveillance—the names of the detectives assigned to the subversive Red Squad and the identifying numbers of their informants.

Scanning the pages, I feel a kind of odd out-of-body sensation: I'm reading someone else's words, seeing through someone else's eyes, but the people and the places are familiar to me. I was there. The years at the top, ranging from the late 1960s to the early '70s, are the years during which I was heavily involved in radical social justice movement work. These were the years of J. Edgar Hoover's **COINTELPRO** crackdown on dissidents. Each report details some objectionable event or activity that apparently demanded surveillance. In some of them an informant, pretending to be one of us, reports back to the police what he or she saw and heard. In others the police themselves are posing as activists amid us, at our meetings, at our protests, in our homes . . . watching and listening.

In each report my name appears somewhere, misspelled ironically, also in all caps: **JOANN CAROLE CASTLE.**

I'm not alone, of course. In one, from some of the early days of the Ad-Hoc Action Group Against Police Brutality, the agent reports that Sheila Murphy led a discussion about the reality of policing in the ghetto, how the only concern for police is the protection of property, which the people do not have. When the people riot to let the world know they've had enough of how they're being treated, the police move to protect the property and kill the people. I was there taking notes. Sheila was describing how to identify unmarked police cars.

"You can tell by the small radio antenna in the rear window," she noted.

"They're taking our license plate numbers," I said. "We should take theirs."

"Yes," Sheila agreed. "Watch out for any and all unmarked police cars that you see, such as at police headquarters and precinct stations, and get their license numbers so that a list can be made up for the membership of Ad-Hoc and any other interested groups.

"Next week," Sheila continued, "we'll be having a session on photography. Don't forget to bring your cameras. We're going to do some police watching." We were training to be body cameras forty years before the concept was introduced.

The police knew who we were. They put tickets on our cars when we parked in front of the Ad-Hoc building. They would ticket Sheila's car every two hours all day long when she was in her office. When there were meetings at my house, they would boldly park out front and take the license plate number, as well as note the address of registration, of everyone who came inside. There, at the bottom of the page, among the people whose attendance is worth noting, is my name.

In another report, the police are monitoring an "unannounced meeting" at 630 West Boston Boulevard, Detroit, Michigan. Or, as I knew it for many years: my home. The date at the top identifies it as being in August 1971, making it just after the four-year anniversary of the Detroit Rebellion—the moment that changed my life forever.

Police "red squads" have been used to target and destroy organized political dissent in America since the mid-1800s. They became fixtures in urban police departments in the early 20th century, driven by anti-communist sentiment. During the 1960s, red squads targeted anti-war and civil rights movements through infiltration, sabotage, and outright violence. Their brutal tactics, often employed without concern about constitutional protections, helped destroy numerous movements for social justice, as well as many individual lives.

Upper right: The Spirit of Detroit by Marshall Fredericks, dedicated in 1958. Center left: The Gleaners Temple, built in 1908, was the 1969 headquarters of the Ad-Hoc Action Group Against Police Brutality.

There's my name, as always. Sheila's is there as well, as are others. They've noted the license plate numbers and the makes and models of the cars. Looks like Sheila was driving a fairly new Chevy—this is Detroit, after all.

Ironically, nothing of any great interest really happens in most of the memos. There are no violent revolutionary conspiracies, no destructive anarchist plots. We hold meetings. We talk. We strategize about how we can make our dissenting voices heard. Our message is that we are citizens. We have rights. And we will no longer be ignored or repressed by the powers that be. Our actions reflect our tests and our testimonies. We refuse to go silent in the face of injustice after injustice.

It's not what's in the memos that is of interest. It's that they exist at all; it's knowing that there are dozens, if not hundreds and thousands, more. They reflect the time and place, the people and the actions. They are proof that what we were doing was enough of a threat that powerful interests conspired to work against us, day and night. They signal our resistance. They are proof that we were being watched, spied on; that people were plotting our demise even as they walked among us, calling themselves our friends and comrades. They show that the belief that not all of us would make it out alive was a rational one. Those who infiltrated our ranks sought to exploit our weaknesses and divisions, even while marching alongside us and sharing a meal at our dinner tables.

These documents reflect a different time in my life, in the life of my city and the life of this country. These records are testaments to the past, but they are also warnings to the present and the future. They are glimpses into what lies ahead for those who dare to answer the call for social justice, those who are moved by their consciences to act. They're badges of courage, reminders of the importance of the work that was done, as much as they are notes from which activists of today can easily crib. They are evidence that the past has lessons to teach.

WE OLDER ACTIVISTS watch the motion picture of our lives unflinchingly and examine those frames that led to our fully becoming ourselves. Played all together, they tell a narrative of risks and contradictions that accompany choosing to embrace all of life's possibilities.

I clearly see times when I had more courage than wisdom. My bold moves were sometimes ill advised, but my commitment to justice knew no bounds. Many of my decisions involved taking risks, but they were based on my fundamental values. Other decisions were undertaken with less forethought than I like to admit. But I have never regretted anything that I have done with the intention of improving the lives of those who have intersected with mine.

I came to consciousness at the moment in our history that gave birth to the civil rights movement and the black self-determination movement. None of us had a road map. Those years were a period of inspiration and devastation in a movement that had power and passion, but our path was untraveled. As the movement gained steam it grew and multiplied, and so did our detractors. We had to find our way. We were creating a new vision of society that grew out of our collective efforts, never imagining that we would also watch its decline. We were bone weary and even with the best of intentions watched our zealous efforts give way. But we were not done—it was not over. We knew that if we didn't persist, freedom would become a word we uttered but not a life we lived.

At that time, I had no concept of the hold or the toll that movements take on the activists who put their lives on the line to fight for a better world. Such radical action is often taken at great risk to the physical and psychological health of the activists themselves, as well as their loved ones. There can also be legal repercussions. Social justice stirs a passion in the marrow of their bones. Take it from me: once you give yourself entirely to this fight, it is an ache that never goes away.

When I first became involved, it would have been a priceless gift to have had some upfront understanding of social movements. But we had no in-the-trenches mentors. We were confronting forces that were new in the world, and often we didn't know how to respond. The crisis and turmoil that were exploding in our own backyards, in our country, and around the globe were all-consuming.

How could I explain the profound nature of my internal calling to others when I could rarely find a vocabulary to explain it to myself? All I can tell you is that I had no choice. Or was it that my choice had already been made, and there was no going back on my word to God or to myself? My high school homeroom nun was correct about my calling: I was called—not to the convent, though, but to the community.

The burning idealism of the moment, the passionate belief in the righteousness of the cause, the incandescent vision of the scope of change that could occur—these are what drive us into the movement and give us the fortitude to stand in the face of tremendous resistance. Almost invariably the change that actually occurs falls short of the ideal. But to interpret that outcome as failure is to misunderstand what movements are for and why we must continue to join them again and again.

Social change is never instantaneous. It always comes out of somewhere. It is the sum of efforts, sometimes over many years, by individuals and communities, often in the face of tremendous resistance. Always, it is about building on the sacrifices of the past to create a better future. Sometimes that future is far off in the distance. This means that success cannot simply be measured by how many demands in a manifesto can be checked off, or whether a law gets passed or a candidate elected.

Social change requires each generation to take up the banner anew, to ensure the gains of the past are protected and the promises of a better future move ever closer to becoming a reality. The abolitionists' success in defeating slavery wasn't an end but the beginning of the next chapter. Likewise, the legal death of segregation after the civil rights movement didn't mark our final victory; it was instead the start of the next struggle. Real social change is incremental; measurements must be made accordingly.

Perhaps most important, success is not predetermined. And we understand that better today than at perhaps any point in the last generation: losing what we've gained—slipping backward—is possible. But it is only when we stop, when we fail to resist, that we will truly lose. Marching in the streets, organizing in the community, and standing up to the forces arrayed against us is not just about drawing that better day closer. It is equally about fighting to keep it from being pushed further away.

Today, a new generation of activists is feeling that call. The election of Donald Trump has mustered radical right-wing forces unseen since the revival of the Ku Klux Klan (KKK) in response to the civil rights movement. Civil unrest hangs in the balance, related to the wanton murder of unarmed black and brown civilians at the hands of our nation's police forces. A long list of social ills is burdening our communities, from gross economic inequality to the destructive practices of mass incarceration, from the targeted violence and oppression of immigrant communities and LGBTQ communities. These challenges are spurring a new rise to activism among the people.

My heart was lifted recently by the explosion of activity around these issues. The hundreds of thousands of women—mothers and daughters, wives and sisters—pouring into the streets in cities and towns across the country and around the world the day after Trump was sworn in as president of the United States was akin to the spontaneous actions that flourished during the civil rights and anti–Vietnam War movements. As were the responses to Trump's executive order banning Muslims from entering the United States, when thousands of protestors descended on airports from coast to coast, and the outpouring of anger at congressional town halls across the country over Republican plans to shred health care for millions. These passion-filled, often quickly planned shows of resistance are vital first steps in response to the political tragedy playing out under President Trump. In between flash points, critical work is being undertaken to fashion new, long-term strategic plans to fundamentally reshape society into a more just, sustainable, and equitable place. Both kinds of initiatives—spontaneous and strategic—are necessary parts of the next wave of activism blossoming today.

It's much easier to talk about the valuable and righteous nature of social movement work than it is to *do* that work. The focus is so often on the figures and personalities who become leaders of the movement that it can be easy to forget that the movement really consists of people and their communities, all working, in their own imperfect ways, toward something greater. That work can take a heavy toll.

Generations raised to expect conveniences and machines that literally think for them may have difficulty when they discover that life does not offer the neat solutions posited at the end of a one-hour television drama or a competitive video game. It is important that young activists learn some critical lessons about how human beings battling for power behave. They need to learn that no matter how sophisticated the devices that surround the game board, they must always anticipate both tribute and treachery and protect themselves from the stress of the unexpected. In the end, knowing before they go can not only ensure their physical and psychological safety—it can save their lives.

Recently, I was watching a Black Lives Matter march in Chicago after a police shooting of a young, unarmed black man. I observed three young millennials moving with the crowd—fear etched on their faces, arms around one another—chanting over and over the words from a Kendrick Lamar song: "We gon' be alright." Yes, hang tight, young folks. You gon' be all right, but only if you are wise enough to arm yourselves with knowledge and understand that you can control your actions, but you cannot control the outcomes of your actions.

These realities about life as an activist inside movements for social change rarely crop up in the accounts by and about the leaders who come to symbolize the social struggle. The stories tend to focus, rightly, on how a normal person overcame extraordinary odds and circumstances to help bring about significant social change. These books seek to inspire us, to give us insight into greatness, and to motivate us to believe that change is possible.

Very few people ever rise to the ranks of identified movement leaders, and even fewer to the level of civil rights icon. But for every civil rights leader, however great or small, there is a small army of committed activists working day in and day out, building the infrastructure that both supports the message and propels the messengers forward. All those individual efforts largely go unnoticed on their own, but without them there is no movement.

THE FIFTIETH ANNIVERSARY of the Detroit Rebellion—which coincides with this moment of new national mobilization—provides a unique opportunity for me to reflect on my own five decades of activism and to consider what those of us who stand up for justice, truth, freedom, and progress face in the days ahead. My commitment to the movement came with a cost, as it must for all of us. But that cost also delivered clarity. Over time, reflecting on the experiences I had and turmoil I went through—both personally and as part of the movement—allowed me to see more clearly, and understand more deeply, the lessons I learned.

These lessons, hard-fought for each and every one, are what my story is about. Like most stories, mine also is, in part, about a place. It is impossible to understand me, or anything I did, without understanding the place where it happened. During those amazing years, we knew—everyone knew—that Detroit was fertile ground for a revolutionary black-conceived, black-organized, black-led vision for a new society. Our world was in chaos, our task urgent. We saw a parallel path in the successful freedom struggles of the Third World. Significant gains were made, but the personal cost was often tremendous. My journey sometimes unfolded in a sea of inner and outer turmoil. I had little guidance. There were times when I failed spectacularly, but I got back up and kept on fighting.

The emergence of black power in Detroit was an extraordinary time in the revolutionary movement. There had been many successes here that demonstrated that black power and black self-determination were important weapons for change. Yet the support of whites and community coalitions cannot be overlooked. Each step in radical consciousness took us deeper; more was needed and more was asked. Community coalitions that crossed racial lines were a remarkable component of our unique efforts.

Detroit personified the belief that the old order was ending and that change was possible. People looked to Detroit; people even moved to Detroit, where blacks were forging an autonomous identity and demanding change. There should be nothing surprising about this. Black communities in Detroit have long resisted the inequalities forced on them by American society. During those racially charged, fraught years at the end of the 1960s, riots broke out all over America. But Detroit's civil uprising was the largest, the most destructive, and it resulted in the greatest loss of life.

There was, of course, precedent to 1967; twenty-four years earlier a race riot broke out that saw thirty-four people killed before it was over. The riot of 1943 was notable because here in Detroit, blacks fought back. And this wasn't the first time blacks fought for their rights in our city. Some years earlier, Dr. Ossian Sweet, a Detroit physician, purchased a home in an all-white neighborhood; he was accused of murder after using armed self-defense when a white mob attacked his home. Dr. Sweet was acquitted, setting a legal precedent and winning a huge victory for the black community. It is my belief that these examples, among others, paved the way for black self-determination and the power and success the movement garnered here in Detroit in the 1960s and '70s.

When I first began to absorb city life as a child, Detroit—once a cosmopolitan city of art and finance—was developing a reputation worldwide as the thriving capital of the auto industry. I knew my city as a bustling community with safe transportation and large downtown department stores. I also knew it was a very segregated city. Detroit began to lose its population in the 1950s, but it remained a city where blacks migrating from the South could get a good job in a factory and move into the middle class.

Factories began to move out of Detroit when they retooled after World War II, abandoning outdated structures and leaving vast tracts of polluted landscapes within our city limits. White middle-class Detroiters headed for the hills of suburbia, where jobs were plentiful. Government housing programs offered low-interest mortgages on postwar ranch-style homes with spacious backyards, in areas African Americans could not access. By denying them bank loans through real estate lobbies and barring them from neighborhoods by writing legal restrictions against their ownership into deeds, blacks were intentionally excluded from these opportunities. At the same time, blacks fleeing the South's Jim Crow laws were streaming into the city in record numbers.

By 1950, federal funds were allocated, and Detroit's urban renewal plan—extending highways and clearing land to build a strong city for the future—began to take shape under the direction of Mayor Albert Cobo. Cobo's plan called for the destruction of historic cultural communities like Black Bottom, Paradise Valley, and 400 black-owned businesses which decimated the core of black music and arts that stood so strong in Detroit. Poor communities west of the city's center were also destroyed. This thoughtless renewal wiped away the soul of black communities and left poor people homeless or in crowded tenements like the Brewster and Jeffries Projects, creating ghetto-like conditions, or prisons without walls. That's where the black people lived.

All of this would set the stage for what was to come—not only for the city and the country, but for me as well. It has informed every aspect of my life, even if I was unable to understand or recognize it at the time. The story of my life played out against the backdrop of Detroit, its history, and its people. It's about as improbable a story as there is: a naive, white, working-class Irish Catholic mother of six young children taking a stand against society's racial inequality. My journey as a white woman, and later as an anthropologist, taught me to understand and confront white privilege, and prepared me to become an ally to the black freedom movement. I was a foot soldier using my left hand to advance social justice and my right hand to love and sustain my family. It's a story that begins and ends in the only place I have ever called home.

My story is a Detroit story.

PART ONE

In the Name
of the Father

IRISH STEW

Life is like a cup of tea; it's all in how you make it.
—IRISH PROVERB

THERE ARE TWO COMPETING QUALITIES IN MY HERITAGE that rule my life: the warmth and sensibility of my maternal Irish grandmother and the distant practicality of my father's German ancestors. One has gifted me with compassion and the ability to walk in another's shoes; the other has instilled in me the cold determination to distance myself from pain and move forward. It is my drive to survive—a rich Irish stew with German potatoes.

My parents, Esther Jorn and Barry Reschke, were third-generation immigrants of Irish German descent. Their kinfolk were well integrated into the fabric of the midwestern single-family homes and working-class communities so characteristic of Detroit. Although my parents were married, my father—a dapper lady's man—was still living with his mother. From what I later learned of those years, my mother was equally unprepared for a child. But Mother's reticence was trumped by Grandma's open arms and warmth.

Grandma saw the world with different eyes. Cathleen Boyle Shuell was her own person. Unlike the obedient flock, she practiced her Catholic religion in her own unique way, uninhibited by stifling rules and traditions. Freedom to be herself was in the beat of her heart and the marrow of her bones. Although I lost her physical presence when I was a child, my grandmother's determination and energy has, like an invisible current, suffused every aspect of my being, informing every part of who I am or, at least, who I aspired to be.

Being raised Catholic was both a blessing and a curse. From an early age, my pure faith was my shelter from the storms of life. The women in my family, my mother and her sisters, relied completely on its teachings: mass on Sundays and lifelong suffering would bring us eternal life. On the good side, having the Church as my guide and protector instilled in me a powerful moral compass in an environment devoid of security. Yet at the same time, the Church was largely responsible for my unhappiness. Its overbearing presence and eternal gloom siphoned all the joy out of my life.

The Church was also the binding force between my mother and me. My parents had violated their Catholic consciences by marrying outside the confines of her faith, and in my mother's eyes—as well as those of the Church—their state-sanctioned marriage meant they were simply "living in sin."

Mother took me to Sunday Mass each week as far back as I can remember. Failure to attend was a mortal sin that could send you to hell for all eternity. We would stay until it was time to consecrate the host for communion—the sacred bond between the Church and its practitioners. As the altar boy lifted the little bell to signal the beginning of the transformation of the host to the body of Christ, she would burst into tears.

At this point in the service, with all eyes upon us, she would grab my arm—little tot that I was—and drag me along the center aisle to the huge heavy wood-carved doors of St. Bridget's. There we exited from her state of hope for forgiveness, and returned to her self-imposed martyrdom and the immaculate keeping of my father's house. No words were ever spoken about the spiritual and emotional pain she endured. Yet each Sunday, I knew, we would return to repeat the ritual once again.

I was a serious child, and I took on the responsibility to win God's favor for all of us. My church taught me that we are all sinners and that I should get down on my knees every night to ask for forgiveness. The concept of an all-knowing God who threatened eternal damnation frightened me. He already had my mother in His grasp. I learned to say the rosary, and I kept mine in my pocket at all times. I learned that I had original sin on my soul when I was born and that I had to worry about my mother going to hell. I even slept without a pillow at an early age to cause myself suffering, which I offered up as self-discipline in atonement for my sins.

Ironically, there was no discussion of religion, no prayer, no Catholic icons in our home. Perhaps my father would not allow them. Dad objected to old-world practices. To please him, the decor of our house was serene and scrubbed clean. We ate no vegetables with our meals of meat and potatoes because Dad said that they would "make our house smell like a foreigner's." My mother served applesauce in place of vegetables at every meal.

Growing up with my parents, nothing was ever certain. There was no way to get a grip on who we were or what we believed. Even the air around me seemed tentative. I never felt secure. I longed for a life with love and purpose. As I grew older, I could see families who laughed and played and interacted with interest in the world around them. My parents laughed with friends—not with me, and not with each other. I never saw them hug or hold hands.

I don't believe that Dad ever intended to marry my mother, but my forecasted coming and my grandmother's broomstick deemed it otherwise. My parents were both twenty-one when they were married by a justice of the peace in Orchard Lake, a little town near my mother's parents' cottage. Clearly there were extenuating circumstances.

When I was two, Mother and I moved to Dad's mother's house so she could live with her husband. Part of the bargain was that she would be his mother's housekeeper. That didn't work out so well. Finally, we moved again, this time as a family, into a small upper flat on Detroit's near West Side. The house sat forlornly at the intersection of Meyers Road and Schoolcraft, overlooking busy traffic and the local bus stop. There was only one bedroom in our small flat and no place for even a small child's bed. My crib was in the dining room. I slept in that crib until after I started kindergarten.

That first year, I became very ill with scarlet fever. There were no antibiotics in the late 1930s, and being confined to one's bed was the typical directive in response to serious illness. I lay in my cramped crib for weeks, ultimately being diagnosed with rheumatic fever.

The illness left me weakened, with virtually no strength in my legs. Once I was strong enough, Mother—small as she was—would lift me out of the crib and place me in a chair. From the chair, she would slide my legs to the floor and support me under my arms as I learned to walk again.

These respites of a mother's concentrated care were few and far between. My parents' marriage was filled with strife, and our upper flat abounded with tension. In the evenings, they argued.

"So, where were you?" I would hear my mother's voice, the pitch rising to a crescendo ahead of a shriek: "Now, tell me the truth, because I found these two movie stubs in your pocket."

I softly interrupted, doing my best to stall the flow of the all-too-familiar pattern. "Mommy . . ."

"Go to bed—now," my father's voice commanded. "No dinner for you!"

The scenes were endless, my punishment for simply existing was always the same: "No dinner for you!"

As an only child for many years until my younger sister, Karen, was born, I was lonely. In keeping with the tenor of my home life and its uncertainty, I was shy and had no self-confidence. We had little contact with the outside world. There were no books or newspapers in our house. Dad wouldn't read the paper because he claimed that it made his hands dirty. I knew nothing of other peoples' cultures or experiences. My days were framed by my mother's unhappiness and insecurities and my dad's rigidity and emotional distance. My physical being reinforced my inadequate feelings. I was sickly, long-limbed, skinny, and pale. My hair was straight and thin; Karen would get the pretty hair. I had "weak ankles" and was kept in high-top shoes until I started school. I was a frail-looking child searching for my place in the world.

One of the things I loved to do was to lie on the floor and try to imagine how different life would be if I lived on the ceiling. There would be things in the way, like light fixtures and heating ducts, but if I was careful, perhaps I could find enough free space to create my very own world. In my world I would dance on the ceiling and be happy.

I spent a lot of time alone, avoiding my parents, usually playing outside our door on the stairway that led to the first floor, where our landlord lived. A little light shone through a small window on the landing. It provided just enough light that I could play house with my paper dolls. I don't remember having any toys. I was careful not to make noise and disturb the landlord below. And I longed for Wednesdays to come.

ONE DAY, I OVERHEARD MY MOTHER on the phone with a friend.

"Sorry, I can't," she said. "Every Wednesday, my sisters and I go to help my mother clean house."

That was a gross misrepresentation.

On Wednesdays, Mother and I took the Grand River bus to Grand Boulevard and walked two blocks south on Larchmont Street to meet my aunts and cousins at my grandparents' house. As a child, there was no place I would rather have been.

My grandparents lived in an unpretentious white frame house with a big front porch. Their street was narrow, though wide enough for the ice man to come with his horse and wagon. It was during the Depression, and no one in this working-class neighborhood had a car. Two wicker rockers and an old-fashioned glider graced my grandparents' kid-friendly porch. Big maple and oak trees kept the neighborhood shady and cool on summer days. In the backyard, Grandma had a Depression garden where vegetables grew between the leaves of fragile bleeding hearts—my favorite flower—which symbolized a symphony of tenderness and pain.

Inside, Grandma had a player piano, around which we gathered for comic relief from the woes of the Depression, for solace during the war, and for a brief respite from the rigid lives the three girls had married into. Sometimes, at her expansive dining room table, Grandma read her daughters' fortunes in the tea leaves left in their cups as they discussed their troubles, their burdens softened by the light from her Tiffany lamp and my grandma's wisdom.

Wednesday was a free-for-all at Grandma's house. Cleaning would have been impossible with the five of us cousins screaming and chasing in circles, spinning around the small pillar that separated Grandma's living and dining room, tearing through the kitchen and down the long hallway that led to the bedrooms then back again. When the adults eventually shooed us out of the house, we would have races on the front-porch glider.

In the afternoons, we walked through Grandma's backyard and across the alley, then through the gate into the yard of the house behind. My older cousin Jack would lead the way past this house to the sidewalk on the other side of it and across Tireman Avenue to the drugstore on the corner, where we would buy penny candy. It was only about forty yards from my grandmother's back door to the drugstore.

Then, quite suddenly, things changed. In 1943, when I was six years old, we were told that we couldn't cross the alley anymore.

"No candy," we were told. "Stay on the porch or in the yard."

We were jumping up and down, impatient to leave. The candy store for an after-lunch treat was the highlight of our day.

"Why not?" we pestered. "Please, please, pretty please!"

"No! It's too dangerous. We have to stay with our own people," my mother answered nervously.

What we didn't understand was that there had been a race riot. On Sunday, June 20, 1943, a fight had broken out on Belle Isle, a beautiful island park nestled in the Detroit River. Rumors spread among blacks that white men had killed a colored woman and thrown her baby into the Detroit River and, among whites, that colored men had raped and killed a white woman in the park. Neither rumor was true, but thirty-four people were killed during the two days before the violence was quelled.

Isabel Wilkerson writes in *The Warmth of Other Suns: The Epic Story of America's Great Migration,* that the 1943 Detroit riot was the first in the country in which blacks fought back when attacked by whites. Historically, when there was trouble between the races, whites simply solved the issue with force. Many towns in the South were burned, and many innocent people were lynched in the wake of racial conflicts. But Detroiters are not conformists.

I had little ability to grasp what was happening around me. My parents never talked to me about race, but my mother read me the story of *Little Black Sambo,* and I knew who Aunt Jemima was. In school games I learned to chant, "Eeny meeny miny moe, catch a n'gger by the toe. If he hollers let him go . . ." I had no idea of the racist origins of what I was saying. This was simply the deplorable norm in many white communities at the time.

Even so, the riot caused enough of a social disturbance that as I grew older I became aware of its impact. I began to notice that different types of people stayed inside certain neighborhoods, avoiding others unlike themselves. I noticed that black people kept their eyes down when they passed white people. At first, I thought it was because they were poor and ashamed.

With the migrations north during this period, the black population in Detroit was quickly expanding. Tireman Avenue, the street behind my grandmother's house, had long been a dividing line between black and white neighborhoods. Soon after the riot, my grandmother's neighbors moved. The color line was broken when a black family moved in next door.

I watched my grandma's response to events in her neighborhood, and I understood that in her heart she had equal space for all mankind. Grandma saw the world with different eyes. She loved people for who they were and believed in racial equality during a period when it was very unpopular to do so. Grandma's independent nature and her Christ-like spirit were my first exposure to the lessons of humanity that shaped my life as an adult.

Grandma may have been physically small, but her essence, like the lavender scent she sprayed on her pillow, was as intoxicating as her warmth. Standing barely to my shoulder when I was twelve, she conducted her life and touched the lives of those around her with a unique assurance, authority, and grace. Her Irish skin was pale, almost translucent; her face was wrinkled with wisdom like a fine parchment paper. She wore her hair, a silver gray, short and softly curled. But most striking were her kind blue eyes, which reflected her generous Irish heart.

Grandma had all the qualities most admired in the Irish. She was witty, nonjudgmental, straightforwardly honest, and engaging. Most of all, Grandma loved life. She told jokes, laughed at herself, and sang at her piano with total abandon. Sometimes her unruliness embarrassed her daughters, but she was a humble woman in dealing with others. Mostly I remember her unconditional and often-expressed approval. It was warm in Grandma's arms.

If the riot in 1943 did anything, it was to firm my grandmother's resolve. Around that time, I remember standing at Grandma's side as she chatted with the new black family who'd moved next door. Grandma was as relaxed as always, talking a mile a minute. The lady she spoke with was pretty and seemed warm in her manner. But I could tell something was different. Things had started to change when we went to visit.

"I'm right here," she was saying to the lady. "Let me know if you need anything."

As they talked, my aunts and my mother stood uneasily in the doorway. "Joann," I heard my mother call, "come in the house."

Trips to the candy store were now completely forbidden.

One Wednesday during this same time period, Grandma and I, along with my mother and her sisters, were on the Grand Boulevard bus on our way downtown. I sat next to my grandmother. The bus became crowded as we traveled closer to the city's center. As we continued along the route, many dark-skinned people were standing. The bus lurched forward, and a lady with a small baby lost her footing. My grandmother quickly reached out her arms.

"Here," she said warmly, "let me have your baby so you can hold on."

The woman cautiously handed her baby to my grandmother. I heard a gasp. All eyes were fixed on the two women. My grandmother paid no attention. She sat the baby on her lap and began to play with her. The baby smiled, but the baby's mother looked uncomfortable with her hasty decision. I didn't understand the dynamics of the situation at the time, but the exchange registered and lingered in my awareness. It was such a small thing, but Grandma's gesture was genuine and humane.

There was something about Grandma's presence that was hauntingly clear and inspiring. Today, as I revisit my memories of her, I am struck with the feeling that I have spent my life searching for the quality of her character in others—in friends and lovers. My connection to her gives meaning and moral substance to my life and stands as my incontrovertible guide in a complex world. Sometimes when I look in the mirror, I see my grandmother's eyes.

I was twelve years old when my grandmother died as a result of bloodletting, which was then used as a treatment for hypertension. Her death closed the door on this aspect of my consciousness for more than two decades before I became deeply involved in the civil rights movement. But in that short time I knew her, Cathleen Boyle Shuell's spirit burned a course in my consciousness that changed my life and runs through me to this day still.

THE SUMMER BEFORE I was to enter eighth grade, I decided that I wanted to go to Catholic school. A boy in the neighborhood whom I was sweet on went to grade school at St. Scholastica's parish, adjacent to the campus of Our Lady of Mercy High. I thought I could ride the bus with him.

I structured my argument like a seasoned lawyer.

"I'm not learning anything at public school," I told my mother. I paused and decided to press my argument one step further. I aimed for her sweet spot: "Catholic schools are stricter, and I think I would learn more about my religion."

Mercy High School was an upper-middle-class girls' school that I was determined to attend because the graduation ceremony took place next to a man-made lake complete with a grotto, a small protected cave where one could pray. During the ceremony, the girls wore long white gowns and walked through a long rose arbor to place flowers at the feet of the statue of the Blessed Virgin Mary.

There was a class divide at Mercy. Girls from the upscale community near the campus were placed in the college-prep classes and took art and sculpture as their electives. I took two buses to reach school, and girls like me—from the other side of the tracks, literally—were put in commercial classes that prepared us for work in an office. Most of these subtleties escaped me. I was happy just to be there.

In my homeroom class I was elected Sodality leader. Sodality, founded in the 1800s, was a Catholic Church society for young ladies founded on four components: religion, purity and virtue, charity, and social activities. Young women joined this society in eighth or ninth grade and remained members until they married or entered the convent.

As the head of Sodality, my responsibility was to organize and encourage the girls in my class to be involved in good works and mission activities. I learned that I had some capacity for leadership, but in truth, I didn't like to stand out in a crowd. I had inherited some talent for being diplomatic, and I was honest to a fault, which only contributed to my virtuous image.

One day when I stayed after class to finish my Sodality responsibilities, I realized that money from a collection came up short. I had been careful in accounting for all the money, but then I had briefly left the box in the care of another. By the time our homeroom nun returned, I was visibly upset. She sat next to me in the otherwise empty room as I tearfully told my story. She wasn't angry. In her wisdom, or perhaps in her experience, she said, "Joann, you trust people too much. Someday you're going to get hurt."

As a young teen, I thought a lot about moral responsibility and set a high bar for myself. So when the Little Sisters of the Poor sent a note to our principal asking for high school girls to assist in the care of the frail, elderly women living at their home for the aged across the street, there was little question I would volunteer. In fact, I was the only one who did.

This home for the aged, an architectural jewel topped with a quaint copper bell tower, was set back from the road and situated among the trees. Its exterior appearance suggested a peaceful and serene retreat. I soon discovered that the beautiful outside was a stark contrast to the dim halls and foul, end-of-life stench on the inside. After one of the sisters took me on a tour of the wards, we stopped in a picturesque chapel with sunlight streaming through red and blue stained-glass windows. It was a welcome relief from our depressing rounds. Sister was talking about how God provides, using me as an example.

Then she blithely told the story of a recent time when they were short of food for the elderly in their care.

"One morning," she said, "I arrived right here where we are standing to find two bushels of potatoes sitting in the center aisle in front of the altar. It was a miracle."

She bowed her head and crossed herself. My thoughts were a bit more pragmatic. Someone had to put them there, I thought.

"Now," sister intoned, "God has sent you to us."

I wasn't feeling as confident. But two days a week, after my classes, I dutifully began to volunteer at the home. It wasn't long before I was assigned to help a group of aged ladies take a communal bath. The good Sisters assisted six deformed and depleted bodies in disrobing and getting into a huge vat filled with tepid water. It was my job to keep them safe and assist them as they bathed. I was fifteen and had come into puberty at a later age than most. I was still getting acquainted with the changes my own body was undergoing. The sight of a body at the end of life was shocking and troubled me greatly.

Flesh seemed to disappear. Skin was hanging from bones. One woman intent on cleaning herself in the now rancid water impatiently tossed one breast over her shoulder to get it out of the way. I was undone. The scene would work its way into my dreams over and over. I had no preparation or counsel for this. I began to make excuses on my days to volunteer and soon stopped going altogether. I buckled and deserted, even as guilt and shame ate away at me. I have thought of this many times during my life, when my lofty efforts to accomplish something grand turned out to be beyond my reach. These are the moments that keep us humble.

Despite my imperfect record, some of the nuns at school felt my commitment and willingness to help suggested I had a vocation. My homeroom nun approached me.

"Joann," she said. "I truly believe that you should consider going into the convent. I think God is calling you."

The Church shaped and directed large parts of my life. But Jesus' love was not enough for me. I wanted to be touched and held and comforted.

I had a boyfriend, Jim. He was a caring and good-hearted guy who helped me feel good about myself. He went to Catholic Central, a boy's school that paralleled Mercy's educational and religious training, and we shared Catholic values. For my sixteenth birthday, he gave me a sterling silver rosary in its own cross-shaped box. Jim offered me what I was missing from my parents—comfort. Our time together was markedly different than my life at home and the constant criticism I received there. Most of all, he made me laugh.

Jim and I continued to date on weekends throughout high school and during his first years at the University of Notre Dame. During this time, I became friends with his best friend's girl, Barbara Schneider. When the boys drifted off into their own lives and activities, Barbara and I talked about our common desire for adventure.

At the time, I was reading novelist Pearl Buck and anthropologist Margaret Mead. Pearl Buck, who grew up in China with her missionary parents, introduced me to peasant life in *The Good Earth*. Margaret Mead wrote about the lives of women in traditional cultures in the South Pacific and Asia. I was impressed to learn that people on the other side of the world had similar experiences and feelings as I did, even though our belief systems were completely different. I longed to experience a larger world and to understand the cultures of other people. I researched going into the Foreign Service and thought I could get a job as a secretary in some distant land like China or Asia.

Walking in the shoes of others became a reality at home during my junior year, when the U.S. Supreme Court ruled that school segregation was unconstitutional. By my senior year, five black students were integrated into Mercy High. This happened with great fanfare. Before the new students arrived, our principal, a nun, visited all the classrooms.

"We are pleased that some young Negro women will be joining our student body," she told us. "God created everyone equal, and I want you to welcome them in the spirit of a loving Christ."

Once the students had been with us for a couple of weeks, Sister had to visit the classrooms again. Our reception had apparently been a little too warm.

"You are smothering them with love and attention, and that is a wonderful thing, but I ask you to back off just a little and give them some space," she said. "They don't want to be treated differently; they just want to be normal girls. Let them get adjusted like any other new student."

I was proud of the goodwill and warm welcome we showed to the black students. It was clear, after the Supreme Court's decision, that this wasn't happening everywhere. I was beginning to take notice of the inequities between races. It seemed that the South was poised to wage a new civil war. The spark, lit by the court's action, would soon ignite a firestorm.

This gathering storm of events gained enough momentum and speed to penetrate the self-absorbed fringes of my teenage life. I well remember Rosa Parks and her role in the Montgomery bus incident. Parks, a seamstress and highly trained black activist, was on her way home from work when she refused to give up her seat on the bus to a white passenger. She was arrested, triggering the bus boycott, which inspired the black population into solidarity. The boycott lasted 381 days. According to Parks, she was just tired of giving in.

I didn't know much about the South, but I couldn't imagine telling blacks in Detroit that they had to sit in the back of the bus. This period was my first real awakening to events outside my small world.

A broader social movement began to coalesce with a series of cataclysmic events that began in 1955 and barreled into the 1960s. The first was the unspeakably brutal murder of fourteen-year-old Emmett Till and the subsequent acquittal by an all-male, all-white jury of the two white suspects identified by black witnesses. I knew little about the South, but the names of many southern cities would soon become all too familiar: Little Rock, Greensboro, the Freedom Rides from D.C. to New Orleans, and the little girls at Sunday school in Birmingham.

I lived in a white world where such things were not discussed, yet the news kept delivering the grim reality that existed outside our bubble. I went to school and afterward worked in an insurance office located in the basement of a family home. I would get back to my own home late in the evening, do my homework, and go to bed. My mother and I never talked about real life. Karen, my chatty sister, was ten and filled our house with her antics. My dad was seldom home and never engaged with me in any way.

I heard, I saw, I hurt—but everything felt very far away. My life was bonded to my faith. As news continued to come from the South, my conscience was stirred by the reported injustices. I wondered where the hatred against Negroes came from and how those who saw it could allow it to continue. I no longer felt free. I felt weighed down by an inexplicable burden. I knew that injustice needed to be addressed, but I didn't yet know how to do so.

High school graduation arrived. I was an excellent seamstress, and I made my long white gown, patterned after a gown I had seen in a shop window. On graduation day, carrying my long-stemmed roses, I walked in all my glory through the rose arbor at Mercy. Jim came home from college to be with me and share in the joy of the day. He was preparing to become a journalist, and we would soon go our separate ways.

THREE DAYS AFTER GRADUATION, I received a call from one of the nuns at school. She had recommended me for a job in the Personnel Department of Ford Motor Company. My long-held desire for security beckoned, and my response was automatic. A door opened, and I quickly walked through, without a thought of where I was heading. I entered the world carrying a basket full of inexperience and naïveté.

Motherly Ever After

More than in any other human relationship, overwhelmingly more,
motherhood means being instantly interruptible,
responsive, responsible.
—Tillie Olsen

Today, Gen X-ers raised on *Sex and the City* and digitized millennials who've come of age watching *Girls* may be incredulous to discover that, in the 1950s, the dominant social programming confirmed that a woman was not expected to have, let alone voice, her own opinion. When I was young, Jackie Gleason's popular TV show, *The Honeymooners,* reflected our society's "woman as second-class citizen" worldview. Gleason played Ralph Kramden, a working-class Brooklyn bus driver, whose wife, Alice, displayed troubling signs of independence. Gleason's signature response to Alice's rebellion unleashed a flood of pure adoration from his audience.

In each episode, Alice's resistance would inevitably rouse Ralph to raise his fist and threaten: "Alice," he would call out in exasperation, then he'd turn to his friend, Ed, to cosign the check. "One of these days, POW, right in the kisser!" Now it was time to cue the laugh track, which was accompanied by Gleason's smacking one fist into the other and performing some fancy footwork. Then he landed the punch line: "And send her right to the moon!"

Audiences howled in approval, much like audiences howl at Donald Trump's disrespectful mockery of women today.

I fill with pride as I witness millennials and women of all ages express their resistance to the assault on our democracy in nationwide protests on the streets and harness the new cultural media online. I am heartened when twice a week I receive my online feminist communiqué *Lenny*, its email tagline announcing: "Dismantling the patriarchy, one newsletter at a time." The minimagazine portrays the reality of our country's cultural diversity in life, art, and politics and boasts over 500,000 subscribers. This increased presence "on the streets and in the tweets" demonstrates the essential role of women as change agents who appreciate the distance we have come but also realize how far we must go. Today, there is much work to be done and an infinite number of ways for women to complete that work. But when I graduated from high school, there was only one legitimate option—so-called women's work.

IN THE 1950S, college was unheard of for a working-class girl. It was expected that a young Catholic girl would meet a man and marry soon after high school. The rest of her life depended on where that man would lead her.

I met Don at a Young Adult Club meeting at St. Suzanne's Church. He was the president, brisk and efficient. Shorter than I, with sun-streaked, light brown, unruly hair, he had a commanding presence and a biting sense of humor. I learned that he was in a work-study engineering program at the General Motors Institute in Flint, where he rotated between six weeks in the plant and six weeks on campus. This schedule was intended to lead ambitious young men into management-level positions at General Motors.

Early in the meeting I could feel him looking at me. I was flattered but then embarrassed when I asked a few questions to impress him and felt my face flush. Don quipped some witty response, making me feel stupid and prompting the others to laugh. I've always had a problem with blushing; there is just no way to control it. I knew I was vivid red. Don approached me after the meeting and asked if I wanted to go to the state fair with him on the following Saturday. I looked into his dancing eyes and accepted. He was both smart and clever. I liked that.

Don always possessed an unimpeachable air of maturity and self-assurance. I learned later that he had been deserted by his mother and passed from home to home as a foster child.

"It's hard to believe in love when my own mother didn't love me," he told me one day as we were window shopping outside a downtown Detroit jewelry store.

After Don's birth mother died, a relative of his mother's fiancée, whom he called Grandma Bet, was awarded guardianship, and she sent him to a military boarding school. He was back living with Grandma Bet when I met him. Rootless as a youth, Don began to construct his identity as a young man. He applied and was accepted for membership in Mensa International, the largest and oldest high-IQ society in the world.

By contrast, I was young and immature, just one week beyond my teens when we married in June 1957. Somehow, I thought that becoming a wife would result in a storybook life. When I told my mother that I was getting married, she had one piece of advice for me: "You have to pretend you're helpless or you'll end up like me, responsible for everything."

My mother did all the repair work in the house as well as the painting. She cut the grass with a push lawn mower and kept a flower garden. These were the skills I learned from her. I didn't know how to be helpless, but I also didn't possess the skills Don would expect me to have. I had always been an independent person who had handled responsibilities without complaining. Unfortunately, my mother's advice was not going to help me.

I understood from the very beginning that Don and I were different; it was part of the magnetic attraction. He was the time-and-motion-study engineer, and I was the virtuous and compliant Catholic girl who admired his intellectual prowess and would give him beautiful children. As soon as we were married, our relationship changed, and we began to argue. Don was a self-made man and staunchly independent. He didn't need a partner; he needed a skilled homemaker who was organized and efficient. He was impatient with my inability to fulfill that role. His witty remarks soon became sarcastic. I believed my husband loved me as an object but not for who I was. Maybe I didn't yet know who I was.

This all made getting set up in our own home hard. I had no housekeeping skills, and I came home from work tired. I could sew up a storm, but I never liked to cook, so preparing meals took me a long time. Don was often grumpy and hungry after his drive home. He would ask how long before dinner and would then sit and read a magazine while I struggled to prepare the food; sometimes he set a timer to see how long it took me. This was dispiriting. At the time, I believed my lack of skills was the problem. I was hurt and felt incompetent in his presence.

I blamed myself for expecting more from my husband. My dad was a working-class man, a reliable provider, but he never lifted a finger to help my mother. In fact, I don't think in all the years of my childhood that I had ever seen my father in the kitchen. My life, it seemed, would be no different. In the 1950s, women were expected to carry the full burden of keeping house and caring for the children, even if they were working outside the home. In the fantasies of the era, being a housewife was a very easy job.

Don's critical behavior toward me wasn't confined behind closed doors. There were times when friends and neighbors would ask me how I could let him speak to me in such a disrespectful manner. They didn't dare say anything to him. He was intimidating.

At one point early on, Don decided we should play bridge with a neighbor couple, a brainy exercise for his stifled mind. I tried, but I just couldn't master the game. I was so afraid of his reactions that I couldn't make confident decisions.

"Your play, Joann," my neighbor Joy said.

"I know," I said, but I didn't want to play. I didn't like the game, and I was desperately trying to remember if the Jack of Spades had already been played. Engaging in a competitive game of cards didn't interest me. I loved the social engagement of an evening spent with our next-door neighbors, but learning a card game with high emotional stakes was simply too stressful.

Don mumbled something about my stupidity, and Joy raised an eyebrow.

I could feel Don glaring at me; we were losing. An exasperated look on his face, he drummed his fingers on the table. I had been hurt and humiliated before by Don's demeaning comments in front of others, so I pretended I hadn't heard.

BY THE TIME WE HAD BEEN MARRIED THREE MONTHS, I was pregnant and sick as a dog. I dragged myself to the bus stop, four long blocks from our flat, to get to work and home again. All morning and into the afternoon, I struggled with morning sickness, running down the hallway to the ladies' room to heave up that awful green bile. My employer soon asked me to quit my job. In his view, I was spending too much time running back and forth to the restroom and wasn't producing enough work. There were no maternity benefits in those days. I was fired because I was pregnant.

Staying home and being sick all the time did not help my house-keeping or my cooking skills. The smell of food made me throw up. To be fair, Don and I never really got to know each other as people, nor did we become friends. I was a sheltered young woman with no idea who I was or where I was going in this world, except that the destination seemed to require housekeeping skills, which I didn't have.

It was obvious that we needed to move from our small upper flat to a place where we could raise children. We were just start-ing out, and our modest income didn't qualify us for a mortgage. Don found a little house on Wohlfeil Street in Taylor Township, a semirural area lying southwest of Detroit on the western edge of the downriver communities. At the time, Taylor was known as Taylortucky because many people—mostly truck drivers from Kentucky—had settled there with their families when they came north looking for work.

This was not really an area where I would have wished to raise my children, but it was a viable option for us. The owners' mortgage was in default; we could assume it for the balance owed under the original low GI terms. There was no need for approval. We could simply take over the existing mortgage and start making payments. Our baby was due soon, we needed a house, and this was the only one we could afford. We were elated that the house was brick and, feeling like the wise little pig in the storybook, we moved in immediately. I felt grateful that we had a home, and my dream of a large family was upon me.

When the real estate agent was driving us through the neighborhood, we noticed that the house behind us was destroyed. Windows were broken, the aluminum awning above the front porch was twisted, and the front door hacked.

"What had happened here?" we asked.

"Oh, these people sold their house to Negroes," he said, "so the neighbors destroyed it. It's all over now—they're gone. Bet they won't come back here."

IN SEPTEMBER 1957, shortly after I discovered I was pregnant with my first child, Little Rock, Arkansas, made the news. The nation watched as Governor Orval Faubus sent his National Guard troops to Central High School to defy desegregation orders from the federal government. Standing at the schoolhouse door with bayoneted rifles, the Arkansas Guard refused entry to nine black students known as the Little Rock Nine.

Three weeks later as the Guard drifted away, angry whites took their place, taunting and shouting obscenities, spitting at the students, tearing their clothes, and demanding they be lynched for pursuing their legal right to attend high school. The situation was quickly out of control. Forced to act, President Eisenhower explained his reasoning in a televised address to the nation, and the next morning sent federal troops into Little Rock to enforce antisegregation laws.

Increasingly, tales of racial conflict were becoming a daily part of our lives. I was sick to think that humans could do this to others. The South was exploding in chaos in full view of the watching nation. Blacks in the northern states developed stations of support for the Southern Freedom movement, sending money and supplies and offering respite in northern homes for weary civil rights soldiers.

Most whites in the North had been hesitant to commit to the fight for civil rights because they felt no immediate threat. Segregation can be quite comfortable for whites. While some supported civil rights as a moral issue, others didn't yet perceive how equal rights were necessary to the future of America. Even today, there are whites who perceive the black radical movement as a threat to their quality of life. Emotions run so high that whites tend to avoid the topic. It's easier to get along with family and friends. It follows the same principle as the "never wake a sleeping giant" rule, taught to our children from an early age in "Jack and the Beanstalk."

While turmoil grew outside, Don's and my rocky home life continued with the addition of our first child, Ken. He had a wretched experience in my womb, and he entered the world tense and colicky. He was also prone to croup. I spent many nights sitting in the steam of the shower pleading with him to relax and just breathe.

"Breathe, baby, breathe," I would whisper as I gently rocked him.

WHEN I WENT INTO LABOR with my second child and had no one to watch Ken, who was barely one-year-old at the time, I called my mother, who had become a salesclerk at Hudson's Department Store around the time Ken was born. "We're having friends over this evening," she replied. "It's too late to change my plans."

Babies were just not her thing. Over the years, Mother would occasionally call, but I seldom had time to talk. I was consumed by the day-to-day responsibilities of my growing family, and we drifted apart. Mother just didn't see herself in a supportive role, and she never reached out to help me. Don had no family, so this situation didn't seem unusual to him.

With Don's engineering background and his history in military school, combined with my rigid upbringing, our child-raising approaches were trial and error, and there were a lot of errors. This was prior to Dr. Spock. I just didn't know. My parents had taught me nothing about demonstrating love, and I didn't know how to show it. I was too young to understand that I had inherited a contradictory nature. I had a warm Irish heart, but the distant German side of me prevented me from demonstrating the love my heart held.

In 1959 and 1960, Don and I produced two more healthy boys, Greg and Jeff. Shortly after Jeff was born, I was diagnosed with a thyroid tumor and had surgery. The tumor was benign, but in the years after I came to fear it had a bigger impact than I initially realized.

Carolyn, our fourth child, and Michael, our fifth, were both born with vision impairments and are considered legally blind. We noticed early on that our daughter was visually impaired. Her development was different from that of our other children.

"Carolyn doesn't look at anything," I told the pediatrician as I watched him examine her eyes with his penlight.

"You're right," the doctor said. "Her vision centers are covered with a speckled pigment. It almost looks like measles. I want you to consult a vision specialist. Right now, she can't see, but it's possible the tissue will thin out over time."

Hearing his words, my heart was racing. I didn't know if I could bear this. I was hurting for my baby; I was hurting for myself. Dear God, please make this be temporary! Suddenly, I remembered my grandfather's blindness. He was no longer living, but his struggles and the vacant look in his eyes now haunted me. It's not fair for a baby girl never to see the green trees and the blue sky.

How would we cope? Where would we find the strength?

"Return in six months," the doctor said.

"Yes, of course, Doctor." I was numb.

Michael, our fifth child, born just a year later, had a similar eye condition but faced even greater challenges. He needed a special diet of bland and strained foods. He was also late to talk. My pediatrician gently suggested that I prepare myself, as these symptoms could be indications that Michael was what he called "mentally retarded."

Michael remained nonverbal until a summer vacation just before his third birthday. We drove all the way from Michigan to Washington, D.C., pulling behind us a collapsible sleeping trailer on wheels that we had made from a kit. With so many children, camping was the only way we could afford to get away. Unfortunately, the heat in D.C. was suffocating, and it was a miserable place to be in the depths of summer. We had envisioned educating the children about our seat of government, but we would never make it into the city.

The ranger at the campgrounds had to take Don to the emergency room with heat stroke. I was trying to keep the kids entertained and stress free. We were marching around on the campsite trails singing when Michael suddenly joined in the song—with complete sentences and all the words: "With a knick-knack paddy whack, give the dog a bone. This old man came rolling home."

Tears of joy were running down my face. My child was mentally whole. All of a sudden, our trip became a joyous one.

I continued to seek services and resources for Carolyn and Michael. I was relentless. I took them to the Low Vision Clinic at Sinai Hospital. During the evaluation, the doctor handed Carolyn an $8^{1}/_{2}$-by-11-inch typed card and asked her to read it to him. She just stared at the card, holding the writing upside down without realizing it, as I held back tears. My heart was broken.

Each morning this extraordinary little girl went off to school and never complained. How hard she must be struggling to function. How could I help her? The doctor concurred with earlier advice that a regular-school environment, rather than arrangements for the disabled, would be best for both of my children in the long run. I didn't coddle them. I wanted them to be independent, resilient. I taught them that disability means different, not less than. I always reinforced that there were many roads to success, but there was only one path that could guarantee a loss in life: giving up.

Because of his limited vision, Michael depended on clues from his other senses to navigate through life. He absorbed existence on so many different levels and was sensitized to small nuances that the rest of us missed. Nothing went unnoticed or unreported. Forced to spend his childhood inside because he was blinded by bright daylight, Michael often occupied himself in his room, collecting, analyzing, and organizing things he could manage.

Early one summer morning, Jeff called me to come outside. He put his finger over his lips, signaling that I should be quiet. The sun was beginning to crest the rooftops. Long shadows still covered the ground around our house. There in the morning shade were math problems written in chalk all around the perimeter of the house. "It's Michael," he whispered. "Look." Chalk in hand and lost in thought, this seven-year-old child was writing times tables that we had no idea he comprehended. Michael may have been disadvantaged in some ways, but he was abundantly gifted in others.

One summer, when the children were in high school, I learned that Michigan's Services for the Blind offered special training in mobility skills. Michael attended a day program. Carolyn participated in an on-campus program at the University of Detroit. She loved living on a college campus for a week and sharing life with others who had similar visual limitations. Both children learned how to make their way around the city walking with white canes and using city bus services. It was an excellent experience in learning how to be independent, and it allowed them to approach their futures with more confidence.

As our family quickly grew in the early 1960s, the demands at home, and the social expectations for a young white suburban housewife, meant I rarely got out. Even so, the discord growing in the outside world managed to find its way in. Scenes of high school teens in Birmingham being hosed and attacked by dogs possessed me. What if these were my kids? These children had mothers. I learned of sit-ins at Woolworth's Five and Dime in Greensboro and of the Freedom Rides that followed throughout the South, and I was amazed at the courage on display.

In June 1963, shortly before I became pregnant with Michael and two months before the March on Washington, Dr. Martin

Luther King, Jr., an advocate of Mahatma Gandhi's belief in nonviolent protest, led a march of 125,000 people in Detroit's Walk to Freedom. At the time, it was the largest civil rights march in U.S. history. It was there that Dr. King gave his first "I Have a Dream" speech, testing his message in the warmth of an increasingly black city that supported his mission.

The changing world was also being felt inside the Church. John XXIII was pope during the years I was developing as a social activist, and he was a hugely popular father figure in the world. He was a man of humility who led the Church with a vision of change. Believing that it had become stagnant, Pope John pushed the Church to play a broader role in the world. He was a human rights activist who demonstrated his beliefs through actions and was involved in the sociopolitical events of the time. Pope John's convening of Vatican II in January 1959 set the Catholic Church on a radically new path.

We all know that Italians appreciate expressive gestures. It was reported that when the pope was asked to reveal his intentions, he simply moved to a window and threw it open, to let in a draft of fresh air.

Vatican II was a timely message to people of conscience in the United States. It was time to take a stand. Violence by whites around school integration was incomprehensible to me. As Washington sent troops, it also became clear that these events had the potential to explode out of control. History is filled with tales of ethnic wars. I began to feel protective of my family in a way that was unknown to me before I had my own children. I started to follow events more closely. For the first time, it occurred to me that as a Christian, I had a responsibility to assure that basic human rights for all people were protected. I had no idea how I could make a contribution, but the compulsion to help was heavy on my mind.

Then Father Bill Cunningham arrived at St. Alfred's Catholic Church. Father was about thirty-five and in the prime of his life when we met him. He was a brilliant speaker, with a rich voice and a commanding presence. He was intense, bigger than life, and he loved every minute of it. Stocky but fit, with dark eyes and a shock of black curls, he usually wore the traditional black suit and priest's collar, but he was as comfortable in jeans and sweaters or his leather jacket when out on his motorcycle. Father Cunningham was a rare breed who took great pleasure in laughing at himself and the ironies of life. He was as at ease with people on the street as he was with elite officials.

The first time I heard Father speak, he eloquently painted a picture with his words of how urban renewal was devastating black neighborhoods.

"Rather than support the poor we are bulldozing their homes and destroying their rich culture." With emotion, Father quoted words from the last supper: "They know not what they do." His strong voice filled the church. He stood before us at a small lectern in front of the altar in St. Alfred's. Father was wearing his colorful mass vestments, his face intense. The pain in his eyes was penetrating my soul.

"We have no clue what we are creating," he said softly.

Then his voice rose in a crescendo: "You live in the suburbs, and when you have business in the city, you drive in on smooth subterranean roads walled by green lawns and flowering trees that block from the view of white suburban travelers the inconvenient sight of the miserable plight of blacks. We as whites and our leaders have chosen to ignore the poverty and hunger and lack of adequate services provided to our black brothers and sisters in Christ.

"In the calling of Vatican II, Pope John has challenged us to open our hearts and open our eyes to see the challenges of our lifetimes. It is time to wake up and see that Christ is in our midst as he walks in the shoes of our black brothers."

I was transfixed.

Even as I was awakening internally with the desire to get involved with the struggles unfolding around me, my life at home continued to pose its own set of challenges. I felt as if I had gone from the isolated home life of a child to the isolated life of a young married mother of small children, and I had no time to myself to think or be. My anger grew. I let it out like my parents did. I slammed doors. I threw things. I screamed at the kids. I tore the wall phone off the wall with my bare hands when its incessant ringing kept interrupting my ability to get things done. I curled my hair when Don was at work so I could look appealing when he came home. I changed to clean clothes and even put on lipstick as suggested in a *Woman's Day* magazine article on "how to keep your man."

Outside, I dug a little flower garden next to our front step to make our house look cared for. Few homes on our block had gardens.

"I love your flowers," my neighbor Joy remarked one day.

"I wish I had more time," I said woefully. "It feels so good to get outside. It even smells good when I dig my hands into the wormy earth."

I savored the thought of ignoring my duties for a moment of pleasure outside, plunging my hands into the good earth and breathing in the fresh air.

"When the flowers bloom, I feel like they're thanking me for the care," I said.

"I know," she concurred. "We don't get many thanks for what we do."

Don and I both wanted a large family. We had been lonely youngsters and were eager for a rollicking chaotic household. But the children were coming too fast. Being good and devout Catholics, we went to a priest for counseling, but I was told that my concerns were simply those of a weak woman.

"Once these difficult years pass, you will laugh about your present troubles," the priest said in response to our concerns. I tried to hide my tears as we left.

Few other options were afforded us by the Catholic Church at the time. One was the rhythm method, where a woman checked her basal body temperature every day before rising, to determine when she was ovulating, and then abstained from sexual relations during that period. Our only other option was just plain withdrawal during intercourse. Neither was healthy for building a loving relationship.

I went to my OB/GYN to ask for help in mastering the rhythm method. My pencil and paper charting of my daily temperature suggested that I ovulated twice a month. He proposed a medical test to confirm my ovulation patterns. This meant that we needed to abstain from sex for a full month. I begged Don to understand.

One wretchedly emotional month later, I returned to Oakwood hospital to get my results. All the children were with me. The nurse called me into the treatment room to give me my results.

"I'm very sorry, Mrs. Castle," she said, "but the test results are inconclusive and will have to be repeated."

"You're kidding!"

"No. Here's the paperwork," she said. "You can call the laboratory on the pay phone in the waiting area and make another appointment."

"I can't do this again. Not now," I said, as emotion welled up in my throat. I tried to push it down.

"If you want reliable results, you'll have to call the lab and make an appointment. The pay phone is right around the corner in the patient waiting area."

I returned to the waiting room in a daze. The children had worried looks on their faces. The pay phone was free for calls made within the hospital, and the operator put me through to the lab.

"Please hold and we will be with you shortly," a voice said.

I could feel that I was losing control and was soon overcome by a flood of tears and anger. I began beating my fist on the wall of the phone booth and screaming as the pain inside me found an escape. There was a commotion outside the booth.

I heard a nurse say to the receptionist at the desk, "Call the social worker; I'll take the children."

I dropped the phone and ran for my kids.

"Don't you touch my children!" I literally growled like a beast. I began walking toward the elevator, kids in tow. "Don't touch my children and don't try to stop me."

The mental stress and the physical strain were taking a toll on me. But I was compliant in concert with my beliefs. I did love my children, but this life was so hard. I let myself be inspired by movies of the day like *Cheaper by the Dozen*. It made me laugh, and I wondered why I couldn't be lighthearted about our challenges. I resolved to try again. I threw myself into my family. There would be more challenges ahead, and I needed to become strong. My children were depending upon me. No weakness; no whining.

MY MUNDANE DOMESTIC ROUTINE of those years was interrupted twice by life-altering events. The first was when President Kennedy was shot. The second was Selma, Alabama. It was Sunday morning, March 7, 1965. Breakfast was over, and I was busy cleaning the kitchen. Don was watching TV in our bedroom.

I heard him call me, his tone urgent. I dropped what I was doing and joined him. Chaos was unfolding in Alabama. I was aghast at live footage of peaceful marchers being attacked and beaten with billy clubs and tear-gassed by Alabama state and local police. Some of the officers were on horseback and charged into the defenseless marchers swinging their clubs. People were lying injured on the street.

I sat down next to Don on the side of the bed, speechless at what I was witnessing in real time. "Why?" I asked. "Were they peacefully marching?"

"They were beginning a march from Selma, Alabama, to the state capital in Montgomery to demand the right to vote." Don turned his head, and I saw the tense expression on his face. "The state troopers attacked without provocation. This is not going to end well."

He stood up, clenching his fists the way he always did when he was upset.

Led by Hosea Williams of the Southern Christian Leadership Conference and John Lewis of the Student Nonviolent Coordinating Committee, the group was only six blocks into their walk when they were attacked as they passed over the Edmund Pettus Bridge, heading east toward the interstate highway. In the chaotic melee, fifty demonstrators were injured and John Lewis nearly died.

It was overwhelming to realize these horrific national events were on view live in my bedroom.

Two days later, Dr. Martin Luther King, Jr. led a ceremonial march of twenty-five hundred protesters across the bridge without incident, but then they stopped. Later that day, segregationists attacked three white ministers who had come to support the marchers. One of them was James Reeb, a white Unitarian Universalist minister from Boston. Reeb was initially taken to Selma's public hospital, where he was refused treatment. He was then driven to a university hospital two hours away. He died two days later. People across the country began to organize.

One of those people was Father Cunningham. He had been with Dr. King on the day of the second march. He stood in front of the congregation the following Sunday holding a copy of *Time* magazine open to a picture of those who had crossed the bridge with Dr. King. Father delivered a moving sermon on the need for Catholics to witness their faith and live the Church's teachings with the courage of Christ.

Father Cunningham's sermons were changing my outlook on the world around me. My consciousness of the impact of racism on our society was soaring. His intellectually stimulating sermons on topics of the moment were falling on me like rain on a thirsty plant. I was coming alive. I know Don was affected also. Don was a hard-liner in many ways and not very sentimental, but he had a good heart.

I felt driven to do something, anything, to help. I leaned over to Don as we sat in the pew with our children around us, baby in my lap, and whispered, "I want to do something. We have to do *something*."

Don and I approached Father in the church vestibule after Mass. Don stepped forward, extending his hand.

"Don Castle here," he said, his voice strong and his manner direct, "and family." He gestured to include all of us.

I was dressed in my Sunday best—a little hat with a veil, white gloves, and high heels—with our baby Michael enveloped in my arms. Don held Carolyn, still a little tot in her Sunday bonnet. Greg and Jeff were between us, bumping hips, competing for our attention. History suggested it was best to get to the point before this serene family portrait burst into noisy, individual photos. And today, I felt emboldened.

"We were moved by your sermon," I began, uncharacteristically taking the lead. "We want desperately to do something to contribute to the civil rights struggle. As you can see, we have small children and can't travel to join the protests. Is there anything we can do here that would be helpful?" Unknown to anyone, including myself, I was taking my first baby steps on my road to becoming an activist.

"Many families like yours have approached me this morning," Father said, patting Ken on the head. Ken, almost six, glanced his way but said nothing. "I'm suggesting that we all get together to discuss how people like yourselves could have an impact," Father continued. "I have some ideas."

We readily agreed and left church that morning excited that we might play some small role in making a difference. This was the beginning of our involvement with Father Cunningham's Christian leadership training. I don't believe that he knew yet what he was going to do with all of us.

I WAS NOT THE ONLY ONE watching Selma unfold. Viola Liuzzo, another white woman and mother from Detroit, was also horrified by the images at Selma. She attended a local demonstration against the brutal police actions at Wayne State University, where she was a student. There, Viola made a connection and headed to Alabama to help, as did scores of other sympathizers—spiritual leaders of all races and religions, and hundreds of other people of conscience from across the nation.

On her way, Viola telephoned her family and told them that she was going to Selma to support the marchers. Viola arrived in Selma on March 21, 1965, the night before the third attempt to complete the Selma-to-Montgomery March. She parked her 1963 green Oldsmobile with Michigan license plates, and entered the Brown Chapel AME Church, where she offered to help serve food to marchers.

"Hi, my name is Viola," she said, and put on an apron.

By the next morning, the number of marchers had swelled to eight thousand. Viola worked the nursing station for four days during the fifty-four-mile march. On March 25, after completion of the march and celebration in front of the state capital in Montgomery, Viola offered to shuttle some of the marchers back to their cars along the route to Selma. She was tired, but she was headed that way anyway.

Thousands of marchers were in Montgomery, and their cars remained wherever they had joined the swelling protest. For Viola, one shuttle ended up being two. After dropping off her second load of marchers, Viola was driving back to Montgomery, accompanied by a black teenage volunteer named Leroy Moton, when they were pursued by a car of Ku Klux Klan members. Viola tried to shake them off for twenty miles, sometimes exceeding eighty miles per hour, before she was run off the road. The thirty-nine-year-old Detroit mother of five young children was shot twice in the head and left to die in her car on a lonely stretch of Alabama road. One of the KKK members was an FBI informant who later bragged that he had been the shooter.

I heard the news the next morning. Until that moment, I'd felt as if the events had been unfolding on the fringes of my life. But Viola's death hit home—hard. Like her, I was a mother of five small children. I, too, was a Detroiter who had been raised Catholic. Viola had made her own decisions and had stood up for what she believed in. Through her, I learned that a mother with children could fight back. My religion taught me that we are our brother's keeper and that all people are created equal. I wanted to stand up for what I believed in. I could be more and do more. And I *would* play a role.

It was an historic moment. It was also *my* moment to consider the role of whites in the civil rights struggle. Race was dividing the country into passionate opposing positions for and against the rights of blacks to fully participate in our society. I needed to let it be known which side I was on. That was my moral responsibility as a Christian and as a human being.

Father Cunningham's inspirational sermons were birthing an existential crisis in my life. I was struggling with the meaning of life, who I was, and how I was going to infuse my children with moral values. Not only was I responsible for myself but I was also the primary reference point in my children's development. There was a lot at stake here; I needed to get my feet on the ground and show them the way. I didn't know anyone at church, and I had nothing in common with my neighbors. Taylor Township's residents were not, by and large, supportive of civil rights. Since Don and I had never learned how to share our deep inner feelings, I had no one in whom to confide this moment, nor did I necessarily expect to.

My counsel was the innocence on my children's faces. Every moment, every action on my part was shaping their future life and the world in which they would live. I felt a huge responsibility to educate them in the realities of the world. I didn't want them to grow up being naive and afraid like I had been.

Somehow, in the most contradictory way, I wanted to protect them from harm by becoming involved. Clearly, I didn't want to die, but Viola had demonstrated that mothers of five could be more. She was a student, an activist, and she had been making a difference in the world. I longed to be like her. My uninformed strategy was to involve my kids in the struggle, educate myself in order to arm them with knowledge, teach them to be strong, and show them an example of a meaningful Christian life.

That afternoon my parents stopped by, and I was still spinning at the news of Viola's killing. I knew my mother's position on race was different from mine, but my heart was bursting with pain.

"That poor woman," I began.

My mother was adamant: "That woman had no business going south when she had small children at home. She was mingling with all those Negroes; she was asking for trouble."

I found myself taking the other side of the argument. "But Mother," I started, "racism needs to be confronted. Aren't all people equal in the sight of God?"

"In God's sight, her role was to be with her children," Mother stated flatly.

But just being home with my children wasn't enough for me. I was struggling to give shape to my side of the argument, to give words and actions to my feelings. "How could anyone not be moved to action under these circumstances?" My heart took me one step further as I mused out loud. "Think of how things would change if *everyone* acted."

My emotion ran over. "Why *isn't* everyone acting? Are we not called on to support a more noble cause?"

By this time my mother was totally dismayed. "Barry," she said to my father, "I think it is time to go." In silence, I watched them leave, then slumped into a chair near the front door and continued thinking about the situation.

Famous people attended Viola's memorial, including Dr. King, Michigan's lieutenant governor William Milliken, Teamster president Jimmy Hoffa, and UAW leader Walter Reuther, but the spate of respect was short-lived. Viola was killed on a Thursday, and by the following Sunday, our church lay silent in its response to her sacrifice.

Viola's killing, unbeknownst to us, was targeted by the early work of **COINTELPRO**, J. Edgar Hoover's FBI Counterintelligence Program aimed at surveilling and disrupting the civil rights and other political movements at the time. Within days of her death, the newspapers began to smear her reputation. Viola and her family were under attack. Her six-year-old daughter had stones thrown at her at school. Her family members were called "nigger lovers" by their neighbors. Racism, usually subtle in the North, unleashed its fury on her family.

Three KKK members were arrested but ultimately acquitted after their assertion that Viola was an interloper with a feverish lust for black men, a drug user, and mentally unstable. Years later, the Liuzzo children would discover Hoover's thirty-seven-page FBI file that spread outrageous lies about Viola.

I couldn't get these tragic events out of my mind. Father Cunningham's sermons had taken me to a new place in my soul. He was pouring gasoline on the flames. Was Father's courage rubbing off on me, or was I just digging deeper into my soul? I wanted to be more and do more, but the reality I was living kept pushing me back. I was learning that the world often deems those who fervently care about injustice to be unworthy and un-American.

"My country 'tis of thee, sweet land of liberty," I silently cried out. For whom, a chosen few, based upon the color of their skin? How does a black child pledge allegiance to the flag and say the words, "with freedom and justice for all"? I was obsessed with the need to do something. I wrestled with the question: What leads one person to walk away and another to lie sleepless over injustice? Was I naive? Was everything I had been taught about our great country a sham?

I began to realize that I had married when I was still a child. Now, I was struggling to grow up fast and learn about the real world. I longed to affect the world my children were growing up in, and I regarded it as my duty to enrich and prepare them with knowledge and experiences that I had never had.

Events assured me that the call for action was not to be taken lightly. What kind of role model must I be for my kids, who would need courage to survive in such a world? My life was at a turning point—I was evolving from an eager but green Catholic housewife into a woman ready to collaborate with others in the broader world, bent on creating a future where all people have dignity and respect and are afforded equal opportunity.

Deep inside, I felt a kinship with Viola, and I understood why she had been compelled to go to Selma. Perhaps by participating in the movement and picking up the freedom baton on her behalf, I could be counted among those who had finished what she had started. Through my participation and others like me, Viola would not have died in vain.

IN SEARCH OF A MOVEMENT

Never doubt that a small group of thoughtful, committed citizens
can change the world. Indeed, it's the only thing that ever has.
—MARGARET MEAD

IT WAS 1965: the world was on fire, and here we were in Taylor
Township, a predominantly redneck community with little sympathy for the plight of a distant city—whether Detroit or Selma.
Father Cunningham was intent on changing these attitudes by
casting his sermons in the light of Christian responsibility. He
loved living on the edge of controversy. I did not know at the time
that he was getting death threats for his passionate embrace of racial equality. It never slowed him down or reduced his willingness
to take risks in pursuit of racial justice. Father Cunningham's sermons about the obligation of Catholics to support the civil rights
movement opened the door for Don and me to become involved
in activities that forecast the onset of a fledgling radical Catholic
movement.

Our request of Father Cunningham to find some way for us
to get involved led us to the home of our neighbors, Eleanor and
Don Josaitis. Father was a regular guest of the Josaitises when
he spent Sundays at our parish. Their family lived in a three-
bedroom newer ranch home on the other side of Telegraph Road,
where the nicer homes were. Don Josaitis owned a hobby store

with his brother, and Eleanor stayed home with their kids. She was also helping Father set up weekend activist retreats.

After the trauma of Selma, Father's group of Christian soldiers from Taylor gathered in Eleanor's finished basement. When Eleanor answered the door, I expected a warm neighborly greeting, but her manner was cool. She would prove to be all business, which is what every visionary leader like Father Cunningham needs.

I searched her face for a connection but then decided she was preoccupied. Eleanor looked a few years older than I, plain, small-framed, and serious. She directed us downstairs where I knew no one. As we took our seats, I turned my attention to a friendly woman named Gloria, who asked me how many children we had. This was a Catholic gathering—we all had a lot of kids.

As our formal discussion began, we introduced ourselves one by one around the circle of chairs positioned for inclusiveness. When it was Eleanor's turn to speak, she talked about how seeing the fire hoses turned on teenagers in Birmingham had brought her into the movement.

"I was watching television," she began. "I saw images of young people attacked by police dogs and ravaged by blasts from fire hoses. Those were teenagers, children. I couldn't believe what I was seeing. I was outraged and knew I had to do something. When I heard Father Cunningham speak of how Catholics should step forward and be involved, I knew I wanted to play a supporting role in his work."

I understood things more clearly when I listened to her speak from her heart. It was clear that she had a gift for speaking in front of a group. She had a way of catching people's eyes, engaging them in her message—and that voice: calm, reassuring, yet commanding our attention. "All my life, I have experienced a deep religious faith," she said. "As a young girl, I wanted to be a nun, but my father wouldn't allow it. He wanted me home to help my mother. I believe in Father Bill's work. I believe he's making a difference."

Eleanor was also the mother of small children. At the time, we both had five. Although we never discussed it as such, I sensed we were being called to similar life paths. We were both very moved by the dedication of Father Cunningham to his mission and felt the need to contribute our support to the civil rights struggle going on across the country. Eleanor's life had reached the point of no return as she'd watched the children in Birmingham get blasted by fire hoses; my own activist no-exit clause had been cemented by Viola.

As we got to know each other better during that time, Father Cunningham called Don and suggested that we assist him with a mentoring program for students on the campus of Eastern Michigan University. Don loved to be in the spotlight, and he said yes for both of us.

"But how could you answer for me," I said when Don told me. "I don't know anything about college kids, except that they experiment with drugs, dress crazy, and talk in a language I don't understand. At our last meeting, I heard someone say there had been suicides on campus. These young people intimidate me. I don't know what I'm going to do when our kids become teenagers."

I could already tell it was a done deal, but I had a need to express my feelings.

"Don't make such a big deal of it," Don said, bored with my response. "Just get a babysitter."

It was a thirty-minute drive from Taylor to the Eastern Michigan University campus in the city of Ypsilanti. We found the Pope John XXIII Ecumenical Center on the edge of campus. Father Bill hadn't arrived yet, and we were welcomed by another couple. It turned out they had nine kids yet still found time to dedicate to helping others.

"We often speak at retreats for high school and college kids," the woman said. "We have fun doing this together. You'll see."

Other people with big families are active outside their homes, I thought. Maybe I am going to enjoy this experience. My brain was suddenly awake. I could use a challenge that was greater than endless meals to fix, dirty diapers to change, and conversations to conduct in baby talk. For at least a few minutes, I might be seen as a person who had something to give to others—experience, perhaps wisdom. Now, I just had to become wise . . .

Father Cunningham showed up at the last moment to give us a short orientation: "The purpose of the mentoring program is to give these kids a chance to express their fears and talk with couples in successful marriages. For most of them, it's their first time away from home. All at once, they're confronted with drugs, sex, drinking parties, student protests, and the like. They need to talk to stable adults in successful Christian marriages."

Father looked at us, his face expressing a glimmer of humor.

"You, in your experience, can help them chart a path through the challenges they face. They're young and their generation is totally destabilized. After a couple of weeks, you'll get to know these kids and begin to build relationships." He laughed. "You always wanted teenagers, right? Well, now you've got 'em."

I groaned. But Father was right. The students were open, trusting, and eager to bond. Once inside, Don started off with a series of witty remarks that softened his audience. I was more sensitive to getting them to reach into their deeper selves, where they could meaningfully explore who they were amid the chaos.

"We're open to discussing anything that's on your mind," I said, before pausing to slow the tempo down. "What did you hope to learn when you walked through that door today?"

They responded by asking about choosing a mate, having children, and dealing with health issues. I began to talk about what it had been like to discover I had two visually impaired children.

"It was hard to accept at first," I began. "Our first little girl appeared to have been born blind. I wanted to fight the doctor for confirming this was true. I didn't want to accept it. My heart ached every time I looked at her, but it was something I couldn't fix. Finally, I decided that I would do all in my power to make a good life for her. It helped when I stopped fighting God's will. I was the only one who could turn this burden into a blessing."

I saw one young woman in tears as I spoke. I had been afraid that I had nothing to offer these students. She was expressing her sympathy for me and what I had gone through. We were both learning, one from the other. I was touched.

We met regularly with the students over the course of a number of weeks. Our conversations began to broaden my horizons. This was my first experience in sharing such intimate details with others. It was a reflection time. It led me to explore my feelings in new ways. As I sat at Don's side and we talked with these earnest young people, I realized something else. I was learning how much he and I differed in our outlook on the world.

When it was Don's time to talk, I often found my mind drifting. Don and I had a communication pattern in our daily lives, I thought: he played offense, and I played defense. He wanted a wife to take care of his house, his kids, and him. I couldn't meet his expectations. I wanted to be someone and something more. I was happy to be a mother, and I loved my kids. If I ever relaxed, it was when I was with them. They amazed me. But I was not a very good wife. I never had a chance just to be a wife and lover.

I would look at Don and see him as the showman, always in character. At one point during one of our sessions with these young people, I heard him laughing about keeping me "barefoot in the winter and pregnant in the summer." This made me feel that I was no more than a baby machine.

"Funny to you," I commented lightly, adding a smile because I didn't want the students to think we were feuding. But I was offended.

"How did you go about choosing a wife," one of the young men asked Don.

"I'm short," Don quipped, "and I thought a tall woman would make me look successful. When I was at her house, I checked out her mother to see what she would look like when she got old."

The students were laughing. But it became clear that, for Don, it was all about what I could do for him. Was the role of a wife simply to reflect her husband's needs? Is that all there is for the wife? For me?

It is said that when a man gets married, he always hopes that the woman will remain the same, but she seldom does. I was beginning to realize that, in our marriage, I was, in fact, changing. I was seeing our relationship differently, with fresh eyes. All around me people were seeking the freedom to re-create themselves and the world they lived in. For the first time, I realized that in my youth, I was so eager to be independent that I traded one dependency for another. I never had a chance to discover who I was as a unique person.

As the semester ended and the students left for home, I knew I would miss them. Father Cunningham had introduced me to a new world. He offered an opportunity for me to learn that fear needed to be faced if it was to be conquered. Not only did I learn that young people are not to be feared, I also discovered that I could effectively speak in front of a group and that people would listen and learn from me. I learned a little about courage. I faced my own shyness and acknowledged that overcoming it would still need some work. I also looked in the mirror of my soul and saw that I was growing into womanhood.

FATHER CUNNINGHAM was working hard during this period to create even more opportunities for us to learn, grow, and prepare. He began a weekend program to train Christian leaders based on his own experience taking part in Cursillo, a worldwide retreat movement then popular in the Catholic Church. The Cursillo movement (the name means short course) originated in Spain. The method consisted of speakers of wide-ranging perspectives giving presentations to help the other participants become aware of their uniqueness and creativity. The format was designed to strengthen conviction and encourage participants to share their skills and insights to benefit society. The ultimate goal was to teach laypeople how to become effective Christian leaders and then send them back out into the world.

In replicating the Cursillo training back in the States, Father Cunningham was laying the foundation for a movement. He hoped that participants would become socially active and work with him and others to address some of the social ills, particularly racism, in our city.

Don and I were privileged to be invited to the first of these trainings. It was located west of the city, in what appeared to be a church retreat facility in the woods. With its log cabins, bunk beds, and dining hall, it had all the trappings of a summer camp. There were fifteen to twenty attendees who stayed the night, ranging from lay folk like Don and me, to seminarians fulfilling a real commitment to church-centered activism. Much of what we experienced was relevant to the deepening racial crisis in Detroit. It was, in reality, an awakening that proved to be our first giant step in becoming social activists.

Father Cunningham's energy and dynamism were infectious. We experienced two full days of self-actualization and Christian fellowship with a focus on Pope John's intent, as part of Vatican II, that the Catholic Church become pertinent to people's lives in the changing conditions of modern times.

The civil rights movement was in the air, and we felt a sense of urgency to support equality. In Detroit, racist policies over the last several decades and white flight to the suburbs had isolated blacks in decaying areas of our city, promoting fears and distrust from both sides. In the metropolitan area, this was a growing social problem of critical proportions.

We spent the weekend discussing the responsibility Christians have to be socially active in their communities, and more specifically the obligation we had to support racial equality in our area. We heard from an array of people working on social justice issues. One presenter was Neal Shine, the publisher and editor of the *Detroit Free Press*, a friend of Father Cunningham's, who came to talk to us about the realities of life for blacks in Detroit. Some of the participants would go on to become instrumental figures in the movement we were on our way to joining. They also became dear friends. Among them were musicians and artists Patrick and Rosemarie Mason, whom we'd originally met at the Eastern Michigan retreats, and whose home in Detroit would become a key rallying point for us going forward.

I also met Walt Hardy, a black man and friend of Father Cunningham's. Mr. Hardy was one of the speakers. He spoke movingly on the ways racism impacts black families, the destruction of their neighborhoods, and the covenants that limit where they can live.

It sounds peculiar now, but this was the mid-1960s, and up to that point in my life, I had never had a conversation with a black person. Blacks were not welcome where we lived. At the end of the afternoon, we all held hands in a circle. I was next to Mr. Hardy. I looked at our hands together, two shades of the same skin. There was no more physical difference between us than a brown egg produced by a brown chicken and a white egg produced by a white chicken. I don't know any white people who demand to know if the cooked eggs on their plate came from a brown or white shell. It's ludicrous. Our differences lay in our cultural history, in the way one of us had exploited and oppressed the other. Color is a convenient means of profiling people, and I couldn't help thinking that if people all over the world would simply do what we were doing, what a different world it would be.

OUR NETWORK of like-minded and dedicated friends expanded throughout this period. Our new friends Patrick and Rosemarie opened their home to us. Together we shared new ideas and had deep conversations. The music they made accompanied our commitment to building on our faith in action. Patrick and Rosemary had just cut a record geared to young people about changing social values and appreciating the benefits of living a simple Christian life. Pat was an artist and composer. He played the guitar and Rosemarie sang.

We were spending the evening at their home, a small group of Catholic activists sitting on the floor in the sunroom of their auspicious old house, searching our souls for our place in the movement. Father Cunningham occasionally attended our evening discussions. Our distinguished gray-haired "grandfather," Father Berg, who had been by Father Cunningham's side in Selma, was a regular. He was warm and gentle, with a hint of dry Irish wit that enlivened our conversations. Father Casimir Paulsen, a young and restless Mariannhill missionary, also joined us regularly.

"I'll be transferred to South Africa soon," said Father Cas, as we called him, "to a place where apartheid is the law. My job will be to spread Christianity. I'm not sure how I can work within the law and still be a Christian. It's keeping me awake nights."

I saw Patrick pick up his guitar and look at Rosemarie. "Try this," Pat said to Father Cas, tuning his guitar. He began to strum the chords to "Easy Come, Easy Go." Rosemarie moved next to Pat, her long black hair glistening in the candlelight, her black eyes beaming with pleasure.

"Let me tell you a story," Pat said strumming. "Rosemarie and I were on a trip in the Allegheny Mountains when we passed a hitchhiker alone on a mountain road. 'Did you see what I saw?' I asked her. 'A man holding a lamb? Let's go back.' And we did. The guy was traveling the country with a lamb wrapped in his poncho," Pat said incredulously. "We picked him up and listened to his story. He told us that he gave up his worldly possessions to live as a wanderer on the road for Christ. Perhaps he was Christ, who knows? Our wanderer inspired this song."

Pat began strumming, and Rosemarie picked up the lines: "Easy come, easy go, in winter and in snow. Up and down all around this universe we go."

We spent many evenings in Pat and Rosemarie's living room, lights dim, candlelight reflecting off the gold frames of Pat's many oil paintings, listening to his musical compositions. "Here's a new one I'm working on," Patrick would say.

Father Cunningham watched over his flock, offering us a community of support for our work. Father's efforts were having a particular effect on me, opening my eyes to the practice of my faith when many contradictions were on my mind. I was noticing that my ideas on womanhood and marriage were rapidly changing, while my responsibilities as a wife and mother did not. This inner turmoil was complicating my life. I was beginning to believe that the Church was mistreating women, but the thought of such widespread abuse in the name of God was frightening. It was true that the Catholic Church viewed women much as they were seen in the Middle Ages, when women were baby machines producing workers for the fields. As a woman, I was beginning to realize how not only the world but especially my church had misused me as a human being.

There was more: I began to understand that the Catholic Church was the province of men. Women's voices were unfairly silenced, belittled. In marriage, women promised to obey their husbands, who were keeping them "barefoot in the winter." Of course, there were times when I was feeling overburdened and distraught, when my new self failed me. In these times, I fell back into thinking that I was weak and inferior. What would happen if no one scrubbed the hearth or educated the children? What would become of them? I was searching for my place in a world that was wobbling on its axis. Who was I anyway? I didn't even recognize myself. In my new circle of friends, I was beginning to feel loved and recognized as a human being. Was that so wrong?

I loved my children. I couldn't imagine life without every one of them. I wanted to raise my children on solid ground, not only because of my obligation to God but also because I wanted my children to have good and full lives and to be happy. In so many ways, I was privileged. How could I complain? Yet I felt compelled to extend myself in other ways. I knew some of the questions, but I didn't yet know the answers. And I needed to discover my own self-worth. Surely, I was worthy.

I was forming a new vision of my spirituality. I wanted to become active, not just a passive believer on my knees praying for forgiveness for some mundane fault. I needed to demonstrate my faith in action. I now believed that Christ was alive in everyone, and that belief was beckoning me to act.

The retreats with Father Cunningham and the new, dynamic circle of friends and allies began to propel each of us, and, like a breeze that blows through an open window, we felt free to make decisions about how to practice our faith. Without permission, we planned an open-air Mass for our families in the Orchard Lake area, in a space generously provided by a priest from our retreats.

I promised to bake unleavened bread that we could use for communion services. The children watched me shape the dough.

I talked about communion as I worked. They took turns holding a saucer while I cut the dough into a round shape to make a host that could be held up for the participants to see. The boys quickly reappeared when the buzzer rang to take it out of the oven.

"I thought it was supposed to be white," Greg said. Slim and blessed with his father's head of blond, wavy hair, Greg was never still. He was bold and funny and loved to live life on the edge. Even at six years old, he was our little adventurer.

"It looks like regular bread to me," offered his five-year-old brother, Jeff. "It's just flat." Jeff was a gentle child with straight sandy-brown hair and a more robust build, like my dad's father. More relaxed in his manner than his brothers, Jeff was sensitive to others' needs and profoundly generous.

"Can we taste some?" they asked in chorus.

"Nope," I answered. "This bread has a special purpose: it's for Sunday Mass."

"Can we have some then?"

"Only those who have made their first communion," I said, thinking that I should put this loaf out of reach of little fingers.

Unfortunately, our joyous Orchard Lake ceremonies were short-lived. We were told to desist in our unorthodox activities. The reaction of the traditional Church against our newfound freedoms was having an impact felt throughout the wider Catholic community. As the Church pushed back, many priests and nuns left their church assignments to become actively involved in the civil rights movement, some to marry and raise families. Like them, I was beginning to question the faith that had been the foundation of my life.

DURING THIS PERIOD of growth and questioning, I found that I was pregnant with my sixth child. When I told my mother, she didn't share my happiness.

"Joann, what are you doing to yourself," she asked. "Why do you think I had only two children?" Mother's tone was curt, and it sliced through me.

I didn't answer the question. I wasn't unhappy about this

pregnancy. Despite my parents' distance and unwillingness to be of help all these years, I felt supported and had friends in our church circle who cared about me.

My new pregnancy was different, and I was not ill. But our small house was bursting at the seams, and Don's and my relationship was disintegrating. It seemed like the more social interaction we had, the more dissatisfied I became with our marriage. He was having a great time with all our interesting new friends—we both were—but it wasn't improving the slog at home. Maybe it wasn't Don I was angry with; maybe it was my plight as a woman in the Catholic Church.

Christine was born in October 1966. I was twenty-nine years old and had six children. Then God sent me a friend.

Deacon Jim, who served at our church, was training to be a priest and counselor. About twenty-five years old, his large frame and smiling eyes were topped by a head of light blond hair and just as sunny a disposition. He was the kind of guy to whom anyone could tell their troubles. We first met when he brought me communion in the hospital the Sunday after Christine's birth. After I was released from the hospital, he began to stop by regularly to chat with Don and me. The three of us became friends, and he became known to us, simply, as Jim. The children adored him.

As we began to plan our new baby's christening ceremony, Jim brought her a tiny white embroidered gown, accented with delicate lace trim and streaming white ribbons. I was joyful at this new life who had been given to us. As I looked at her tiny face in all its angelic innocence, responsibility for another life tugged at my heartstrings, but at the moment I felt strong. I was beginning to know myself and to respect my own voice. I had come to understand that when a child depends on me, I feel strong, but when a man depends on me for things he can do perfectly well himself, I get angry.

When the day arrived, Father Cunningham baptized little Chrissy. He, with Patrick and Rosemarie, presented me with a big rocking chair in which to rock her to sleep. My father and my sister were godparents. My mother and her sisters joined us for dinner. It was a blessed day.

Jim was a trusted friend who continued to stop over often. We talked about all manner of things that I had never shared with anyone before. I explored a lot of feelings about marriage, raising a family, and the world. Since his role as a priest would be to counsel couples, it was an opportunity for him to learn about marriage.

We enjoyed an equal relationship. I was the ready student and he was the teacher and coach, and then we switched. My talks with Jim filled me with self-confidence. I was ready and eager to come back into the world. It snapped me out of the malaise of a downtrodden wife. His ready laugh and upbeat disposition were contagious. Coming from a large family, he knew what my life was like. He was unlike any priest I had ever met.

One day, Jim was at our door.

"Want some coffee," I asked.

"I just came to ask you something." I motioned to a seat at our kitchen table. He sat facing the outside window, his face eager to share his question.

"I'm planning a conference at the seminary," he began. Jim was in his last year of training for the priesthood at St. John's Seminary, the graduate-level training college for Catholic priests in the Detroit area. Next year, he would be ordained and assigned to a parish.

"The topic is 'Women and Love,'" he said. He looked at me for a reaction. "I'd like you to speak."

I was thinking of all the conversations we'd had. I was pretty sure that I could adapt the general tone of those to a larger audience: stress, babies, changing ideas about love, disillusionment, physical exhaustion, and trying to find yourself when obligations take precedence over the healing you desperately need.

"By the way, I've also asked Sister Agnes from the school," he said. "You'd be on the program together . . . Many of the guys don't have the opportunity to talk with women," he added, not yet knowing what my response would be. "By next year, we'll be in parishes counseling and hearing confessions." He laughed. "They don't teach us about marriage or women in our classes."

THE BELL TOWER of the auspicious redbrick seminary could be seen from a distance as Sister Agnes and I exited the freeway. We turned into a wide expanse of rolling green hills and small ponds. The square tower projected a heavy masculinity as it reached for the sky above the trees and flowers on the sculptured grounds.

The resplendent chapel had rich stained-glass windows and a wide marble floor with pews on either side that lead to the altar, which was framed by a huge organ. Walking to the gymnasium where we would speak, Jim paused at a wide doorway and with a formal sweeping gesture at the door frame said, "You, my ladies, are the first women to cross the cloistered threshold in the history of the seminary."

I thought of Pope John, who had instructed us to open the windows of the Church, and here we were boldly stepping through the door. Were we going too far?

In the gym I noted sixty or so priests in training. They were seated around the wide gleaming floor of the basketball court. In the center of the floor were two folding chairs and a microphone. Jim opened the session then motioned for me. I had prepared my remarks on the topic of love and marriage, mustering the best attitude I could about the day-to-day struggle of maintaining a relationship while juggling the demands of work and family.

As Jim handed me the microphone, it crossed my mind that it was dishonest of me to agree to speak on this topic. I really didn't know a lot about love, other than that I was still seeking it. My life was more about obligation.

"I'm afraid I don't know a lot about love," I began, surprised that I was not giving my prepared talk. "Women are raised with the idea that love is romantic," I continued. "You'll be kissed by a prince and live happily ever after. But life gets in the way. Instead, life offers us crying babies, unending meals to be cooked, dirty clothes, ironing boards, sick kids, and demands for sex even when we're exhausted. There's never a moment to find ourselves or to get a grasp on who we really are. I'm certain that you'll encounter a number of distressed women during the course of your work."

I ended with a caution: "You need to keep in mind that women are not getting a fair deal in their marriages or from their church."

When I finished, I handed the microphone to Sister Agnes, a third-grade teacher at our parish school.

"I know about love," she confessed, "because I'm in love with a priest in our parish."

Even I was shocked. Sister talked for a few minutes about how love was fulfilling her life. Suddenly, someone shouted out, "Why are we listening to this nonsense? Since when do we need women to tell us about life?"

There was a rumble in the crowd in response to the interruption. I noticed the protestor was a young black seminarian, the only black person in the room. I had to think about his reaction. Perhaps he disagreed with changes in the Church; perhaps he craved stability; or perhaps he was in love and didn't want to admit it to himself. Then another thought came to my mind: perhaps we really had no business being here. The session was terminated.

RACIAL TENSION WAS PALPABLE IN DETROIT. Around 1966, Father Cunningham proposed a radical idea, an outreach program for white families from suburban parishes to meet and become acquainted with black families from Catholic parishes in the city.

Father wasn't timid in his ideas. It took guts to imagine that blacks would be willing to go into white neighborhoods and knock on someone's door. Conversely, it was also dangerous for whites to go wandering around black neighborhoods where they might not be welcome. But Father was firm in his belief that if people of different races got to know each other, they would see beyond color. Because of his charismatic personality and marketing skills, Father Bill was successful in many things that others could not pull off.

This was no Archie Bunker versus George Jefferson script but a meaningful reaching out. The people who volunteered did so out of the earnest belief that it could make a difference. The effort was announced from the pulpits in Catholic churches. Suburban and city parishes were matched up, and families signed up for the reciprocal visits.

On the appointed day, a group of three young black nuns came to our house in Taylor. I was disappointed because I had hoped to receive a family with children who could play with mine. After I thought about it I understood that that had not been a very realistic hope. These young nuns were barely more than girls and looked like missionaries in their black habits and veils.

It was a beautiful warm, sunny day. We had tea and cookies, and my children brought toys to share. The next thing I knew, the nuns were eagerly joining the kids in play then getting a tour of their rooms. After our visit, we lingered outside, chatting and laughing, in full view of our Taylor neighbors. After the nuns visited our home, the rumors began to swirl. A neighbor phoned to ask if we were selling our house.

When it was our turn, we visited a family in the Cathedral parish in Detroit's North End neighborhood. The address led us to a neat little white house with shingled siding and a covered front porch that sported two red metal chairs, perfect for engaging with neighbors or watching the afternoon traffic. A middle-aged man rose from one of the chairs to greet us.

"Please come inside," he said, "we've been waiting for you."

Our host introduced himself as Benny. As we stepped over the threshold, he told us, "I want you to know that you're the first white people ever to enter our home, and you're welcome here anytime."

"Thank you for hosting us," I said as the men shook hands. "This is also a first for us, as we've never been in a black home before. We're so glad to meet you."

I looked around and felt comfortable. There was a calendar with a black Jesus on the wall in the dining room and a picture of President Kennedy on the far wall. There were photos of children in small frames on tables that were covered with neat white linen doilies. I asked about the photos.

"Grandchildren?" I inquired. Then I moved to a family group photo: "Tell us who these people are."

Benny stood next to me pointing out people in the photo. "These are my two sons and their kids. This is my daughter. She recently left home. She moved south to Georgia and lives with my sister. She hopes someday to go to college."

We took seats that were offered and began a conversation about our families and the parish-to-parish program that Father Cunningham had begun.

"I think it's a great idea," Benny said. "It's a bad time now, and there's a lot of tension. This helps. We need to see beyond our fears. Father Cunningham, he's a great man."

We wholeheartedly agreed.

Father Cunningham's program to reach out and meet our city parish neighbors happened over a relatively short time, but the results were lasting. The goal of the program was to reduce fear and build friendships that could have an ongoing effect on our lives. I know those who participated were changed by their experience.

Eleanor and Don Josaitis were the first of Father Cunningham's Taylor followers to decide they wanted to move out of the suburbs and into the city. Eleanor was now working with Father Bill to develop a program to combat hunger in the city. She and her husband put a down payment on a home on West Boston Boulevard near Father Bill's father's house, where Father Bill had an office. The home Eleanor and her husband chose was a grand old house in a once beautiful neighborhood that had been abandoned by white flight. It had three floors, thirteen rooms, three fireplaces, a library, and a huge backyard. The land was first deeded in the late 1800s, at the time of the great fire in Detroit.

Eleanor and Don's plans were thrown into crisis when Don's older brother and business partner threatened to sever Don's role in the family business if they went through with the move. He claimed to be protecting his brother's children. Eleanor's mother threatened legal action to take their children away.

When the Josaitises were forced to abandon their plans and were about to lose their down payment, it occurred to me that the city was the perfect place to raise our six children in a "real world" microcosm, observing different classes, races, and cultures. I wanted them to be citizens of the world, to understand people other than themselves, and to make decisions about their lives in that context. I was impassioned about this opportunity. Yes, I knew that my kids would be among a handful of white kids in the parish school, but kids are generally open-minded; surely they would develop friendships no matter where we lived. Besides, our current house was only about seven hundred square feet, with tiny rooms. The four boys were sleeping foot to foot on a stacked set of bunk beds.

Don had no family to object, and my parents were so uninvolved in my life, I didn't believe that it would matter to them. Besides, my mother and dad were in the process of purchasing their first-ever home of their own. They were pretty excited and caught up in getting ready to move.

In the city, with a big house to share, perhaps I could take in foster children. In essence, I believe I was seeking a way to make a valuable contribution to the world. Foster child care was something that I could do at home and still take care of my kids. I longed to do something bigger with my life, something beyond my obligations. I also thought a bigger space might reduce some pressure and improve our marriage.

I expressed these thoughts during one of our gatherings at Pat and Rosemarie's home. We were discussing the Josaitises' potential loss of their down payment when I heard myself saying, "I wish there was some way that we could buy the house. I want my kids to grow up in a real-world environment. We're bursting our seams as it is . . . Anyway," I said, my voice dropping, "I would really like to be in the city."

It was silent for a moment then Father Berg quietly responded. "I'll loan you the money, if that's what you really want to do. You can pay me back over time."

I looked at Don. It wasn't like we hadn't talked about moving to the city. As it was, we were already spending a lot of time there visiting Patrick and Rosemarie. We admired the way they lived so simply in that big old house with their family.

"I can do that," Don said thoughtfully. It was an enormous decision we made in that moment. So the Josaitises got their down payment money back, and we got the house. My heart leaped. Patrick and Rosemarie lived a block farther down our same street. Bill Cunningham's father had a home at the end of the new block where we would move, and he served as our real estate broker. We would continue to stay in touch with Mr. Cunningham over the years after we moved to Detroit.

We also had friends among the priests and nuns in the city who were committed to the cause. My deacon friend, Jim, had transferred to the cathedral after being ordained. We would have a community ready and waiting for us.

One day, as we were preparing to close on our new home, I was in the area and drove past one of Patrick and Rosemarie's teenage sons walking down the block with his arm around a young black girl. I startled, suddenly overcome by a blast of fear that I had gone too far. I felt a pain that started in my chest and ended with a thud in my gut. What had I done? Did I have a right to bring my children into the fray? Was this the right thing to do? My compulsion to do more in the broader world would have consequences in the lives of my children. While I sought to add dimension to their lives, I was realizing that I could complicate their lives in other ways, ways that could ultimately include interracial relationships.

I worried occasionally that the children would not be able to run free and play. I looked at my seven-month-old in her stroller and thought carefully about the step we were taking. Would she be able to play outside safely, to develop freely, to reach her potential? What about my children's education? Would life in the city limit my children or spur their growth and maturity? Was a suburban life and perspective the only norm by which success was judged? Was I thinking only of myself? I buried these thoughts next to my unshakable resolve, never dreaming that I would be the first in my family to have an interracial relationship.

PART TWO

Rebellions

THE 1967 DETROIT REBELLION

The most dangerous creation of any society
is the man who has nothing to lose.
—JAMES BALDWIN

SPRING BLOOMED IN MAY 1967 as it had every other year, but this was not going to be like any other year for us. Once the house on West Boston Boulevard was officially ours, we packed up our belongings and departed Taylor. We took the I-94 freeway downtown and then switched to the Lodge, moving right to exit at Hamilton-Clairmount, where we shed the safety of the highway and followed the surface streets to our new neighborhood.

As we approached our new home, I took it all in. It was a three-story Dutch-style brick-and-stucco colonial, painted gray with little white shutters. Its history reminded me of a storybook I used to read to the children. It had been built as a large farmhouse, surviving the decades during which the city grew up around it. The original front and back porches had been enlarged and enclosed, and big front windows had been added to better conform with the stately neighborhood, which once housed the auto barons—the Fisher, Briggs, and Dodge families. Few vestiges of that long-lost neighborhood were left.

What remained was the broad green island planted with stately elms and shorter birch and blossom trees that officially made the street a boulevard. An inviting long brick sidewalk with asymmetrical steps led to the front porch of the house. There were stoops on either side of the porch steps, perfect for sitting outside to enjoy the shade provided by the beautiful elm trees. When we arrived, our new home looked like a big hug. I hoped that was a good omen.

We had been settled for less than two months when my high school friend Barbara, her husband, Jerry, and their two small children came to spend the night. They had just sold their family's inner-city home and were moving out of state. Their former house on the near East Side was in the neighborhood of the Kercheval incident, a small but significant civil uprising in 1966. As urban renewal took its toll, poor blacks living in deplorable conditions lashed out in response to the glass-walled, upscale high-rises emerging from the bulldozed landscape of their communities and the Tactical Mobile Police Units that patrolled their streets. As Father Cunningham had warned us in his sermon, "They know not what they do." Kercheval 1966 was the first sign that all was not well in Detroit. While I was counting my blessings, my friends were eager to escape the city. They were heading to the West Coast, not yet sure where they were going to land.

Sunday afternoon, July 23, 1967, was sunny and peaceful. I'd heard the bells in the cathedral tower ring out the Angelus at noon. Standing in the kitchen, I gazed out the back screen door and reveled in the good fortune that had brought us to our new home. Though it had been hot for the past few days, there was a breeze stirring the full leaves on the trees surrounding our house. The spires of our new parish, only a block away, were visible through the swaying branches. The people who lived here before us had planted a circular rose garden in the yard, edged with raspberry bushes. Daylilies lined the side of the garage. What an amazing space for kids to grow and play. And what a contrast it was to the just-beneath-the-surface racial tensions in the surrounding neighborhood. Racial tensions were on the rise in many urban cities around the country. Police were cracking down everywhere, and Detroit was no exception. Looking back, I realize how insulated and intoxicated we were in our bubble of white privilege.

The children—my five oldest and Barbara's two young boys—were all playing in the yard. Baby Chrissy was upstairs having a nap. Suddenly, the children's voices changed. They were rushing around the yard, squealing and grabbing something out of the air. As I approached the back door, I could see them excitedly chasing small bits of charred paper that were falling into the yard. When I walked outside, I could smell smoke. To the west of us, the sky was completely black. Then I heard the sirens and realized that something big in the nearby neighborhood was on fire.

The smell of smoke was becoming heavy. We took the children inside and sent them upstairs to play. I steeled myself. No one knew what to expect. Don slipped outside and turned the car around in the driveway so it was facing the street ready to make a quick getaway, should that be necessary. When he tried to get some news on the radio, we discovered there was a news blackout.

Unbeknownst to us, the conflagration had started in the early-morning hours of Sunday when police raided an after-hours club at 12th Street and Clairmount, fewer than ten blocks from our home. Raids on this social club happened often, but this time, according to Thomas J. Sugrue, in his foreword to the book *Detroit 1967*, "The police officer who directed the raid decided to arrest all eighty-five people present." By four o'clock in the morning, a large crowd had gathered outside, and there were shouted allegations of police brutality; tempers rose, and bottles and rocks were thrown. Black residents pushed to the edge by ongoing police violence, economic depression, and social marginalization soon took their anger and frustration into the streets. Looting began. Fires were lit. The social rage, pent up for so long, became a bellows stoking the literal and figurative fires in the community. By four o'clock in the afternoon, the flames were engulfing the entire vibrant heart of the 12th Street community . . . and spreading.

"Let's fix dinner," I said as cheerily as possible, and everyone fell to the task. I put chicken in the oven to bake. "Barb, can you make a salad?"

"Sure." The look on her face was tentative, but she moved to the refrigerator, lifted out the salad greens, and started to chop vegetables. Jerry was wandering about looking agitated, his mouth voicelessly forming words, his arms involuntarily moving in unexpected directions but he said nothing.

I caught Don as he left the kitchen and spoke quietly. "Can you take Jerry somewhere and talk with him," I asked. "Calm him down."

Like sailors preparing for a storm, we put together a meal and called the children down to eat, avoiding talk of an impending disaster in front of them. Somehow, we got through dinner and shooed the children out of the kitchen and upstairs to play once more. Then we soberly sat down to discuss our situation. Riots had taken place in other cities over the past few summers. Newark had been on fire just five days before. Our friends had sold their house because racial unrest had erupted in their East Side neighborhood the past two summers and they had been living in fear.

Don left the table to try again to get some news. There was only music on the local stations. Jerry's agitation grew, and he was unable to sit still in his chair. I was struggling to stay calm in the face of his anxiety. At first, our conversation was thoughtful and controlled. But then Jerry lost it. He sprang up and moved quickly to our kitchen window. A stream of racial epithets burst from him.

I knew I had to take control. This was *our* house. I couldn't let this happen.

"Motherfucking animals," he was screaming. "Monkeys . . . idiots!"

"Stop!" I leaped to the window, fearful that he would be heard. "Stop," I cried again as I slammed the window shut against the hot summer night. My emotions were overflowing—fear of what was happening only blocks away and rage at Jerry's behavior were twisted around each other. It was hard to identify which I was feeling at any particular moment.

"You may not speak such language in our house," I said, placing my face directly in front of his, my voice controlled so he couldn't escape my words. "Your language invites violence—and I will not have it in my house! Do you understand? You'll endanger all of us."

"Jerry, don't lose your cool," Barbara said, and took him by the hand. "We're going upstairs." She led him out of the room.

I was seething. I didn't know where Don had gone. I was afraid of Jerry's uncontrolled anger. And the children were calling; I could hear urgency in Greg's voice: "Mom, what's going on?"

The kids understood that something bad was happening. How could I explain it when I didn't understand it myself? I left the kitchen, dishes undone, to settle the children in bed.

"What's happening, Mom?" Greg asked again as I made it to the top of the stairs. Barbara and Jerry were settling their children on the sleeping porch at the back of the second floor. My kids were huddled in the upstairs hall.

"Into your beds now, my kiddies. It's time to get some zzz's." I tried to be lighthearted and ease their fears.

I knelt down next to Greg's bed, rubbing his temple in a soothing gesture I had found effective in calming the children.

"We don't know yet," I offered, "but we're together and we'll be fine."

I kissed them all and tucked them in, going from room to room to assure they were comforted. My voice was calm, but my insides were bursting with confusion and fear. I was grateful once they were all asleep.

We struggled to get information about what was going on. We didn't have a working television, and the reports coming over the radio were vague. We were largely in the dark about the extent of what was going on around us.

Later that evening, an unfamiliar car pulled up in our driveway. Don watched it with some trepidation until he recognized Deacon Dennie Moloney getting out. Dennie was a small-framed, tough, and tenacious red-haired Irish guy who had grown up in the city. We had met him just a few days before at a party in Detroit's downtrodden Cass Corridor. "I know your place," he'd ventured when we were introduced. "I know the folks who live next door to you." I thought he seemed like a down-to-earth guy.

We never dreamed we would connect again so soon.

Yet here he was, standing on our porch. The neighborhood air was dense with smoke and it was increasingly difficult to breathe outside; the sound of sirens was relentless. Don and I invited Dennie inside, and we settled at the kitchen table.

Dennie relaxed for a moment and then began to tell the story of how he had ended up on our doorstep. "My family has a home on Dexter Boulevard at Montgomery," he began. "I hope we have a home," he added wearily, his voice trailing off. "That's where I grew up; my mother and my younger brothers still live there. The area has been hit by police gunfire and snipers as well as raging fires. My mom called to say that she and the kids were headed to my uncle's cottage north of the city, leaving their home vacant."

I prepared a cup of coffee and set it on the table in front of him. "After I finished my work this afternoon at my St. Clair Shores parish," he continued, "I decided to drive to the old neighborhood, hoping to look after the family home. As I approached the city, I could see that the smoke-filled sky over Detroit was being fed by ten or fifteen plumes of fire rising over areas of the city, mostly on the West Side. That's where our home is."

We listened attentively as Dennie continued: "I decided to approach Dexter Boulevard from the south. As I turned northwest onto Grand River, I encountered a scene that was the stuff of nightmares. Whole blocks were engulfed in flames. Hundreds of looters, both white and black, were on the streets. Glass and debris were everywhere. Firemen trying to reach the inferno were being pelted with rocks and bricks."

My mind was racing as I tried to assess what kind of danger were we in as well as understand what Dennie was going through. His story moved relentlessly on. "All around me, the raging flames spewed black smoke skyward, blotting out the remaining sunlight. The heat from the flames was so hot, I had to drive on the wrong side of the street, away from the burning buildings, just to pass. My stomach was weak by then.

"And reaching our home proved impossible. Police had already closed off Dexter ahead of the curfew. I tried to get to the block from another direction. Block after block it was the same: stores, homes, community businesses—all in flames. It was just impossible to get through."

"I was feeling such a sense of dread, and worry about our home. Night was falling and the curfew was in effect. I was running out of options. Then I remembered you guys and where you lived, and I just headed here."

"You are so welcome to stay," I told him that I found it comforting to have more people in our home that night. Dennie would also be close to his neighborhood. I felt less isolated and alone as I adopted the position that there was safety in numbers.

I thought to pray, but somehow, I didn't think that God was going to change the minds of the enraged young people in the streets and influence them to accept their fate. I prayed instead that I would find the wisdom, the courage, and the foresight to make good decisions that would keep my family safe.

Throughout the night, we listened to the sound of gunshots ring out. I was startled initially and forced to consider the seriousness of our situation. I had never heard real gunshots before. At first, I tried to convince myself that it was something else. But really, I knew. The enormity of our situation was overwhelming. I hardly knew how to think about it.

Don and I talked until late into the night. It was reassuring to have him there. He was capable of handling stressful situations. Finally, restless and exhausted from emotion and fear, I slept.

DETROIT FREE PRESS, MONDAY, JULY 24, 1967:
"Mobs Burn and Loot 800 Stores; Troops Move In; Emergency Is On"; "Looter Killed, 724 Held as Riot Spreads"

When we woke in the morning, my friend Barbara and her family were gone. I never heard from them again. Dennie announced that he was going to volunteer at the fire station near his home and left in his car. We were alone once more.

Later in the day, Father Al, a good-natured but nervous priest friend of Don's from our suburban parish, was at our door, knocking with some urgency. He looked as if he needed a cup of coffee, which I quickly prepared. He seemed relieved to finally wrap his hands around the warm mug.

"I volunteered," he began. "I've been over to Visitation parish all day, and I need a place to sleep nearby. I have to return to the parish in the morning." I assured him he could stay with us.

"We need news—what's happening? How bad is it now?" I asked him. My questions came all at once.

"The area where the fires began is totally disrupted. Snipers are on top of buildings, shooting at police and firemen. The anger is contagious, and it's still spreading," he said. "Supplies are coming into the area in an effort to get people off the streets and back into their homes. I'm working with a distribution center to get families basic necessities like milk, canned goods, baby formula, and diapers; to address the portion of looting that's related to legitimate need."

It was a job that suited him. Al was chatty, able to connect with others through his self-effacing laugh, his priestly collar, and his good heart. His manner was strangely endearing. He was both qualified and uniquely comfortable with the process, something that few whites would have been able to pull off.

He paused, laughing in a self-conscious way before continuing. "You won't believe what they've asked me to do. I'm supposed to go into people's homes to check their cupboards and refrigerators to make sure that they're not hoarding, that they really need the things they're asking for."

Father seemed to be struggling to explain, to himself as well as to us: "Well, you can't just let people walk away with stuff and then not have enough to go around to those who really need it. I went to one lady's home today and had to turn her down."

Throughout the day, the boys ran around the house playing "riot," as it was being identified on the radio, never tiring of the droning sounds of sirens. We were destined to make our way through this crisis dependent solely on our radio for news. I'm convinced now that seeing the visuals in real time might have been much more frightening and disturbing to the children.

Don heard that a child peering out a window had been shot dead by a sniper. We pulled Christine's baby crib away from the window and told Jeff to move from the top bunk in his room and, for the time being, sleep with Michael on the bottom.

In between hearing bits of news and trying to keep the children occupied inside, I noticed something else: the bells in the cathedral tower lay silent.

DETROIT FREE PRESS, TUESDAY, JULY 25, 1967:
"Paratroopers Roll into Riot Areas as Gun Battles and Looting Spread; 14 Killed; Damage $150 Million," "LBJ Approves All-Out Drive to End Strife"

An article appeared in the newspaper Tuesday morning: Angry blacks, it said, were targeting homes on Boston Boulevard for attack. Up to that point, the violence and looting had been on the other side of the freeway. Our immediate neighborhood had been spared. We had remained alert, weary, and concerned; now fear became part of the equation.

Don and Patrick had a conversation, and the men made a decision: Rosemarie and I, along with all the kids, were to leave. But how? Why? I didn't want to leave my home.

Then our phone rang. It was a neighbor from back in Taylor. I didn't know these people well; they had moved in next door to us shortly before we moved away. She said she'd been seeing the news of what was going on in Detroit and thought of us. They were on vacation out east—did we need a place to stay? She could tell us where the spare key was . . .

It was amazing that they would think of us. Perhaps this was divine intervention. I hadn't talked with them since we'd moved. Though I was reluctant to leave, I didn't want to refuse a God-sent offer. Yet leaving nagged at me. It just didn't feel like the right thing to do.

"I don't want to leave my home," I told Don emotionally. "How could we possibly take enough clothes and supplies for all the children? Baby bottles? With Rosemarie and her kids, there'll be nine children and two adults. That's eleven people, in a tiny house. This is nuts!"

I was pacing, rubbing my own temples this time, and twisting my hair. I was torn. I was fearful of staying, but it was not in my nature to run away.

Dusk was falling when Rosemarie appeared at our door. I was still dragging my feet, but it was clear that the men were not going to relent. Rosemarie was driving their Volkswagen van, and her kids were in the van waiting. There was no time for preparations; we just grabbed our pajamas and piled in.

There was discontent among the packed-in crew, especially Rosemarie and Patrick's older boys. Rosemarie was having none of it.

"You kids shut up in the back," she scolded them. "You have no choice."

My children were a little younger. I was watching them. They were quiet, inhaling the strangeness and feeling insecure. I needed to mind my words so as not to inflate their fears.

Rosemarie was a city girl and unflappable in the face of urban distress. We were both upset that we had been sent from our homes. I had to admit that I had some apprehension about the drive because there were rumors of cars of blacks on the freeways heading toward the suburbs.

"Look around us," Rosemarie said as we surveyed the highways. "The roads are deserted. Does this make any sense?"

Had we become unwitting pawns in panicked white flight? Our husbands' fears, stoked by the media's nightmarish portrayal of exaggerated black threat, confirmed the effectiveness of the Armageddon propaganda. It made me question our position. White families always had the option to leave Detroit for an outpost of suburban whiteness. But where could our frightened black neighbors flee? Where could they go?

White suburbanites huddled at the edges of the city, even farther from the actual unrest, steeped in their worst assumptions and prejudices. My friend Eleanor Josaitis would later describe the paranoid mood back in Taylor. Vigilante groups were proposed to stand guard on the overpasses, lying in wait for the hordes of black rioters who never arrived. Eleanor said she was told to learn how to shoot a gun, and to stock her basement with food in preparation for more rioting, which was sure to come. "You turned on the television and thought you were in some foreign country that was on fire," she later wrote.

As Rosemarie and I continued along the empty highway on our way to Taylor, it became clear that our place was back home, where we had a community—a mixed community of blacks and whites that was solidly united. Our neighbors watched over us, and we watched over them.

"Let's go home first thing in the morning," I suggested to Rosemarie.

"My thoughts exactly," she replied. After this experience, I vowed never again to allow the media—or any man—to overwhelm my gut instincts.

We had a terrible night. It was a small house, and the kids were sleeping on the floor with any blankets we could find. We didn't have enough food to satisfy them, and Rosemarie's older son was constantly whining. My kids didn't sleep well, and Chrissy, who was just nine months old, cried in tune with everyone else's discontent. In the morning, we fed the kids cereal and milk, piled them back in Rosemary's van, and drove home.

DETROIT FREE PRESS, WEDNESDAY, JULY 26, 1967: "New Gun Battles Shatter Riot Truce; Troopers Seal Off Nests of Snipers; Death Toll Grows; Copters Called In," "2,600 Jailed; New Riots Hit Outstate Area"

During this period, our neighbors and the clergy who stopped by filled us in on what was happening on the ground—sometimes offering their own unique takes.

Mr. Siegel, our eccentric, aging next-door neighbor and a well-to-do entrepreneur, began producing and selling T-shirts that read **SOUL BROTHER**. He claimed that he had ordered a truckload of guns for us to protect ourselves, but the truck was commandeered and the guns confiscated. Mr. Siegel was a hapless storyteller, and we never quite knew how much of what he said was true. But if there was one thing I didn't want responsibility for, it was a gun.

Far more in the know were our neighbors across the street—Phil Gordon and his brother, Lincoln. It was Phil who kept us truly informed.

Phil, a tall, friendly man with a pocked face, worked for the National Association for the Advancement of Colored People (NAACP), where he was responsible for keeping an eye on the neighborhood. He walked every day, all day, taking the pulse of the streets. As a community ambassador, he was tasked with talking to folks, making friends with young people, and reporting his findings to his agency. When the disturbance broke out and others were fleeing, Phil walked toward it to learn what was going on.

Don noticed him returning home after one of his rounds, and we went outside looking for an update.

"The area is cordoned off," he said. "One of the cops recognized me and called me by name. 'Hey, Phil,' he said, 'what are you doing on the outside? Why aren't you in here, helping us corral these young bucks? We need you to get in here and reason with these jerks.'"

Phil knew a lot of young people involved in the violence. He remained inside the barriers all afternoon talking, listening, and advising the young men who were caught up in the fray. Phil was one of the most down-to-earth people I have ever met. He was humble, a good listener, and he saw things that others didn't see.

"It's bad," Phil said. "These young people are angry at the police and their lack of opportunity. They're trapped and they won't listen to reason. They've been pushed too far, and they have nothing to lose."

As the three of us were standing on the boulevard's island, peacefully chatting, a police car slowly pulled alongside us. "Return to your homes; the city is under curfew" came loudly through their megaphone, startling me. "No gathering is permitted."

The cops knew Phil from his community work. He walked

closer to the police car to explain the need for our conversation, but they weren't interested in making exceptions.

It was through these conversations with neighbors that my understanding of what drove the disturbance began to evolve. It was not simply racial. That was what the media accounts would have had us believe: that it was simply the black community lashing out impulsively, which just served to reinforce the idea that what was happening was a riot—that these were simply lawbreakers, troublemakers, "no-good doers." But that was a misconception. In reality, this was an outburst of oppressed people against the police. This was, in fact, a rebellion—against the police, yes, but also against the system that the police protected, a system that denied decent housing, essential services, good jobs, and safe communities to blacks in Detroit. The police were the primary instrument of oppression. It was just a matter of time, though; people can be pushed only so far.

I began to understand that there was a deeper need for social justice that responded to the realities in the black community, justice that considered the plight of blacks at the hands of the dominant race and the law-and-order, racist police who ruled over their communities. The fires rising into the skies signaled that they were done with waiting. They were taking matters into their own hands.

DETROIT FREE PRESS, THURSDAY, JULY 27, 1967:
"New Tactics Flush Out Snipers; Army Chief Feels Battle Is Won," "White Looter Is Killed; Death Toll 36"

By Wednesday, we heard on the radio that the National Guard had been summoned and would soon enter the city. In truth, they were already there. The rumbling of the tanks could be heard as they approached in the darkness. By morning, we adults were quietly watching out our windows as the National Guard took up positions in our community.

The sight of soldiers and tanks on our streets was surreal. For a time, one tank was installed on the front lawn of the elderly next-door neighbors to the west of us, giving their home the over-whelming look of a fortress. As tanks and armored personnel carriers rolled down the streets, we became eyewitnesses to history. The city of Detroit, with soldiers posted on every corner, had become a community under military occupation. I was intent on keeping the children free from worry. I don't believe they really understood what was going on. They were young and don't remember much of this. That is probably a blessing.

In the coming days, order—or, perhaps more correctly, control—was returned to the streets. During this uprising, forty-three people died, most of them shot by the cops and the Michigan National Guard; more than seventy-two hundred people were arrested and incarcerated on our beloved Belle Isle. According to Thomas Sugrue, the police were especially brutal, beating arrestees. In a well-known incident, three police officers raided the city's Algiers Motel and executed three young black men, none of whom were participants in the uprising. Thirteen hundred buildings were burned, and five thousand people were left homeless. Detroit was just one of the many cities where civil disturbances erupted that summer.

Those of us who lived through the uprising emerged stronger and more tightly knit than before. We were part of a network of committed individuals driven by ideals. We were also part of a united neighborhood community of blacks and whites who cared about each other. I believed we were all put together for a purpose.

Finally, the violence subsided. A few days later I opened our drapes to the world, as we attempted to regain a sense of normalcy. While I could again open our windows without fear of being hit by a stray sniper's bullet, without being confronted by the sight of an armed soldier standing at alert in front of a tank on our neighbor's lawn, the world outside had been changed forever—as had I.

I knew I had a role to play in the city's recovery. I just didn't know what it was going to be until I noticed Father Jim coming up the front walk with a young black child about five years old. Eyes wide with curiosity, the little girl looked up at our big house, taking it in, then searched my face inquiringly, assessing, it seemed, if I could be trusted.

"I want you to meet Chandra," Jim said. I opened the door and invited her inside. She stepped gingerly into the front hall. Really, it didn't even take a moment: Chandra was immediately engulfed by my children, and they were off to play games. I noted that Chandra was not at all shy.

"Chandra's mother is in the hospital with a mental breakdown," Jim explained, gazing at me. "They've lost everything. I don't know how long it will be; her mom is completely out of it. The child had been staying with the nuns at St. Theresa's parish, but they told me they can't keep her any longer. I thought, maybe . . ." He grimaced.

He shouldn't have feared. It was natural that he would bring her to us, and natural that we would take her in. This was why we had moved here, to help where help was needed.

BEFORE TOO LONG, Father Jim stopped in again to check on Chandra. "How's she doing?" he asked.

"Everything's fine," I said brightly. "She just runs along with everyone else. She's eating and sleeping well. She's sharing the big bed with Carolyn in the girls' room. I think she's having a good time."

Jim sat down at the kitchen table as Don joined us.

"I think it's important that you apply for a foster care license," he said. "That would protect you legally, in case any issues come up. It looks like her mother will be in the hospital for a while. There'll be a court hearing about her mother's competence. If you're going to keep her, we need to have things in order."

"I'm happy to keep her," I said without hesitation.

"Why don't you make an appointment," Don said, looking at me. "Pick up the paperwork, and I'll sign whatever I have to and you can send it back."

That sounded like a plan.

Catholic Social Services was just two blocks from our house. I applied for a foster care license to keep Chandra with our family. I felt good, realizing this was one more step forward in my longing to do more in the world, the life I wanted to live. Chandra was the first of many children to come with us. Our house was getting full. My activism was fueled by my belief that I could make a difference by helping to keep the struggle for equality alive. I was still carrying Viola's baton.

IN THE EARLY MONTHS AFTER THE REBELLION, social activities in the broader neighborhood ceased. People stayed close to home. Our house, our yard, our church, and our neighbors were the foundation for our physical and psychological needs during this period. The unrest had opened a social fissure. The old social order was exposed for its inequities. This tear in the social fabric opened greater possibilities for individuals and communities fighting for social justice. I was ready to become involved.

As I walked around my community, I became very aware of my surroundings. I learned to walk, talk, and meet peoples' eyes in a way that made an impression, so as not to look vulnerable. Don bought a police radio, and when things got tense, we would listen to police calls and communications late into the evening, thereby monitoring what was happening around us. Sometimes both fear and danger lurked under the surface of the life that we were living. But I had learned that fear is less frightening when it's faced. I resolved to keep my kids close. I felt obligated by my good fortune to be where I was and my desire to be of service to others. My commitment was a prayer of thanksgiving for finding a meaningful place to give back.

My cousin's husband, Joe, was a policeman in Detroit. One afternoon in late summer, he walked in our open front door, knocking after he entered. The children were playing in the yard. We had hung an old tire we found in the garage from the branches of a big sycamore tree, and I could hear the boys' carefree voices. I invited Joe to sit down, but he was too agitated. His tone and manner were urgent. He was wildly gesturing as he spoke.

"You've got to get out of here while you still can," he said. "These people are animals."

His tone of voice betrayed his inner emotions, which were at this moment out of control. He spoke in front of Chandra, who felt insecure and came to sit behind me.

Calmly, I sat down and tried to deescalate the whirlwind he ushered through my front door.

"This is my home now," I flatly told him. "And we intend to stay. All of us," I added, looking at Chandra. We took care of Chandra for about eighteen months. During that time, we also hosted visits from her mother, who was sometimes given a furlough from the psychiatric hospital on weekends.

He looked at me incredulously. "You're nuts," he said, and he turned on his heel and left.

FATHER CUNNINGHAM LATER SUMMED UP his followers' response to the rebellion in this way: "Out of the violence, tumult, madness, and confusion of that historic revolution, a remnant of us, black and white, from Detroit and its suburbs, of every economic and religious background, joined together for intelligent and practical action."

Detroiters are not quitters. Don and I never talked about leaving Detroit. This was our home; this was where we wanted to be. We were part of a network of committed individuals driven by ideals; we were also part of a united neighborhood community of blacks and whites who cared about each other. Still, there were instances in this new reality when I was acutely aware of what my whiteness could represent.

Our neighbor Phil's brother, Lincoln, had something to do with the black entertainment business. Miriam Makeba, a legendary South African singer, was coming to town for a concert at Cobo Arena in late 1967. Lincoln and Don got along well, and for some reason, Lincoln decided to give Don and me tickets to the concert. At the time, Miriam was engaged to the black power leader Stokely Carmichael, and the couple planned to spend the night at the Gordons' house across the street from us. Don was interested in her music, and we decided to go. We were unprepared for the atmosphere in the arena.

As the evening progressed and Miriam captured the emotion of blacks in her South African freedom songs, the crowd began to get unruly, shouting antiwhite slogans, urged on by the evening's onstage master of ceremonies. The power of the audience was terrifying. The arena was literally shaking with rage.

"What should we do?" I quietly asked Don.

"Sit still," he responded. "Don't get up and make a spectacle of being here."

I can honestly say that I was frightened. I kept thinking we didn't belong here. I hoped to live to not make this mistake again.

Suddenly, Lincoln stood in front of us with a few other men. "Follow me," he said, and we were quietly ushered out a side door of the arena. Lincoln walked us to our car. Had we learned something? You bet.

I made every effort to make the community my own, but I wasn't trying to be a hero. One day I was walking down Second Avenue, coming home from the grocery store, when an apple whizzed by my head. I looked for the source. A small boy, eight or nine years old, continued to pelt me with apples from his backyard tree.

"Whitey," he screamed as he threw. Luckily, he was small, and his aim was bad.

I knew what I represented to angry blacks, and I understood why they felt that way. White privilege made my life different than theirs, but if children are hateful and violent at such an early age, how difficult it will be to solve our racial divide. The fissure between the races requires all our efforts, whites and blacks, not only to mend but to work for a new way forward together. And, because of history, whites need to listen and learn to be worthy of trust.

We are not promised anything. An accident of birth made me white. Over time, in the history of the world, power and politics have made that either good or bad. Color is not a biological distinction but a social one. The issue here is not color; it's power. In U.S. society, power brokers use color to divide people, a shameful practice that must be struggled against. Returning power to people in their communities presented an opportunity for a different way of living.

At this stage, events in my life unfolded without notice, like a fledgling sail touched by the wind. Life just happened in the context of our time and place. I was involved in related activities on multiple fronts. While these efforts were distinct in direction, they overlapped and in some cases had an unanticipated impact on the outcome of another. Between my time spent taking care of my children and my sense of responsibility to my community, there was little energy for anything else.

Hourglass

Time is running out to address the underlying causes of racism.
—Hourglass, Detroit, 1968

As the meeting hour approached, people streamed up our front sidewalk. My children were at the window: "There's no place to park on the whole block," marveled one little voice.

I had laid out refreshments on our dining room table, but our house was getting so crowded that once you were in, you weren't going anywhere. The cool early-March air struggled to find space to circulate as body squeezed against body. More than one hundred people were packed into the first floor of our home. But for those in attendance, a little physical discomfort was overcome by a driving sense of purpose that had delivered them to our house that Sunday afternoon.

The children helped me prepare—everyone had a part to play. Five-year-old Michael acted as a communications courier, a role he embraced with an adult sense of responsibility. He would run out the front door, his little feet flying, then around and across the yard to the back door, where he delivered his important message to those of us in the kitchen.

"There's not enough leaflets for the new people that just came in and are stuck by the front door," he breathlessly informed us.

Armed with more leaflets, he sprinted back outside and headed for the front of the house.

Don, acting as the chair, called the meeting to order. His booming voice carried easily across the living area and into the library and the kitchen.

"The name of our organization is Hourglass," he began. "Many of us here witnessed the anger and hopelessness expressed in our city last summer in the devastating riots. We are concerned and fearful. We want to help, we are afraid, and we feel that time is running out to address the ills that have been perpetrated on the black community in our city. Those of us here today are connected by our church community. Other agencies in the city and in the federal government are taking actions, but all of this is slow."

Don paused for a moment as late arrivals pressed into our entrance hall.

"It's time for action," Don repeated for the newcomers. "Archbishop Dearden has suggested that the Church will step forward, but our communities cannot wait. At this point we're thinking that we could help the process along if we were to suggest some actions that could be taken until the Church comes up with a specific plan."

Along with many other Detroiters, my life and the lives of my young children were profoundly transformed by the unprecedented events that had occurred during that swelteringly hot week in July. Racial tensions in the city had continued at a fever pitch. People were working to defuse the situation on all sides. Neighbors in our racially mixed community pulled together to support one another. Our familiar group of church activists continued to explore ways to address the underlying causes of racism in the white community. What could whites do that would have an impact? Did we hold the key to eliminating racism? How could it be done? We were deeply motivated to make a difference and looking for an opportunity.

Hourglass was our first major attempt to create a white organization that responded to the pain and anger expressed by the black community in the rebellion. While we officially kicked off our efforts in March 1968, our roots extended back to the retreats organized by Father Cunningham years before.

AS DON CONTINUED TALKING to those gathered for our first Hourglass meeting, my mind drifted back to early 1966 when we first met Tony at one of Father Cunningham's Cursillo retreats. Tony Locricchio was a Detroit lawyer who was studying to be a priest. At thirty, he was a little older than most seminarians in his class. Winsome and good-looking, with burly shoulders and dark curly hair that fell over his sparkling brown, mischievous eyes, Tony was blessed with a charismatic personality and legal expertise. As we got to know Tony, I observed that he was quite politically astute and walked to the beat of his own drummer.

Tony had experience, we discovered, working with both local and federal government on urban issues around white flight and youth programs. He would go on to work as a coordinator between the Church and federal poverty programs being organized through Detroit's City Hall. Well known to both the leaders of the Church and networks of civil rights activists, his contacts extended far beyond Detroit.

In early summer 1967, a month before the rebellion, Tony had appeared at our front door in evident distress. When I opened the inner door, his back was to me, his posture uncharacteristically disassembled. He was lost in his thoughts.

At the time, we were still in the process of getting settled in our new home, blissfully unaware of the turbulence and change on the horizon. Tony's arrival that night was, in retrospect, a harbinger of the gathering storm that would accelerate through the rebellion, into my work with Hourglass, and beyond.

As I unlatched the screen door, Tony turned toward me, his expression forlorn.

"May I come in?" he asked. "I need to talk."

Noting Tony's distraught appearance, I thought that Don should be part of this conversation.

"Come on into the dining room," I said, gesturing for Tony to follow me. "Don," I called, "Tony's here. Can you join us?"

The dinner dishes had been cleared, and the dining room was quiet; the children were upstairs playing. Don came out of his study and took the seat next to Tony at the table. "Okay," I began gently, "let's start at the beginning."

TONY HAD BEEN WORKING AS AN UNPAID ASSISTANT to Detroit's mayor, Jerome Cavanagh, drafting the terms of the Catholic Church's relationship with the federal antipoverty programs. For the prior two and a half years, the plan funneled federal grants to grassroots programs for the poor in Detroit. The Church administered these programs; the mayor's office provided oversight. Tony, with his legal expertise and clerical ties, provided an ideal link between the archdiocese, with its available facilities and staff, and the federal government, which, under President Johnson, needed an apparatus to administer the funds for his "war on poverty."

In Tony's role as a consultant in this complex scheme to aid the poor, he had access to the chancery, the Catholic Church's administrative offices, where he was assigned as a program development specialist. He also had access to the poverty program's operational staff, housed at the old Felician Academy, located at St. Aubin and Canfield, a couple of miles away. These were the folks who did the work to make the programs happen. Because Tony carried some authority, and certainly because he wore a priestly collar, staff members there were comfortable in approaching him with their concerns about how the program was being administered.

The program had mushroomed into a $3-million-a-year operation, with almost five hundred staff members, Tony said, and it had become total chaos.

"This operation is run by a bunch of priests who have no knowledge of business practices," he said, his voice strained. "They think it can just run itself. The diocese has lost control. Staff members are bickering and threatening one another. The program director's solution to the problem has been to hire a guard, who's walking around with a gun."

How could this be? I thought. I was incredulous.

Tony continued, his expressive hands helping to draw the picture: "The archdiocese badly wanted to be appointed to administer this program. I helped write the original grant, running back and forth to D.C., so I've been around as long as anybody, but I'm just now learning what's really going on at the Archdiocesan Opportunity Program administrative offices, where I was today. The black staff trusts me, and they're asking me for help. There are things going on that are negatively affecting the success of the programs."

Tony's usually buoyant personality was subdued. His stress showed in his slumped shoulders and weary demeanor.

"The staff has told me they have documents that suggest not only financial impropriety, but discrimination in hiring practices and promotions—cases where blacks were being passed over despite their seniority," he said, shifting in his chair. "They also charge that some community programs have become inactive, or even have closed, because funds have been transferred out of the programs and into a bloated administration budget that reeks with nepotism. It's being alleged that some of the priests who are running the program have put their relatives on the AOP payroll."

I noted how Tony carefully used legal language to describe what was going on.

"I have to do something," he said. "The mayor's office is responsible for oversight, but no one is minding the store."

I could see the disgust on Don's face.

The three of us talked late into the night about Tony's deep concern that the Church was mismanaging federal funds. And as the evening wore on, I began to see that Tony had come here on a mission. He finally got to the point. "I need help investigating the staff's allegations," he said meekly, looking directly at me. "Will you help me?"

"What do you want me to do?"

"A little detective work," Tony said. "I need you to go to the chancery offices with me. I need a secretary. We need proof of these allegations."

Did I dare? Don didn't seem to object. My entire life had been a quest to do the right thing. While I didn't want to do anything crazy, I was more than willing to assist in uncovering the truth of the matter. Surely, I could pull off looking like a regular secretary.

Shortly after that late-night meeting, I accompanied Tony to the chancery, he with his priestly collar and casual air, me outfitted in my "secretarial" look. We entered the building with ease. Tony's position as a legal consultant assigned to these grants meant workers were accustomed to his presence. Bringing a secretary seemed consistent with his professional status.

Still, I was nervous as we walked right over to the shelves that held the financial rosters. I watched as Tony nonchalantly grabbed the two hefty volumes, fearing a voice would speak up and demand to know what we were doing. None did, and we quickly took the books into the workroom.

It appeared that the antipoverty program administrators kept two sets of books: one official record for the government auditors and another internal account that tracked how the money was actually being spent. Tony scanned the books for information, and I busily documented the internal account of checks written to people who didn't officially work in the system. Some were relatives of priests and bishops. The size and scale of the abuse was enormous.

It was a sad awakening.

"We should let the archbishop know," I whispered. "This needs to be addressed."

We were able to conduct our clandestine and painstaking hand copying of the records for two days. All the information we uncovered was captured in my notebook. Then, toward the end of the second day, an employee suddenly burst out: "You're not authorized to be looking at those books! You need to leave at once or I'll report you to the director."

Busted, we picked up our notebooks and belongings and hurried out of the offices—with our data intact. In our hands, we held what appeared to be undeniable proof of corruption on a massive scale on the part of the Church.

Before we could take any action with the information we now possessed, the rebellion occurred, upending our lives. It wiped everything out of my mind, including the fruits of our detective work. Suddenly, if it wasn't life or death, *it wasn't life or death*. We were totally consumed by the urgent task that lay before us: that of rebuilding our community. This was our city and we were in deep trouble.

Tony's involvement in my life during this critical time in our community also mirrored a turning point in my evolution as an activist. The three of us—Tony, Don, and I—had already been discussing the appropriate role we whites would play within the movement. It was easy to pick up where we had left off.

"In the Cursillo retreats we talked about white attitudes on race, educating whites about the lives of blacks, and learning what the needs are in the black community," I recall Tony saying at one point in the days after the rebellion. "We're building bridges and raising consciousness. But it's becoming very clear that blacks want control over their own lives and communities. I'm seeing that in the work I do in D.C. That's what President Johnson's initiatives are built on: *community control*."

Our discussions, which had been seeded in the retreats, seemed even more relevant after the rebellion. As we started to brain-storm about solutions in our community, Tony began to stop by our home quite frequently, and our talks continued. The underly-ing theme of blacks controlling their own destiny was consistent with what we were seeing in the world around us. The rebellion was our wake-up call. Programs had to be neighborhood-based, black-controlled, and light on resources. In the urgency of the mo-ment, everything seemed possible.

Tony suggested one empowering idea based on his experiences. The Church had many properties in Detroit, abandoned by white flight, that could be used for community events. At the same time black Catholic communities were suffering as churches, schools, and community centers closed and parishioners moved to the suburbs.

"Why can't these buildings be turned over to the communities where they're located?" he asked. "They could be used as commu-nity centers or recreation centers for youth activities that would benefit these communities and keep kids off the streets."

Thus, the idea behind Hourglass was born. We decided that we needed to put together a list of others who had attended Father Cunningham's retreats. We would ask them to help us build a grassroots support group.

"I'm home in the daytime; I can organize that," I said, my enthusiasm spilling over. As I uttered those simple words, I unwittingly made an irreversible leap into direct social action.

AS I GAZED AROUND at the people who packed the first floor of our home, Don was finishing his remarks and introducing Tony. Hourglass had become a reality.

Tony was comfortable before the crowd, looking to convince them of our plan. "Our immediate goal is action that will give black youth an outlet. We also hope it will channel their energy into responsible community leadership. The Catholic Church has the resources to do this," Tony said. "We're proposing that locked-down or boarded-up buildings owned by the Catholic Church be donated for use as community centers for neighborhood youth. We're asking for three sites that can serve their communities this summer. That's the essence of our plan."

A woman in the front spoke up: "What makes you think that the Church will do this?"

"The archbishop has already made a commitment," Tony explained. "We would like to get our proposal in as soon as possible so we can give shape to a plan that could be implemented by summer. We believe that this plan to create community centers would take minimal funds and can be up and running in a reasonable amount of time."

There remained a considerable amount of radical white energy inside the Catholic Church at that time, particularly those touched by the work of Father Cunningham. Our program alone collected three hundred signatures from laypeople in support of what we presented that night in March. They realized they were living in their white world, blind to what was going on behind those grassy walls of the freeway. The rebellion changed all that. Those with open eyes and empathetic hearts got a good look at the results of our willful ignorance about our neighbors' lack of opportunities within the dominant culture. Father Cunningham's activism over the prior two years gave us a base to organize.

Yet what we were attempting meant pushing church leaders in a direction they had yet to turn to on their own. Throughout this period, we were committed to goading the official Church into action. We, the people from the community—blacks and whites—were leading the Church in this endeavor. We knew that we were creating a situation that put them in an awkward position.

On March 20, 1968, I wrote a letter to Archbishop Dearden informing him of the establishment of Hourglass and our purpose, which was "to support the Church in programs fostering black self-determination and destroying racist attitudes in the white community."

Other organizing meetings followed. A board of directors was selected. We developed a logo to represent our work, an hourglass with the sand draining out, which Don had had drawn up in his engineering department at work. We had lapel buttons made featuring a white hourglass on a black background that participants wore to market our project. I did the communications work—writing letter after letter to advance our work, developing a newsletter, and coordinating meetings.

I never had conscious aspirations to be a leader, but I soon learned that I had ideas with merit and that I could organize something in my home with a baby on my arm. I had better-than-average typing skills, which made it possible for me to produce professional-looking communications and regular newsletters. I had what it took to communicate effectively with bishops, community leaders, and the news media. I didn't have any help with day-to-day operations—when the men went to work, I was it. I had no formal training, but I possessed passion and a relentless drive for change.

Getting organized, finding supporters, and developing a plan were, in some ways, the easy part. Next, we had to convince the archbishop and other church officials that they should trust us, believe in our plan, and provide us with the space we sought. This would prove to be a major challenge.

To start, I wrote several letters to Archbishop John Francis Dearden and Bishop Thomas Gumbleton pleading our cause. At the time, letters were the primary form of business communication. Face-to-face meetings were the primary form of personal communication. There were no cell phones or answering machines, no texting or conference calls. To connect by phone, someone had to be on the other end to answer. A significant amount of time was devoted to posting letters at the corner mailbox and then waiting for the postman to deliver a response. Communication was slow and often incomplete because the means were so inefficient compared to what's possible today.

We had reason to be optimistic about our chances. Archbishop Dearden was known as a significant supporter of the Vatican II reforms, having been an active participant in the meetings. To some, he was considered a liberal and progressive voice on Church doctrine, remembered for actively implementing the new practices. He worked with Church elders on an interfaith program that sought pledges from businesses not to discriminate in their hiring practices in the mid-1960s.

Bishop Gumbleton, too, appeared to be a potential ally. Just months after civil unrest rocked Detroit, Bishop Gumbleton became the youngest vicar general of the Archdiocese of Detroit. At thirty-eight years old, he took on the challenging task of healing a community torn apart by violence. He was young and inexperienced, but so were we.

My initial goal was simply to make the archbishop aware of our efforts, while also pointing to words and views he himself had expressed in the hopes of gaining his sympathies. In late March, I noted a letter the archbishop had addressed to the bishop's Commission on Human Relations, where he issued "an invitation to all Christians to bear witness to the depth of concern about our urban crisis by rallying to create programs of action aimed at resolution."

"Our program, Hourglass, has taken your message to heart, and we have a proposal," I wrote, adding that we had a "plan . . .

for raising funds to acquire three unoccupied inner-city church structures to be consigned to the black community at no cost and administrated in the hands of black church leadership."

It was with shock that I received a call a few days later from a very upset Bishop Gumbleton. His speech was hurried and erratic. "You need to publish a public retraction on the letters your group is circulating. And drop the name, Hourglass. It's an attack on our archbishop and an insult to the Negro community," he said emphatically.

I was completely taken aback by the bishop's call and his criticism of Hourglass. What he said next was truly strange, but would later prove to offer remarkable foreshadowing.

He went on to tell me that irreparable damage had been done by our group because we were connected with Mr. Anthony Locricchio. It suddenly occurred to me that the bishop must be aware of Tony's involvement in the efforts to expose the church's malfeasance. Seemingly, my participation had escaped notice.

Actually, Tony had ceased working with Hourglass shortly after helping us finalize our organizing efforts. At this point he had been gone a month. But Tony had left us with a "parting gift." Before going, he had introduced me to Sheila Murphy, a young activist. Sheila would ultimately become a major transformative force in my life, though at first glance, I would never have guessed that.

When I first met Sheila, she was a young and restless nineteen-year-old. She sat in our dining room during those early Hourglass days, twisting her long, blazing red hair and tapping her foot impatiently. There I was, cradling my baby girl in my arms, her bottle nested in the bend of my elbow, while the other children ran around the house. Sheila seemed a bit perplexed as she tried to size me up. I, meanwhile, was wondered how she could possibly fit into our picture.

It was Tony who gambled that I, a mother of six, plus Chandra, and this restless young dynamo, could work well together. Tony knew that Sheila had the experience, foresight, and connections to assist us in engaging the hierarchy of the Catholic Church in our plan.

I found Sheila wise beyond her years, having grown up in her parents' Catholic Worker house in Detroit's Corktown ghetto. She had many of Tony's winning qualities, but her experiences were of a different sort. She knew what was going on in the streets and was connected with a broad sector of folks across the city, from street people to religious figures to politicians. Sheila soon joined us on the Hourglass leadership team. She did a lion's share of the work in helping raise funds and identify resources.

We needed all the help we could get. The bishop's call suggested to us that we were being ignored by the archbishop himself. I sent a letter to the archbishop's home address, notifying him that his staff was refusing our letters and signatures from other white Catholics in support of our plan. It was only after I alerted Bishop Gumbleton to the fact Tony had "other commitments" that rendered him unable to continue with the group that we were told the chancery would meet with us sometime after Easter. I thanked him and noted that we looked forward to the opportunity to talk, but the bishop never raised the topic of Tony again.

It felt as if the tide was turning. Several prominent clergy groups were urging changes not only within the Catholic Church but in American society at large. In April, the Black Catholic Clergy Caucus took a hard line, admonishing the Church for being a "primarily white racist institution" that was "apparently not cognizant of changing attitudes in the Black Community and is not making the necessary meaningful and realistic adjustments . . . One of these changes must be a reevaluation of the Church's attitude on black militancy." The statement also noted, "Black people are fighting abroad for America's freedom—Why is it not moral to fight for liberty at home?"

That same month, the U.S. bishops issued a national statement on the racial crisis, stating: "The hour is late and the need is critical. We must act while there is still time for collaborative peaceful solutions."

The sentiment at the time seemed to be felt by Archbishop Dearden, who pledged $1.5 million from the Archdioceses Development Fund (ADF) for worthy programs to alleviate the Detroit urban crisis. The ADF was an annual fund drive sponsored by the diocese to finance community grants. Pledges were made by parishioners from across the metropolitan area. By May, it was clear that the generous contributions of the faithful would exceed the targeted $1.5 million. The outpouring was a genuine gesture of concern by Catholics for the welfare of Detroit's most dispossessed.

This was good news for us. Hourglass was ready.

"Things seem to be falling our way," I said to Don.

The opportunity for funding from the Church for exactly the sort of programming we envisioned meant quickly refocusing our efforts on preparing a concrete proposal and plan to present to the archbishop. It was through Sheila's deep connections in the community that we found an ally with the perfect program.

FRANK DITTO WAS A COMMUNITY LEADER and founder of the *East Side Voice for an Independent Detroit (ESVID)* newspaper. He was known for working with youth in this volatile neighborhood. At the time, he was working on a political education project—or PEP—that trained young people, ages fifteen to twenty, to become community leaders by using a mock City Hall model. It sought to familiarize black youth with political institutions, teaching that politics, when better understood, can be used as an effective and orderly vehicle for social change.

Ditto's program was already under way in the East Side community, but they needed space. In our excited discussions, we realized this could be a model for a citywide project that the Catholic Church could fund. By our estimates, five thousand young people could be helped by the program. We were lucky to have the resources of a volunteer with business experience and connections who coordinated with Sheila and Don to develop a professional-looking proposal. The finished product had a heavy cover and was bound with a plastic spiral, a format I had not seen before.

When we were ready, we asked representatives of the diocese over to our home so we could make the formal presentation. Bishop Gumbleton attended then stayed on after the formal program to discuss the details. We sat around our dining room table, talking. The bishop seemed impressed; his objections to our efforts had evidently disappeared, spurred on by Tony's absence.

On May 16, 1968, I received a copy of a letter Bishop Gumbleton had written to the archbishop, in which he called our efforts "one of the most realistic examples of a program of real self-determination that I have seen" and offered his support for funding. "After listening to the presentation and looking through the material, I have concluded that this program has outstanding potential for achieving goals which we have come to understand as primary in the effort to solve the problems of our urban areas. For this reason, I would offer a strong recommendation that it be funded with money from ADF."

Only a few days later we received another letter, this time addressed to the full Hourglass board, letting us know the archbishop was "favorably impressed and willing to give it his backing and has authorized its submission for funding to the committee set up to determine allocation of ADF monies."

We were cautiously optimistic; our first foray into concrete civil rights movement activism appeared to be achieving real results. There was, the bishop's letter noted, one issue, which appeared on its surface to be an administrative issue. While the archbishop was unwilling simply to give us permanent control of a building—like one of the empty schools we'd been eyeing—he was willing to provide support, on a yearly basis, if we could find a parish community that would embrace the program.

One of our board members, Jim Hanna, suggested we reach out to his parish, Annunciation, as a possible site for the potential youth city hall.

"Let's give it a try," he said. "I'll talk with Father Thomas. I know him pretty well." Soon a meeting was set to present the proposal to parishioners at Annunciation parish.

"Well, no celebrations yet, but I'm pretty excited," I told Don. We were feeling good about the progress.

A few days later, on May 15, 1968, Hourglass held a rally at the cathedral to show that blacks and whites in our community were united in the cause of self-determination for the black community. This was our first effort at organizing a demonstration. Mr. Ditto was there with some of the young people from the PEP project. That warm and beautiful Saturday, about seventy-five parishioners and supporters—blacks and whites together—assembled on Belmont Avenue on the north side of the cathedral, next to the school playground. We carried signs identifying ourselves as Hourglass and expressing our unity. A quote from Mr. Ditto set the tone:

> A good house will not give self-determination; a good education alone will not give self-determination. I know too many educated people today pushing brooms who have nothing to say about where they live or what laws are passed that affect their lives on a day-to-day basis. Until they do get that power, they will be administered paternalistic programs with that kind of an attitude from now on. Political power is the most viable and expedient tool that Black people could use at this point, in terms of better jobs, better housing or anything else.
>
> —FRANK DITTO, *EVSID*

The following week representatives from Hourglass, as well as Mr. Ditto and some of his PEP students, were scheduled to present our plan to parishioners. Both Jim Hanna and I talked with Father Thomas prior to the meeting. Things appeared to be moving forward smoothly, and all signs pointed to reasons for optimism. Yet when it came time for the actual presentation to the parishioners, Father Thomas was a no-show. He didn't even send a representative. It turned out that the fifty parish members who had been present were not happy.

I did not attend the meeting, but I was eagerly waiting for Don to arrive home with a report. I knew when he came through the back door that there had been trouble. He entered noisily and was scowling—lips tight, his face red.

"I tried," he finally said. "It was ludicrous! These parishioners should have been briefed, should have had the situation explained to them." He slammed the paperwork in his hands down onto the kitchen table.

"Slow down and relax a minute and then tell me what happened," I said, feeling his anger and disappointment.

"First of all, when we tried to start the presentation, they just kept yelling," he said. "Claude Mayberry was there, a professional black man. They wouldn't even let him speak. We were there a full hour before we could even *start* the presentation."

He continued: "I tried to explain the importance of this kind of positive action between the community and the Church. It's no wonder the black community has no confidence in the white Church. At the moment, I don't blame them. It's a symbol of white society, and they don't want to be part of it. It's not relevant to their needs. This is an opportunity to change that. The parishioners there this morning don't get it!"

"Were you finally able to do the presentation," I asked, wondering if there was any hope.

"A very brief one—after an hour!" Don was still dumping a flood of emotions. "There were three men from the parish who pleaded for some control and consideration for the guests. Then this idiot priest, Father Schneider, asked the group to let us finish, suggesting the parishioners"—Don mimicked the priest's gestures— "just let what we were saying go in one ear and out the other."

"The parishioners were irate at the suggestion of young black people using their parish hall," Don said. "All we wanted to do was provide a brief summary. And these young black kids were sitting right there!"

"I don't understand what happened with Father Thomas," I said. "We need to call him to let him know what happened. Maybe he can find an alternative site."

"I'm not giving up," Don said.

And I agreed—the program was too important.

Don identified a major issue for us going forward. Things went so poorly, he said, because we were unprepared for this kind of pushback from long-time white residents who held a strong emotional stake in their dwindling parish. They had experienced increasing violence and crime in their neighborhood, especially after the unrest the previous year. They were afraid of the black community. Don believed that we needed to do more to help them understand that this project would actually increase neighborhood stability. It was a lesson learned.

The experience left us with a whole new challenge. After a glowing start, we now faced a brick wall. Church officials were unclear how to proceed. After facing the angry parishioners, we abandoned our request to use the targeted facility. Our quest for funds lay fractured and in limbo.

In other areas, our newly defined roles—of working as white allies in support of black self-determination—were beginning to produce results. Shortly after the disastrous meeting at Annunciation parish, Frank Ditto gave Hourglass credit for our efforts, calling it "the first step on the part of white people to support the right of black self-determination. It's a very Christian thing for a man to determine his own destiny," he stated publicly. "It comes from the gospel of Jesus Christ."

Yet Christian charity seemed to be in too short supply when it came to Hourglass's PEP program. After our initial setback, we struggled to get the archbishop's office back on board with our program in a concrete way—and time was running out.

By early June, Bishop Gumbleton felt it necessary to remind us, in a letter, that "it is not possible simply to 'push people around' and make decisions for them," indicating that PEP was just one of the self-determination projects out there that the Church was considering. I wondered if they were looking for a way out, if they were losing faith in the feasibility of our proposal.

I struggled to grasp a nagging inner sense that we had crossed some boundaries in our attempt to speak for the needs of the black community. Over time—and it *would* take time—I began to understand that there is an unspoken, unwritten history in every activist effort. We had to understand our role as whites in the black freedom struggle, and that called for the development of well-thought-out strategies and the acknowledgment that we were allies, not leaders, in this cause.

Not to be deterred by the loss of space within Annunciation parish, we found a new church facility in the general neighborhood, one that was cheaper and more receptive to our plans. We were ready to move. PEP had a late-June deadline approaching— that's when we were to begin our programming.

Don sent a letter to the archdiocese—weeks before the deadline—asking for a response so we could move forward with the plan. We never received a response. We blew past our deadline, and plans for a summer program began to fade. Frustration grew in place of enthusiasm.

At the end of June, I wrote a letter to the editor at the *Michigan Catholic*, and I sent press releases to NBC and ABC, and to the *Lou Gordon Show*, a popular news-focused television show. I urged them to publish or comment on our information regarding the lack of response by the Church to our riot-torn city. To my knowledge, we received no response to any of my letters or press releases.

In late August, I saw Bishop Walter J. Schoenherr when I was walking near the cathedral. I stopped, and we talked over the school-yard fence.

"You're chairing the ADF funding committee, Bishop," I said. "Can you give me an update? Do you think the PEP proposal will be funded?"

"We're still looking over the proposals," the bishop said.

"But last March, the archbishop said, 'Time is critical.' Summer has now passed. For all these months, the needs in the community have been left unanswered," I replied, pushing a little. "This doesn't help people feel that the Church cares about them. When do you think we'll hear something?"

"I'm in touch with a black militant," the bishop said. "He's advising me."

Strange, I thought. That doesn't line up with selection criteria that were described to us.

We continued to wait for word on our proposal, and frustration continued to mount. I was still learning what it means to be an activist. Acting to achieve a specific goal or outcome inspired me. But the conflict between that drive for change and my obligations to my children never left my mind. I wanted both, and I was on a course to prove that both were possible.

One who is considering the life of an activist needs to realize that activists are fundamentally disruptive forces. They are the sociopolitical innovators who believe that there is a better way, but the mission to lead people to achieve that better way always comes with a price. Change and transformation are never free. Someone has to pay the bill when it arrives.

As we worked to raise consciousness in a positive way, our home parish gave us full support. We were determined to engage the Catholic Church in becoming relevant to the lives of real people in the community who were victims of a racist society. There is power in a community of like-minded individuals. Like the weft and the warp of a woven cloth, we understand each other and know where to find strength and support. We were change agents, an extended family rooted in the knowledge that together we could make a difference. We believed we were planting seeds destined to grow into mighty oaks.

Finally, in November, six months after we submitted the PEP proposal, Frank Ditto received a letter. The Hourglass proposal would not be funded. The long-awaited response, signed by a "social planner," was not on archdiocesan stationary, and the Hourglass board did not get a copy.

The letter referenced funding that Mr. Ditto would be receiving from a different source—we hadn't known about that award, yet we were pleased to see the program would get at least some money. But the letter also made mention of funding going to programs with "community control, both in the planning and operation phases." Had our involvement and our "white privilege" been the problem? I wondered how we might have approached our mission differently. Thankfully, however, the work would proceed under Frank Ditto's leadership.

Although our Hourglass proposal was not accepted, the concept of donating facilities for the use and development of black youth remained essential to building strong minority communities. The idea of granting church facilities to the black community in the wake of white flight was not lost and would be achieved in our home parish in the not-too-distant future. At the initiative of Bishop Schoenherr, the humble pastor of Blessed Sacrament, our high school gymnasium did become a youth recreation center, and the old convent became a drug treatment center.

I learned many things through the Hourglass endeavor: when developing a plan, activists need to consider what other forces beyond their control may be at work. Activists must be prepared for power shifts, and they need to be nimble on their feet.

I learned that people look for stability in evaluating proposals for change. They also look out for how your ideas affect their own well-being. When you're not in control, you can't take big leaps and expect people to support you. No matter how much your point of view may be justified, big changes are just not going to happen until the people being affected feel that their needs are being met. Even though the rhetoric and good intentions were in place for our action, the careful consciousness raising and community building that comes through ongoing education and the cultivation of genuine relationships were not. When people have not yet reached your level of understanding, they'll inevitably fight back.

CHAPTER

6

Unfaithful Clergy

These are times to grow our souls.
—Grace Lee Boggs

LIFE-ALTERING EVENTS CONTINUED to unfold—both in the big outside world and in the small world my family and I inhabited. No one was immune to the effects of these changes; nothing was left unchanged.

Amid the smoldering ashes of the uprising no one was thinking about the poverty program. Especially not me. Martin Luther King Jr. was speaking about "curtains of doom" coming down on our country because of our racial divide. In my church community, we believed that our future and the future of our children depended on how whites responded to the rebellion.

In August 1967, Tony provided the *Detroit Free Press* with a copy of the allegations the staff had reported to him. I didn't see a copy of the article then, and I don't know of anyone else who saw it. I found the article years later in the archives. At the time, we were overwhelmed with healing our community after the devastation.

The *Free Press* story that ran on August 17, 1967, reported that memoranda and budget reports—collected by the archdiocese's staff members turned whistle-blowers—supported charges that Church officials had mismanaged poverty program funds. The article further alleged that promising programs were permitted to die and that the organization's accounting practices were questionable. Among the paperwork was a document from an accounting firm reporting that the firm's analysts had been unable to certify the program's balance sheet and that its accounting records were unsatisfactory. It also noted that that Representative James Del Rio (D, Detroit) had subpoenaed the fiscal records.

Disturbed by unfavorable publicity about abuses in the poverty program, Mayor Cavanagh appointed a fact-finding committee to investigate. On October 4, 1968, more than a year later, a public hearing was convened to interview the principals responsible for administering the program. Notes from that hearing published by a Sacred Heart seminarian are housed in our Walter Reuther archives file, along with a diagram of how federal funds flowed into Detroit's poverty programs.

The chairman of the committee was Professor Charles W. Quick of the University of Illinois. During the hearing, the committee interrogated Father Kevin O'Brian, whom the Church had brought in after the program's previous administration was ousted.

According to the documents, Father O'Brian provided shocking testimony stating that the program's administrators had been aware for fourteen months of the program's mismanagement. He admitted that two sets of books were being kept. There were thirteen people listed in the administration, but three times that number appeared on the administrative payroll. An extra $100,000 had been transferred from programs for the poor to cover administrative expenses, which bankrupted some of the programs.

An afternoon session took place in an outdoor courtyard at the Rackham Building. Sheila notified me it was happening, and I rushed over. A stage was constructed and folding chairs set up for delegates. A few of us quietly moved among the crowd to circulate Tony's and my documentation.

At the end of the meeting, I mounted the steps to the stage and handed Dr. Quick a copy of our documentation, which he gladly accepted. He promised to send me his committee's report when it was finished a few months later.

As I headed for home that day, I realized how totally disgusted I was with the behavior of the Church, beginning with their unfulfilled promise from months earlier of making funds available to Detroit's riot-torn communities, funds that Detroit Catholics had so generously donated. Now we were witnessing blatant and reprehensible mismanagement of the federal government's poverty program funds, stolen from the communities that desperately needed them. The Church had known about this for fourteen months and done nothing. My anger was unchecked; these were two blatant acts of fraud perpetrated by the Church. I wanted to see the Catholic Church's unchristian ways exposed, and I was ready to organize the troops.

Activists in Hourglass moved to bring this breach of ethics directly to the archbishop, and we devised an action plan to get his attention. On October 14, 1968, ten days after the hearing, we delivered an open letter to the offices of Mayor Cavanagh and Archbishop Dearden. The mayor was not in his office, so we left the letter with his receptionist. We then proceeded to the chancery building to confront the archbishop.

Thirty-five boisterous souls, Catholics all of us, were there to demand that the Church "come clean" and own up to our findings. We held our picket signs high: **FRAUD! NEPOTISM!** "Turn over the administration of the poverty program to the poor," we chanted. Our outrage intensified as we marched in front of the archbishop's private quarters, which were nestled in a looming granite fortress next door to St. Aloysius Church. Our protest was covered by the local press and watched over by a police car parked close by, just in case there was trouble.

Through some uncanny bad luck for the archbishop—or perhaps it was divine providence working on our behalf—I encountered His Holiness in the elevator when I was on my way up to his office to confront him directly. He was as surprised as I was when the elevator door opened and we stood face-to-face.

"I must talk with you," I said, and moved to step inside the elevator.

He firmly pushed me out of our unlikely meeting place, saying, as the doors began to close, "Yes, but you must call for an appointment."

One week later, I sat across from him at his desk, taking in the scene. At first I felt brazen, accusing, as I spread our evidence on the desk between us. He sat silent, waiting for me to finish. He denied nothing. We both knew it was true. Nervous and awkward, I filled the space between us with a burst of emotional words that seemed to escape from me unbidden.

The distress in my voice startled me as it pierced the air of this dignified male sanctuary. "This is not my church! Not the church I grew up in—where I prayed—where I trusted . . ."

Becoming conscious of the scene I was creating, I stopped speaking, but the sound of my words hung thickly in the austere space. I struggled to regain my composure. The room was dim, sparse, intimidating. No one else was present. The archbishop's hands were folded sedately in front of him. He seemed unaffected. I was restless in my chair. On a mission to seek the truth, I had slid a tape recorder into my bag to capture his words, and then I didn't have enough guts to turn it on. In fact, I was no longer sure that my coming had been a good idea.

It occurred to me, as I searched his face, that the archbishop's seemingly stately and graceful bearing was, in fact, condescending and detached. I was but a mother of six kids, a female parishioner at the cathedral where he celebrated Mass on Holy Days. On the other hand, I had been such a persistent thorn in his side over this past year—with regard to Hourglass and now the fraud scandal—that he had agreed to see me.

My Catholic faith had always been the backbone of my life. My religious beliefs were the glue that held my fractured life together. But here I was, sitting across the desk from the archbishop of Detroit, having accused him and his church—*my* church—of committing fraud with the federal government's poverty program funds.

"So it's true," I prodded.

"Yes, it's true," he confirmed unapologetically. "But you need to know that even if you continue to persist in involving the press, they won't print it."

It was his desk, his diocese, and clearly his terms. I was still learning. I was shocked to realize that a spiritual leader with so much power would offer no response to this grievous injustice but to conceal the scandal from the press.

I don't know what I expected. Maybe I wanted the archbishop to affirm my fantasy that, as a man of God, he would take action and right the wrongs. That those who hurt others in this disgraceful situation would be punished and my world would fall back into place. But that would have been too easy. Instead, my world lay shattered. The archbishop and I sat face-to-face, in a city cast adrift as the aftermath of rebellion and unrest swept over us like waves before a storm.

DURING THIS PERIOD, my involvement in movement work expanded beyond Hourglass. My activist touchstone remained the Catholic Church, at a time when white Catholics were at the forefront of the civil rights and antiwar movements. These two efforts often overlapped, and participants in either would rally to support their brothers and sisters participating in other, like-minded work.

I began to take some of my children with me to antiwar demonstrations at Kennedy Square, the downtown people's square in Detroit. As we did when the smaller children accompanied me to the grocery store, we locked wrists in order to stay together while we snaked through the crowd.

At one boisterous antiwar rally, police rode their horses into the unruly crowd, knocking some people to the ground and causing the others to scatter. Ken was busy taking photos. I wasn't worried about him. He had developed street smarts at a very young age. Take a roll of photos and then hand off the film. Then, if he was confronted by the police or others and lost his camera, the photos would be saved. But this time, the force of the surging crowd broke our grip, and I lost Greg, who had been at the far end of our safety chain. Now, Greg was a child who tended to seek his own adventures, and I was worried that he could wander off and get hurt.

"Where's Greg?" I shouted at everybody and anybody. I could see all the others. The horses backed off, and people were getting back on their feet. "Ken, do you see him?"

By now, I was shaking inside. My eyes scanned the crowd. I saw shapes and colors, but I was too upset to focus on anything. Dear God, please . . .

"Greg!" I shouted again. "Ken and Jeff! Spread out and look for Greg—but I need you both in my sight."

Greg was safely located—a long, harrowing ten minutes later— expounding with glee about his adventure. Losing contact with a child in a crowd is a traumatic experience, something that nightmares are made of. I needed to keep my kids close. Maybe mass demonstrations weren't our best options. There were other ways I could contribute and grow as an activist, through friends such as Father Dennie Moloney.

After his stay at our home during the rebellion, Father Dennie and I fell into a habit of keeping in touch, and we shared several friends. At the time a deacon in the Catholic Church, he was characteristically quiet, reflective, and an independent thinker. When in the seminary, Dennie had majored in philosophy and was an avowed antiwar activist.

I was trying to come to terms with the continued relationship problems between Don and me, and I needed a place for gentle, reflective conversation. I often visited Dennie in his study at the rectory, where we sat on the floor with his books and had long discussions about life and politics. He introduced me to some of the great philosophers of social and political thought, the study of whom is an essential step in becoming an activist. My mind was opening to the college education that I never had. I would also learn some practical lessons about being white in a black community.

During this period, Dennie asked me to speak at a one-day retreat for high school juniors at the school adjoining his parish. Visitation parish was located on 12th Street and Webb, kitty-corner from Metropolitan Hospital and in the heart of the area where the 1967 rebellion broke out. Visitation parish was well respected by its community, and during the conflagration, the nuns at the convent had opened up a food kitchen for displaced residents.

After the rebellion, a lot of residents fled this decimated area of Detroit. Visitation's parish school was closed in 1967 then reopened by the archdiocese as a consolidated high school that incorporated St. Theresa's parish students after their school was closed. The school was renamed St. Martin de Porres High School, after a black saint. At this time, the high school was 99 percent black.

The topic of my presentation was "Living as a Christian in the World," a topic that I had spoken on to young people in other settings. The daylong event was set up in the school gymnasium. I had thirty minutes to speak, and then there was time for questions. The students, who had had white nuns as teachers all their lives, were warm and receptive. We had a lively discussion, and I felt that my presentation had been a success. Some crowded around me afterward to make comments and ask questions. As the group thinned out and the last child moved away, I found myself face-to-face with a stone-faced, furious Joe Doolin, the black principal of this newly opened school.

"How did you get in here?" he demanded aggressively.

Taking in the look on his face, I realized very quickly that I was a white woman in the wrong place. I suddenly became conscious that my pale skin stood out in contrast to the rest of the room. "Father asked me to speak," I responded, shaken. Something was happening here that I didn't anticipate, and I was struggling to understand what it was.

"We don't need any do-gooder white people in here, telling us what to do," Mr. Doolin stated definitively.

The message came through loud and clear. Joe Doolin was a spirited man on a mission to teach black pride to these urban kids. He was throwing them a lifeline in a world that predetermined their fate by the color of their skin. In the subsequent years, Mr. Doolin would earn a reputation as highly talented educator, energetic leader, and tough disciplinarian. He became an inspiration for the kids as the community attempted to rise from the ashes of civil disorder. On the day we met, he made it explicitly clear that he had an agenda, and I was not part of it.

I learned a lesson that day. The need to be sensitive to my presence in the black community required the deprogramming of a lot of inherited white privilege. As a white person, I may have a role to play, but I was not the decision maker. Blacks wanted control of their lives and their community. I accepted that and determined that I would switch my focus to supporting efforts coming out of the community itself. I was not some master architect elected to design the future.

DR. MARTIN LUTHER KING JR., civil rights leader and advocate of nonviolence, was assassinated on April 4, 1968. In Detroit, black youth took to the streets. Employers let their workers go home early. Out our window, I could see Second Avenue clogged with cars trying to get out of the city. Tony came over to our house after he left the University of Detroit, where he taught in the Urban Studies Department. Like many institutions, the university had canceled classes and closed early. Don joined us as we monitored the radio for news. Martha Jean, "The Queen," a local black broadcaster, reported that black youths were roaming the city, smashing windows and burning cars. That night, the news media reported that "120 cities went up in flames." While such reports were overblown, the threat was palpable.

We took a break from our work and went to the upstairs window in the girls' room, which had the best view of the neighborhood. Tony looked reflectively at my young daughter Carolyn, now eight years old, and our black foster child, Chandra, who was five, asleep side by side in the bed.

"It'll take time," he said, "but these kids won't know racism when they grow up."

At that moment, I believed him. But I had no idea just how complicated it was, how deeply imbedded race is in the structure of American society. Racism has always been essential to good order and economic growth.

By morning, we knew that several cities were under siege by crowds of young black men. I called the cathedral and strongly suggested to the priest that they hang the mourning banners over the church doors. They did.

Then I thought about Michelle, a black friend whom I had met through volunteer work at the church. I decided to give her a call. I'll never forget how she responded.

"Michelle, I've been thinking about you since I heard about Dr. King," I said, once we were connected. "I'm so sorry, I know how much his leadership has meant to your people."

"Don't cry for me," she said. "Your people are the ones who just lost their best hope."

I was stunned by her words—and humbled. How could I have been so shortsighted?

Dr. King's death was a turning point, not only in black–white relations but in how blacks saw themselves. Nonviolence had not solved their problems. The black power movement came at a time when society was in the midst of a major social transformation, making it even more forceful. Losing King brought this into stark focus.

Black power leaders Malcolm X, Stokely Carmichael, and H. Rap Brown believed that self-determination and self-defense were the keys to relevant change. Brown had recently been in Detroit and had spoken to blacks from the riot-torn rubble on Dexter Boulevard and Elmhurst. It was time for blacks to set their own agenda, and they did.

This strategic change would give rise to national militant groups like the Black Panthers. In Detroit, the 1967 publication of the *Inner-City Voice* became the foundation for the League of Revolutionary Black Workers, followed by the Republic of New Africa in 1968. Hostility heightened in the streets, and the cops prepared to double down.

After the 1967 riot, city officials had created a special police task force called STRESS (Stop the Robberies, Enjoy Safe Streets), which had the effect of escalating the tensions between the police department and the city's residents. In *Detroit, I Do Mind Dying: A Study in Urban Revolution*, Dan Georgakas and Marvin Surkin call the "decoy" operation used by STRESS officers a patently illegal "entrapment," during which one officer would act like a potential victim in an area where a crime was likely to occur; then, once he was attacked, other officers would move in. In 1971 alone, thirteen young black men were killed in STRESS operations. Conflicts between police and black citizens were intensifying, and black power advocates were gaining ground against the atrocities.

Believers in the philosophy of nonviolence were aware that, without Dr. King, their movement was in danger of collapsing. They needed a strategy that would buy them time to regroup. After Dr. King's death, his widow, a cadre of black ministers, and the Southern Christian Leadership Conference decided they would proceed with Dr. King's plan for a Poor People's Campaign. Led by mules, the campaign moved from city to city, collecting the poor and disinherited and leading them to Washington, D.C., where they would demand a response to their grievances and remain until they were addressed.

As the Poor People's Campaign passed through Detroit, Sheila Murphy was working in the registration area of Cobo Hall, coordinating overnight housing for the weary travelers. She was there when police initiated what became a standoff that eventually led to members of the Detroit Mounted Police clubbing and stomping marchers. Several people were hospitalized. There had been a peaceful march that morning with local dignitaries, union members, and supporters of rights for the dispossessed. Witnesses said that there was no provocation on the part of the marchers. Detroiters were angry about the heavy-handed police action and demanded an investigation.

When Sheila decided to take a stand following the incident, I stood with her. She was still a college student when she organized and led the filing of a citizen's complaint against the Detroit Police Department, creating the Ad-Hoc Action Group. Ad-Hoc was a multiracial activist group protesting police brutality. The first action of the group was a sit-in at the office of the mayor, demanding that he do something about the cops.

As the police cracked down in the neighborhoods, fanning the rage, new alliances were developing among leftists and intellectuals in both black and white circles. It was clear that we would be stronger if we worked together. The brutality of Detroit's nearly all-white police force following a civil disturbance continued to escalate. While any government's first order of business is to sustain itself against attack, the police in Detroit were acting as an oppressor force and seen as the enemy of the people in the black community. It was time for action.

I was involved in the early stages of Ad-Hoc and was listed as an officer on the incorporation papers, but it quickly became evident that this would be a major undertaking, requiring a full-time commitment. At the time, Sheila and her roommate Lynda occupied a lower flat on Gladstone Street, within walking distance from my house. Lynda became Sheila's copilot in this anti–police brutality coalition.

In between fulfilling my responsibilities for my children, I did my best to help. I attended the initial sit-in at the mayor's office, where we demanded a meeting. There, I shared space with people of influence in the city: clergy, professors, intellectuals, activists, and everyday citizens who were concerned about police run amok in their communities. Overall, the assembly was peaceful; folks went about their protest in quiet conversation.

I was with Sheila in various settings when she talked with the mayor, the police commissioner, and the fire marshal. She was completely comfortable, passionate, and fearless. Despite her young age, she managed Ad-Hoc like a seasoned activist, pulling together a powerful group of concerned citizens who were determined to get a response to community complaints.

Many Ad-Hoc members had been active in Hourglass. Others, primarily the professionals, knew Sheila through her parents at the Catholic Worker. They respected her expertise and experience and regarded her as being on solid ground. After two or three days, the mayor finally met with a small group of us, agreeing to dismantle the Mounted Police Division, the ones who had trampled members of the Poor People's Campaign. Although going forward the mounted division did enjoy a lower profile, the mayor failed to keep his word: the disbandment did not occur.

By the summer of 1968, police in Detroit were brutally wreaking havoc in the community. Tactical mobile units of police, commonly known in the community as the "big four" (for their practice of patrolling four men to a car), were present throughout black neighborhoods. In addition, as the days marched on, there were an escalating number of clashes between police and young people in city parks, where the kids congregated on hot summer evenings. Many of these clashes consisted of teens being harassed by the police, who were intent on clearing them from the parks.

Ad-Hoc had a contingent of white middle-class members, mostly women, who volunteered to monitor police actions at local parks and other spots. On the street, our main mission was to record instances of police brutality by taking photos and capturing the badge numbers of the offending officers. Our cameras were our weapons. This was an effort to force the mayor to take action in stopping these abuses.

We developed our photos, which showed police using unnecessarily aggressive tactics, made posters displaying the badge numbers of these policemen—sometimes with a photograph— and then picketed the police station with our signs.

We demonstrated regularly at midday in front of Police Headquarters at 1300 Beaubien Street. There were always bystanders, some of them surveillance cops with cameras who filmed us as we picketed them. Soon blacks began to join us, marching aside us in a separate circle, and the effort became powerful and newsworthy. The separate circles were intended to illustrate that whites recognized that the grievances were primarily experienced by blacks and that whites supported them in their demands for atonement. At the time, I was unaware that Sheila was coordinating the black presence through connections she had in the black community. It was a very tactically astute action, and I am sure the police were troubled by our unity.

Protest work was fully integrated into the pattern of our lives, and I was drawn like a soldier to battle. I somehow felt that my being there could make a difference. I was becoming ever more deeply involved in movement work, which had by then evolved well beyond those early days with Father Cunningham. There was a different feeling on the streets and in the air, and I was moving with it. This meant finding myself at odds with my mentors at a time when what had initially bound us—our mutual faith—had evaporated on my end.

One day when I was downtown, I ran into Father Cunningham as he was signing up people to participate in a biracial, peace-seeking march for unity. On display at his table was the march logo: one black and one white hand reaching toward each other from opposite directions. As we chatted, he admonished me for my militancy and shared his opinion that activities that promoted opposition and bitterness between the races would push a resolution to racism farther down the road.

"I don't care if you are a purple panther, you will not solve the problem by provoking hostility between the races," he told me flatly.

I disagreed and said so. "I believe that blacks must be the vanguard in the struggle for equality, or we'll never reach our goals," I told him "With simple integration, whites still hold all the power."

Who could deny that there is structural racism in our society—then or now? Why is it that black militants who insist on dignity and self-determination for themselves and their communities are seen as provocateurs of racial hostility rather than as human beings standing against the violence being perpetrated against them?

The underlying assumption of those who oppose radical action is that blacks who are the victims of oppression should be grateful that whites accept them into their world and that this will move us closer to a peaceful and equal society.

"Why would blacks ever choose such qualified integration over self-determination?" I asked. "It's not that whites are powerless to address racism—to the contrary. I believe that whites have an equally critical role to play in pushing back against the overt and covert aggressors within our own white communities."

A group of young people approached and asked Bill about his march. I would have liked to continue our conversation, but that was not the time. He was busy, and I left for home. Our disagreement on this principle would continue. It was yet another part of me that I was leaving behind as I abandoned my old ways of thinking in favor of a new life direction, one in which I was solely in control of where I was headed.

I had been betrayed by my church, first by the dishonesty and hostility we faced as a result of our Hourglass activism and then, fatally, by the intentional cover-up of a breach of ethics regarding the administration of federal antipoverty funds. My faith in my religion was broken.

Severing my ties to my religious past pierced deeply into my psyche. I explored my wounds carefully at first. There, in the place where I expected to find a desolate bleeding hole, a fragment of my inner self bubbled to the surface to heal my pain. I discovered that my spirituality remained, independent of the rituals and traditions of my religion. I was free to respond to the call of my deeper self. Leaving the Catholic Church was not the end of my spirituality, and this was a discovery that I was comfortable with—a new beginning.

This rite of passage placed me on the cusp of major change. While I was not yet sure where this new path would lead me, over time my new theology took shape. In my spiritual life, I still experienced my familiar depth of meaning in my daily activities. My relationships were intact. Ordinary events like hugging my kids, communicating caringly with others, loving and being loved, giving selflessly, and holding deep inner thoughts still touched what I called my soul. My spiritual needs were being fulfilled through conscious action.

In retrospect, my transition from Catholic activism to political work was not a huge leap. Those of us who left the traditional Church had reached a new stage in our spiritual lives. We continued our fellowship to garner strength against the greater oppressors, racism, and the war in Vietnam. We believed that we were living the Gospel and felt that the formal church and its rules were no longer of benefit to us.

As I continued to move along my new path, I slowly disengaged from many of my beloved tribe and adopted a new community based inside the civil rights movement. Although I had gained priceless knowledge and experience, which began through Father Cunningham's work to organize us, there was a price to be paid for my all-out effort to force the Church to act on its promises.

I had expended and exhausted myself. Then, as the reckoning came, I gave up my religion, and unconsciously, I began to tear at the remaining ties that bound me to that last part of my old self: my marriage.

DIVORCE

This is the part where you find out who you are.
—UNKNOWN

FATHER CUNNINGHAM was often in our neighborhood during this period, visiting his aging father at the end of our block. One day, he stopped by to show Don and me his new Harley-Davidson motorcycle, a glowing chrome and black beauty. We walked to the curb to inspect his treasure as he revved the engine, showing it off.

"Climb on, Joann, I'll take you for a ride." I hesitated, but he didn't seem to notice. He mounted the great machine. "Come on!" There was a mischievous look in his eyes.

"Well"—I tried to think of a good excuse, but it was clear he wasn't going to listen—"only if we don't go on the freeway," I said, as I timidly slid one leg over the monstrous cycle. I've never quite understood how I could be so bold in the face of adversity yet at the same time so cautious about my physical safety in more routine matters.

Needless to say, with all his style and verve, that's exactly where we went. The roaring machine canted slightly as we rounded the corner onto Chicago Boulevard, sailed down the Hamilton ramp, and drove right onto the freeway heading toward downtown.

We had no helmets; my hair lay flat against my head. The force of the air against my face took my breath away. I closed my eyes to obliterate the sight of the rushing pavement. He was passing cars, going fast. The noise of the engine hurt my ears. I was terrified and holding on for dear life. I kept thinking, Dear God, save me; I'm a mother.

Suddenly, the sound changed to a resounding echo. We were under Cobo Hall, Detroit's convention center, where the roar of the engine bounced off the walls of the tunneled roadway. Topside again, Bill rounded the island at the foot of Woodward Avenue, briefly stopping at a traffic light, where, for thirty seconds, I tried to calm my beating heart.

Too soon, he revved up again and off we sped, now heading north and backtracking to home sweet home. He deposited me in front of our house—me stiff with fear, him laughing uproariously. It was a typical Bill experience. He just swept you up and took you along. It seemed as if this exactly mimicked the course my life was taking.

As people in need continued to come and go and my interest in the community expanded, the atmosphere within our house also began to change. I admit that it was becoming more of a community house than a place for a man's respite. Don started complaining that the house was in chaos when he came home. Sometimes as he entered the kitchen through the back door, he would open the oven to see if it was clean. I was standing there one day when he came in. There were breadcrumbs in the small oven from sandwiches I had made for lunch.

"And what have you been doing all day," he demanded, his face a snarl of disapproval.

Well, let's see, I thought. Today, I have worked as a mom, a counselor, a social worker, a cook, a supervisor, a community activist, a nurse, a housekeeper, a laundress, and more. Kids were underfoot, toys and people were scattered about the house, the dog needed to go out, and I was struggling to get dinner ready. I had succeeded in some of these activities and failed in others, but I gave each a 100 percent, all-fired try. I didn't say any of this out loud, of course. My body was fired up, ready for battle, but I kept it all inside. As usual, Don passed through the kitchen and the living room to barricade himself in his study, his domain:

the room where no one else, including me, was allowed. He remained there until I brought things under control and put dinner on the table.

It took me decades to realize that being a foster mother and taking people into our home made me feel useful and offered me a purpose at which I could succeed. I would guess that Don's leaving for work each day offered him a similar feeling. My responsibility for our six children and our home was overwhelming and impossible to do well. Embracing others was a distraction. It also provided an opportunity to run away from my unhappiness. I was failing at being a good housewife, the only role that society had told me I was fit for all of my life. Service to others was something Don and I agreed on, or so I thought.

By 1968, I began to see that Don was getting uncomfortable. He was no longer eager to be involved. I was happy to have him stay with the children while I followed the movement. I was aware of the spreading decolonization sentiment through my contact with others at demonstrations, and I realized that the turn-the-other-cheek, nonviolent civil rights movement was no longer the predominant tenor on the streets. Detroit was moving toward black pride and black power. Tension was heightening. I was spending a lot of time with Sheila, who was in harmony with the changes. I sometimes went with her as a companion when she was invited to meet with blacks in their communities. I was doing fine with the changing atmosphere, but no doubt Don, as a white male, experienced it differently.

Fifty years in retrospect, I recognize how difficult this transition in our lives must have been for him. At the time he took me as his Irish Catholic bride, neither of us could have imagined the direction in which our lives would go. My culture had programmed me to be thoughtless and obedient, with no aspirations beyond housewife and mother.

During the 1960s, change was in the atmosphere we breathed—not so much for men, perhaps, because they were free to be themselves coming into this period, but for women, the earth seemed to move under our feet, and we changed before our husbands' eyes.

Some changes were more discreet than others, and some women were masters at satisfying men. I was all-in to explore who I was destined to be, like a woman throwing off the mantle of feudalism. It was my time, my interests, my opportunity to grow. There were many divorces in the 1960s, including Pat and Rosemarie's. During these years, the personal growth that resulted in divorce affected a large number of women, even older ones.

Don was patient for a long time—partly, I guess, because he was a just and honest person, and partly because he did not want a divorce. But our differences were proving to be irreconcilable.

The morning after our protest in front of the chancery and my anticlimactic conversation with the archbishop, Don brought in the morning paper. As he read, I saw his eyebrows lift. There I was on page 20 of Section A, plaid suit, sunglasses, and all. The headline shouted: "Mrs. Don Castle Confronts Archbishop." Our home address appeared alongside my picture.

Don was livid: "How could you do this to me?"

"This was not my fault," I retorted. "Nobody asked me my name, and I would have never given yours. They must have gotten the address out of the phone book."

He spun on his heel, and his face was suddenly in mine. "Everyone at work is going to see this!"

"I can't take it back," I said, dropping the topic and walking away. I was preoccupied. I had walked away from my church, severed in mind, body, and spirit. Now I was losing my marriage, becoming my own woman.

Don was a proud man. Having his wife "on the street" was an affront to his manhood and his ability to control his family. Not long after, I arranged to have lunch with him one day after I had been to a meeting. I thought it would be fun to have lunch: two grown-ups with no kids to interfere. I even thought it might be good for our relationship. Was I ever wrong! In his eyes, I looked like a career woman: tailored dress, stockings, high heels, earrings. He did not speak the whole time we were at the restaurant.

"What's going on," I asked repeatedly. But he wouldn't talk with me.

Afterward, I dropped him back at his office in the General Motors Tech Center. As he was exiting the car he finally spoke. "Don't you ever again come to my workplace looking like a career woman," he snapped. "It makes me look like I can't take care of my family."

This was it, in a nutshell. My rise in the world outside our home made him feel like a failure. I'm sorry, I thought to myself, but this genie cannot be put back in her bottle.

IT WAS THE SUMMER OF 1969. When President Nixon was inaugurated for his first term, he promised to wind down the war in Vietnam then did just the opposite. Fashion reflected the mood of young people, who were wearing antiwar military jackets sporting peace signs. The Chicago Seven, indicted on charges stemming from their protests at the Chicago Democratic Convention, were on trial. Watching on Mr. Cunningham's big television set my children saw Neil Armstrong take the first steps on the moon. More than four hundred thousand people showed up at a farm in Bethel, New York, and created the cultural phenomenon known as Woodstock. Clashes between gay rights activists and police outside a bar in Greenwich Village escalated into the Stonewall riots and ignited the gay rights movement. Gas at the tiny independent gas station on Third Street and Clairmount cost 34 cents a gallon, and if I was out of funds, the owner would tell me I could pay next time. I always did.

I was growing more headstrong and more passionately involved in the world that I was determined to create for myself and my children. Don was getting more and more anxious. "There are a lot of people around, and too many end up staying at our house," he protested.

"Yes, it seems we've started something we can't stop," I retorted. "I'm spending a lot of time with people who *like me*, and that's not the feeling I'm getting from you anymore."

My husband wanted me to be a wife. I wanted to be a whole person. Our marriage was falling apart. Too many of our days and nights were punctuated by emotional outbursts. He was suffocating me, wanting to put me back into the package he had chosen for a bride. Don and I drifted further away from each other. One evening when he was out late, I boldly waited up in the study, breaking his rule by entering and sitting in his domain. When he came in, the violation was irrevocable.

"Why don't you just leave," I offered. I felt a surprising lack of emotion.

"Give me three days," he responded, and it was done. It was the first exchange we had had in weeks that didn't end up in a fight.

Don filed for a no-fault divorce. We explained to the children that we would be separating. They were young; they didn't say much. Their worldview was mercifully narrow. Finally, Greg spoke up: "Will I still be able to play with the Chefs?" The Chef family lived kitty-corner from us.

"Of course," we assured him. "None of those things will change." No one said anything else. What were they thinking?

Did the children even understand what divorce was? What separation meant? Ken told me recently that he hadn't realized that Don was *physically leaving* until he saw him putting his things in his car and pulling away. Thinking of my own childhood now, I recall how oblivious my dad was to what was going on in my mind when I interacted with him. Were Don and I the same, focusing on ourselves? Were we repeating the same patterns? Had either of us considered what this would mean to the children? Like too many important things, we simply never discussed it.

Carolyn tells a story today. At the time, she was seven years old. She saw me vacuuming and approached me, asking, "Are you and Dad getting a divorce?"

Carolyn has always been direct in her communications with others. It's a trait that's deeply imbedded in her personality. According to her memory, I said, "Yes," and then, without further comment, simply turned the vacuum back on and continued vacuuming. Possible? Of course. The circumstances were so stressful at the time, I just don't remember.

Don and I had a brief conversation about what he would take with him, which was basically the furniture in the study, his room, the one he loved so much. He suggested that he would pick the children up on the weekends, and I agreed. For the time being, he would make the house payment, and I would work on the further details with Friend of the Court, the agency that negotiated child support obligations. As promised, within three days of our initial conversation about a divorce, he was gone. He never came back for the furniture.

My marriage was restrictive and demeaning and not a healthy place for me. This was not unusual for women who married in the 1950s. Women's liberation had not yet become a movement, but the concept of liberation was part of the essential change echoing around the world.

Our separation was a relief to me. Our constant conflicts—I don't even know what they were about—in front of the children would stop. Everything turned into a shouting match. Wondering where he was at night and feeling reluctant to come home when he was there would be resolved. I was part of a broader community now, where I was accepted and had connections. I had no regrets. I was thirty-two years old, and I fully believed that I could raise our six children as a single parent, as a part of my chosen community. I was ready to move on.

I recognized that I was not without faults. Housework frustrated me. Everything I set right seemed to be undone thirty minutes later. Don even got a housekeeper to come one day a week. I felt sorry for her, as she tried to mop floors and scrub stairs with our kids and their friends everywhere. She didn't last long.

Our doors were open. What we needed was a manager, and I was too frazzled to perform that role. It took two hours to fix a meal and then it was gone within ten minutes. Underneath, I was angry all the time. I just wanted someone in my life, someone to love me and accept me for who I was instead of rejecting me for who I was not.

I don't remember discussing my life with my parents during this period. They must have known that Don and I were breaking up; my sister was aware. But they did not make themselves available. I was overwhelmed physically and emotionally. Actually, it wouldn't have occurred to me to ask my parents for help or advice in any matters concerning love or the lack thereof. My mother would call occasionally, but it was hard to invest myself in a relationship with her because she had no clue about what I was going through. I felt completely and utterly alone.

Things were financially sparse for us after my divorce. We lived on very little. I had a brief spike of bitterness on my first Christmas alone with the kids. I felt impotent because Christmas was so commercialized, and I didn't have the money to celebrate. I took all our Christmas decorations—including the Hummel Nativity Baby Jesus once given to me by Don's grandmother—to the trash and nixed a Christmas tree because I wasn't able to afford gifts for the children.

I promised to take each child out, one by one, for his or her birthday, and then buy a special gift. This was fine for Ken and Carolyn, the lucky ones who had birthdays early in the year. It was less certain for Michael and Greg, who were summer babies, and for Jeff and Christine—only two years old when Don and I divorced—who were born in the fall. It pains me even now to think about the birthdays I might have missed because we were solely in survival mode.

As a family, we hung out at the Art Institute, the Children's Museum, and, when it opened, the Detroit Science Center. These institutions were free for residents and enriching to my children. I often used the Main Public Library and the Science Center as babysitters while I went grocery shopping. I began to take my kids to the Highland Park YMCA, where they were involved in summer indoor activities, fitness programs, and swimming. A priest at the parish once sponsored Jeff at a summer camp out of the area. Christine was privileged to attend a Girl Scout horse-riding camp. Eventually, our divorce was complete, and Don continued to take the children on weekends. The six of them had an active life that kept them out of trouble.

At home, we fell into a rhythm. The house was more comfortable without the screaming fights between Don and me, and we did well. But I had to admit that keeping up such a large and aging house was a challenge. That, in addition to caring for six young children, was sapping my strength.

There was a collective of medical students who lived in a house on Chicago Boulevard, the next street south of us. One day Larry, a medical resident, knocked on my door and suggested that he and his wife, Gail, move in with us and help me maintain the house. He emphasized that he could cook. Everyone in the neighborhood seemed to know us, and the collective was sometimes involved in movement work. These young residents, in their last year of medical training, had an interest in alternative methods of medical care and had once used our house to host a lecture by a doctor from China who was an expert in acupuncture. What Larry *didn't* tell me was that they needed a place to stay was because he had been kicked out of the collective.

Managing all the work the house required—from fixing leaky faucets to cutting our large lawn—was difficult, to say the least. Ken tried, but it was way too much for an eleven-year-old. And having spirited brothers so close in age, ten and nine, didn't make his life any easier. There were constant battles, as is normal for brothers. A lot of times, Ken just withdrew from the chaos.

In addition to his offer to help, Larry offered to pay rent, which would help with my strapped finances. The Michigan's Friend of the Court is the agency that handles child support services. The court determined that Don should pay me $400 a month—a totally inadequate sum—to feed, clothe, and provide health care for six children, plus pay all utilities and make household repairs. When I protested that was not enough, the worker responded, "You can't get blood from a turnip." Our finances were so tight I felt grateful for Larry's offer, and so I agreed. Larry also failed to tell me about their cats and his and Gail's own poor housekeeping skills.

The whole experience was a disaster. Larry never picked up after himself; he spilled food while he was cooking, then walked away. Dirty dishes were everywhere. His cats had free run of the kitchen counter, walking among the dishes and eating off the dirty plates. I had never lived any place where people behaved like this. We had a couple of big blowouts during which Larry informed me his wife was unhappy because I wouldn't be her friend. Who had time for friends? This experiment was over as quickly as it had begun.

In the long run, the experience was a good one. I realized, more than ever, that I needed to organize a system that would allow my children to carry their share of responsibility. Working together, we hatched a joint plan. First, we established an evening "cooldown" before bed. For this, we'd all get into our pajamas and meet in the upstairs hallway. The hallway was wide and carpeted with an aging red carpet that snaked up the stairs from the living room, twisting across the landing and up to cover the second floor hall. On one wall of the large hallway was a built-in cupboard for linens and below this were three large drawers where the children kept their toys. Five bedroom doors, a bathroom, and a door to the third floor branched off this wide spacious landing. The floor space was accommodating to our evening meeting.

We sat in a circle on the floor and reviewed our day. Everyone contributed thoughts about their activities and how they felt about them. One child might say that he had a fight with a sibling. Another might have felt left out by something her sister had done. I was amazed at their willingness to embrace this ritual. We finished with a discussion of what we could have done differently to make life easier for one another, and apologies were made as appropriate. As I reflect on this time, these evening meetings were kind of like a public confession, repentance, and absolution. Things were going well. Then I had what seemed like a brilliant thought. Why not split up the housekeeping?

There were thirteen rooms in the old house. I suggested that each child keep his or her own room clean, plus assume responsibility for one other room that was shared by the others. Excluding Christine, who was only a toddler, that would give everyone two rooms to clean; we all would share responsibility for the kitchen. This plan was a winner!

The kids kept their own rooms mostly to their satisfaction. A few of the children were neat freaks; the others, not so much. I wasn't too hard on them if they made an effort. The genius of the plan was that they seriously protected their second room. If you were going to use Carolyn's downstairs guest bathroom, you had better leave it clean; Greg's study, the same. Both these kids knew how to make it clear that they expected cooperation or the others weren't welcome to use the room. It was hard to get the kids to keep a regular cleaning schedule, so I got them to agree to what we called a "cleaning blitz." I would blow a whistle and each would work steadily for twenty minutes. When I blew it again, they were finished. It was a good plan and worked well.

At this stage of my life, my world was framed by purpose. Adjusting to being the mom in a one-parent family, I worked hard to keep the house and the family intact. I saw myself as a strong woman, one fully involved in the civil rights movement, with her children at her side. Across the country, there was passion and fervor for change. I was simply in the flow. I felt free to be myself and was compelled to serve a greater cause. I was well supported by friends, and, despite setbacks, I felt that we were making gains both in the household and in the movement.

I did not regret the loss of my marriage; instead, it was a load off my mind. But I had not yet assessed what the divorce would mean for the children long term. Even though Don was rigid and the kids were often afraid of him, I was slow to realize how the loss of a father and the distraction of a busy mother would leave damage in their wake.

When Christmas came around again in 1970, we were still struggling financially, but we decided on Christmas Eve to see if we could obtain a bargain tree from Eastern Market. The lot was nearly empty, and a lonely attendant told us to take what we wanted. We searched through the abandoned trees and adopted one that suited our needs. We went home feeling good, giggling that we were giving this abandoned tree a home. Rescuing others was part of our lives. The more pertinent question may have been, however, would we be able to rescue ourselves?

I was learning that motherhood is a daunting task highlighted by historic events and significant locales that frame our children's growth and development. In this context, we make choices for ourselves, and we make choices on our children's behalf. This takes thought and balance, gifts that are not necessarily given to the young. They are skills that must be learned.

PART THREE

Radical Activism: Control, Conflict, and Change

Revolutionary Detroit

Those who profess to favor freedom and yet deprecate agitation,
are people who want crops without ploughing the ground;
they want rain without thunder and lightning;
they want the ocean without the roar of its many waters.
The struggle may be a moral one, or it may be a physical one,
or it may be both. But it must be a struggle. Power concedes
nothing without a demand. It never did and it never will.
—Frederick Douglass

BY THE END OF THE 1960S, America was teetering on the edge of a precipice. Speaking in Grosse Pointe, a suburb of Detroit, in 1968, Martin Luther King Jr., warned that unless "America is prepared to do something massively, affirmatively and forthrightly about the great problem we face in the area of race . . . the problem can bring the curtain of doom down on American civilization."

The American Left was calling for a revolution. The cry first rose up from the Jim Crow South against discriminatory practices, substandard housing, and inadequate services for minorities, and then blew north. Our poorest brothers and sons were being drafted into the war in Vietnam where they were killing rice farmers and villagers who, like them, just wanted to be free from oppression. At the same time, brutal police tactics to contain the discontented masses were resulting in war on our streets at home.

Young people in the United States knew that we wanted a world free from our pervasive social ills. We were consumed by it and outraged by the repressive response of our country to our calls for equality and peace. On the lips of activists everywhere—from the black power movement to the antiwar movement, from the burgeoning women's rights movement to the radical left political movement—there was one word to describe what we wanted: *revolution.*

The word crept into our daily conversations and changed our rhetoric. But there was no unanimity on the task at hand. In the urgency of fast-moving events, the word *revolution* relative to our fight remained undefined. We were so busy with changes that were destabilizing our lives that we had no time to assess the idea of revolution or where we were on the trajectory. It was like being in a storm at sea without a compass.

Looking back, I believe that blacks and whites approached the road to revolution from different points of view, depending on the level of threat to their race. As events rose to a fever pitch, those most affected were largely people of color, who time after time demonstrated their willingness to lay down their lives in response to the call for freedom. Their only hope was that as they fell someone would pick up their freedom banner and carry on.

On the other hand, I now recognize that white privilege played far more of a role in the struggle than we recognized or acknowledged at the time. Whites on the left had the luxury of deciding when and whether to commit. Too often, they became caught up in an intellectual argument for purism. What we should have been debating was whether effective change comes from the bottom up or the top down, the advantages and disadvantages of each, and how to put ourselves in positions of influence. This imperative was impossible for us to understand in the moment. We were only beginning to grasp our roles and our tasks.

Let's face it, whites have a different life experience. The reality was that, as part of the dominant race, they could always walk away and get lost in a crowd. In stating this, I do not mean to diminish the role that whites played in America's revolutionary consciousness—it was a critical role—but the stakes were not the same for them. Whites were ideally suited to play a supporting role for the black freedom movement. There was, and there remains still, an important role for whites in combatting racism among our own people. Without white activism within white communities, racism will never be uprooted at the source.

Detroit was unique in the way blacks and whites worked together in the late 1960s and early 1970s. There are many possible reasons for this, one being the city's working-class history and its strong union base. Another was the early strength of the Communist Party in Detroit and the class analysis portrayed in its slogan: "Black and white, unite and fight!" Black workers in the auto plants generally understood the real enemy.

Radical black activism had a natural home in Detroit. Ideas, even if they were generated elsewhere, found there fertile ground in which they could be planted, tended, and grown into something unique. The efforts around the Black Manifesto were one such example.

James Forman was the author of the "Black Manifesto." He was a veteran civil rights activist, well known nationally for his work with SNCC and its role in organizing blacks to register to vote across the South. The "Black Manifesto" was based upon the theory that blacks were owed reparations for their centuries of racist treatment, exploitation, and servitude in the building of the most industrialized country in the world, and that the Christian churches and Jewish synagogues brought to this country by the colonizers have been complicit in the process.

Action plans for the "Manifesto" called for radical blacks to confront local white Christian churches with demands for $500 million in reparations. The money would be used to empower blacks in various entrepreneurial start-ups, including businesses that would produce written and filmed material that would educate blacks on how they were being exploited. A detailed plan of how this would be done was outlined in the "Manifesto" document.

The concept of reparations has not disappeared and can be found in contemporary discourse. In 2017, a United Nations affiliated group has said that "compensation is necessary to combat the disadvantages caused by 245 years of legally allowing the sale of people based on the color of their skin. The UN group warned that the United States has not confronted its legacy of "racial terrorism."

The report, which is nonbinding, specified that reparations can come in a variety of forms, including educational opportunities, psychological rehabilitation, debt cancellation, and formal apologies. Some institutions have started to take these steps. The call for reparations is also important because it requires whites to admit that they have benefited from slavery and mass incarceration.

Jim Forman initiated one of the first local confrontations, in May 1969, when he interrupted Sunday services at Riverside Church New York City to demand reparations for the Church's role in perpetuating slavery. A few weeks later, the League of Revolutionary Black Workers staged a similar event at an upscale Episcopal church in Detroit's Bloomfield Hills neighborhood.

These activists had been conducting some of the most effective radical movement work since the Freedom Riders, and they focused largely on black-based organizing for black self-determination. Most of them were connected with the League of Revolutionary Black Workers, which was a magnet for black labor activism at the time. People in the League were well known in Detroit for initiating a newspaper, *The Inner-City Voice*, and for organizing the Dodge Revolutionary Union Movement (DRUM) among autoworkers. In 1968, workers from this group gained attention for successfully leading two wildcat strikes that shut down auto production at two Chrysler Motors plants in Detroit. These actions resulted in a major victory in bringing justice to employment practices in the Detroit auto industry.

I was aware of remarkable work being done by the League and those affiliated with it through my own activities, with Hourglass and then later with Ad-Hoc and other movement work. I was growing more radical, more committed to efforts to support black self-determination in Detroit and elsewhere, and through my relationship with Sheila, I soon found myself involved—in a number of ways—with the vanguard work being done by black activists in Detroit.

Sheila Murphy and I were an unlikely pair. I was ten years her senior and the mother of six children. Sheila was a student at Monteith College, a small interdisciplinary college on Wayne State's campus. Her education was supplemented by a wealth of early exposure to community organizing while growing up in a Catholic Worker house. Nevertheless, as my fervor for politics unfolded, Shelia and I formed a deep bond and we became friends.

Tough as nails and a gifted organizer, Shelia earned my respect early on. Her eyes were always on the prize. In her company, I felt accepted and useful. Sheila's and my friendship was totally in the context of the movement. It was her life; it was my love. I loved being on the street with her. She was astute, and I was learning, learning, learning.

That winter I couldn't afford to buy myself a coat or boots. The kids' needs always came first. I was layered under a lightweight plaid poncho, but my feet were constantly wet from the snow and slush. As I arrived at her house one day, wet and cold, Sheila looked me over.

"What are trying to do, get pneumonia? You can't go around like that," she admonished.

"It *is* miserable out there," I said, brushing snow off my poncho, my lower jaw trembling from the cold. "The snow is so wet—my feet are just soaked."

"Why don't you get some boots? Don't you have a winter coat?"

"No to both." I kicked off my shoes. "Got some dry socks? Anything? The kids' needs come first. They're growing so fast. But by the time the older boys' coats get passed down to Michael, they're shot. He's the one getting new clothes. I made Carolyn a coat out of my mother's old wool one. Friends passed on to me a coat for Chrissy. I just don't have the money. I'm doing the best I can."

Fishing through her closet, she handed me a long brown wool coat, more like a winter cloak with a hood, a popular fashion that she didn't often wear. I was taller than Sheila, but it still worked. She also gave me money to buy a pair of winter boots. I appreciated her sensitivity and was grateful for her generosity. The first time I wore the coat in the neighborhood, a black man sitting on a porch turned to his friend. "Well, lookie here," he said. "If it isn't Snow White." I had to laugh—it was true; all I needed was a basket.

As a teenager, Sheila had worked as a staff secretary at West Central Organization (WCO) on the Near West Side of Detroit. The operation was the hub of a citywide effort at community organizing based upon the concept of self-determination and was a connection point for both races to coalesce around this work. Sheila's parents were active in the formation of the organization and served on the board. In the WCO setting, black militants became comfortable working with respected whites. Sheila's talents allowed her to work with one group as easily as the other.

It was there that Sheila met Ken Cockrel, a young black militant law student with a penetrating analysis and a masterful machine-gun tongue. Ken was tall and sleek, with wire-rimmed glasses and a distinctive fluid walk. He was not a man who engaged in trivia. Michele Gibbs, longtime activist and close family friend, tells the story of a meeting she attended at the WCO office when a black organizer from out of town was making a presentation. As discussion ensued, he admonished blacks for agreeing with something that whites wanted them to do. The speaker was startled when Ken Cockrel angrily responded, "This is Detroit. Blacks and whites in Detroit know how to work with each other. We don't need your advice!"

Although Sheila was not aligned with any leftist organizations, she was very familiar with their histories and politics. I began to realize that I was completely ignorant of the long history of radical left politics in the United States. As I moved around the city with Shelia, I was mystified by the various group names and acronyms. This was a new environment for me, and as I watched people interact with one another, discussing events and organizing activities, I felt like a neophyte.

Sheila introduced me to folks across the political left. Conversations with members of some of these groups were constructive, others rhetorical and hard to sort out, but Sheila managed to communicate with everyone. People engaged in some of the more serious conversations I was party to were now alleged to be underground. I kept my mouth shut and listened. I was unfamiliar with these groups' alliances, their prejudices, and their sectarianism, and I was hopelessly outside their rhetoric and theories. I was there because I was drawn in by the state of affairs, and I depended on my head as well as my heart to lead me in the right direction.

As summer 1969 rolled around, another opportunity unfolded. Sheila was acquainted with some leaders of the Black Manifesto. As the power of the "Manifesto" unfolded, we realized that the information Tony and I had about the Catholic Church's mishandling of Detroit poverty program funds might be useful to their strategic plan, which was currently drawing significant press coverage. Sheila made the contact suggesting that the Manifesto group might be interested in the information Tony and I had secretly replicated at the chancery office on the misuse of poverty program funds.

Our meeting with three black leaders of the Detroit Manifesto actions was arranged by Sheila at her office near Wayne State University. Ironically, the space had been donated by the archdiocese for Ad-Hoc's anti–police brutality work. It was early summer, and it was hot as Tony and I walked up the steps. I was a little nervous. We were taken to a sheltered room for this clandestine meeting. They say that women always remember what they wore at significant or life-changing events, and what I wore this day is emblazoned in my memory. At this time, women still wore dresses. Mine was a sleeveless, yellow linen culotte dress with a self-belt. My brown hair was long and straight, which was the style of the day. It may have been pulled back, as I often wore it.

As Tony and I approached the room, a loud conversation was under way about someone who had shot up the union hall at the Laborers' Local. I heard an amused voice say, "Here was this guy shooting in all directions and corrupt union officials running for their lives, which doesn't happen often enough."

It was a rich and commanding voice. "Bullet holes all over the wall," he added.

I took a deep breath. What were we getting into?

In the room were three big guys with afros and a savvy air about them. As we entered, the one telling the story turned. He was chuckling, which at the time I thought was highly unusual, considering the topic. Handsome, he wore black-rimmed glasses and had an approachable quality. His name was Mike.

Sheila introduced all of us, then left the room. Tony and I proceeded to tell our story. We described how the data we had gathered from the archdiocese office confirmed that money intended for the poor was being siphoned off to special interests and relatives of administrators, who were not working in the program.

Tony was a seasoned lawyer and a very charismatic guy. He loved an audience, and he could sometimes become a bit grandiose, as some lawyers are prone to do. He sat next to me; the men faced us across the table. At one point, when I thought Tony was being a little over the top and a bit insensitive, considering whom we were talking to, I kicked him under the table.

"What are you kicking me for?" he demanded as he turned to face me. I never expected he would say such a thing out loud, and I worked hard to stay cool under pressure. Tony stared at me—in good humor—and the men laughed. Ultimately, we answered their questions, gave them our documentation, and the meeting ended soon after.

It wasn't until later that I learned the men had put our information to good use. On August 30, 1970, I was reading an article in the *Free Press* about the Manifesto organization, which quoted one Mike Hamlin, who was discussing plans to confront churches and synagogues across the country with demands for reparations—including the Roman Catholic Archdiocese of Detroit.

"We are in the process of categorizing all the outrageous acts of the archdiocese against blacks," he said, "including alleged mishandling of poverty funds . . . the closing of inner-city black parochial schools, and nondisclosure of financial holdings."

The article described Mike Hamlin as "a big, friendly man with growing influence in the black community and a potential terror in

Detroit white churches and synagogues"—which sounded much like the approachable man from our meeting!

Hamlin continued, "We have to do what we can for the liberation of our people."

The aggressive measures by the Manifesto group quickly brought unwanted results. Federal subpoenas were handed down, targeting Mike Hamlin, chairman of the Black Economic Development Conference, and others in the leadership with allegations that the reparations demand amounted to extortion. Ken Cockrel and other attorneys working for the group called the move by law enforcement a witch hunt and managed to shame them into backing down by demanding the subpoenas be quashed until the attorneys could determine whether the grand jury was composed of individuals representative in race, age, and income.

A few months later I was attending an antiwar activity at a local Episcopal church. At the time, draft dodgers from the Vietnam War were being harbored there in the basement. About two hundred people had been gathering for three days to buffer the fugitives from the FBI, which was attempting to arrest them. When I learned of the situation, I prepared food and hurried over to the church.

I took my food to a marshal, whom I identified by his armband, at the side door of the church near the stairs to the basement. As I walked back into the sacristy, I saw Sandy Stevenson, a friend I knew from Ad-Hoc activities. She called me over to introduce me to "Mike." The tall black man with a mustache, an Afro, and dark-rimmed glasses looked vaguely familiar, but I couldn't place him. He met my eyes and smiled.

"We've met before," he said. "I'd like to talk with you sometime about activities we're working on." Then he asked for my phone number.

"It's okay," Sandy whispered to me.

I gave him my number.

I was a bit distracted that day, so I failed to recognize the same guy from Tony's and my Manifesto meeting, the one with the inappropriate chuckle. Antiwar work was not Mike's normal focus, but I learned he was at the demonstration because, after separating from his wife, he was staying at the parish house there at the Episcopal church. He had stopped in to see what was happening. After the three of us chatted for a moment, I moved on. There were a lot of connections that I was missing.

IN MARCH 1969, my friend Dennie was involved in an action with eight others—including priests, nuns, and a social worker—who would become known as the D.C. Nine. The group broke into the Washington, D.C., offices of the Dow Chemical Company to protest Dow's complicity in the Vietnam War. Dow was well known for the production of napalm and other chemical weapons widely used against the Vietnamese people. The intruders spilled human blood on files and records—generally destroying the offices —and then awaited arrest. They published a statement against the "death-dealing exploitation of people of the third world" by the company.

I later traveled to D.C. to attend Dennie's trial. I was a hometown girl, an unsophisticated traveler. It was a new experience for me to fly into an unfamiliar city by myself. Somehow, I found the church where visitors were being housed and slept with dozens of others on the hard marble floor. I was there in support but helpless to do anything.

Dennie was found guilty of three felonies for destroying property and sentenced to three years' imprisonment. His legal team appealed, claiming the group did not get a fair trial, and ultimately won their case. Neither Dow nor the government wanted the publicity of another public fight with the Catholic Church over Dow's role in the war. The government offered a deal. Dennie was sentenced to one year's probation and was released after pleading guilty to a misdemeanor. Dennie—who would soon leave the Church—was lucky. Many other activists, some with whom I was close friends, suffered much harsher fates after following their conscience and taking action.

I next ran into Mike after returning from my trip to D.C. That time he was with Ken Cockrel, who always spoke first and at such a rapid pace that it took me time to grasp what he was saying, let alone to process it, before he was gone. He moved as quickly as he spoke.

A short time later I ran into Ken again, who made sure to apologize that "the brother" wasn't with him. I was deeply confused.

Not long after, Mike finally used the number I had given him. He'd lost Sheila's number—could he have it? We chatted for a bit before hanging up. Then he called me a few days with the exact same request—he'd managed to lose Sheila's number *again*. Other calls followed. I began to suspect these calls meant something.

Mike would confess to me later that he had learned from Ken, who'd talked with Sheila, that I was recently divorced. He knew there would be enormous risks for me in our developing a relationship, not to mention for him with respect to his work. The effect of racism is a two-way street. He wanted to be sure that I was comfortable. I kept his calls secret.

Being in Mike's presence was always comfortable. Despite his stature in the movement, he seemed gentle and humble. He had a reputation for being able to draw people of different persuasions together and weave their ideas into something that could move the work forward. He listened. His eyes smiled. He chuckled.

One evening, I walked over to Sheila's house to find Mike and Ken sitting in her kitchen. I knew that Ken and Shelia had become an item. Ken was fast-talking, as usual. Mike looked at me knowingly during the conversation. I felt a warm glow from his presence. We sat and chatted late into the evening. By the time we left, it was dark, and Mike offered to drive me home.

On the way, he pulled the car over to the curb at a neighborhood park a few blocks from my home, and we continued to talk. Over the previous few weeks, it had crossed my mind more than once that his frequent phone calls were headed toward something more. But I put off thinking about this because there was such a huge gap between his radical political life and mine as a white woman, the mother of several small children. I enjoyed our conversations, even looked forward to them, but they had never been personal, and it had been easy to put off any thoughts of a relationship. I never dreamed we would find ourselves together like this.

I sat next to him in the car, confounded by the contrasts between us but drawn to his warmth and his passion for the struggle. Our commitments to the broader good gave us common ground. He could have sensed that I was interested in knowing him better, but the fast-moving events of the evening had caught me by surprise.

"May I see you again?" he asked. "Maybe Sheila would let us meet at her place."

"Yes." The word tumbled from my mouth. "I'll ask her."

He pulled me close and kissed me gently. I was a little overwhelmed, but I didn't resist. Now, I had plenty to think about.

Mike was sitting on Sheila's porch when I came around the corner. He had an intense expression on his face which I didn't know how to read. I was slightly uneasy. We sat awkwardly in her living room for a bit. Then Mike picked up the morning paper and began to read the news out loud and ask me what I thought about the issues. We talked about the world, the struggle, and local events.

His demeanor softened, and I soon relaxed as we began a conversation bracketed by our political interests. Who could have imagined that the morning paper conversation that we started that day would continue for the next four decades?

I hung out with Mike at Sheila's for several months. There was a comfortable chemistry between us, and I believed that our relationship was giving him strength and comfort to carry on his fight. What I learned during this period was that Mike's whole purpose in life was the liberation of his people. He was on the Central Committee of the League of Revolutionary Black Workers and would soon become chairman of the Black Workers Congress, a national organization that was composed of the League and other small groups of black workers from around the country. I also learned Mike's close friendship with Ken Cockrel was born out of their both having served in the Korean War.

Mike and I had long discussions on how to motivate more people to become involved in the movement. He believed deeply that working with and gaining the support of whites would offer the League some much needed protection against government

agencies bent on destroying their efforts. During these early conversations, Mike first advanced the idea of a community-based
book club. We began to fashion the concept of a multiracial educational forum built on good books that would unite blacks and
whites and advance mutual goals. The League would take the
lead in choosing the books and the speakers, while white allies
would handle the organizing aimed at liberals and progressives
who were willing to work together with blacks in developing a
revolutionary consciousness. The book author or another national figure of importance would be brought in to lead the discussion. I immediately saw how important the educational focus
could be as a tool for changing attitudes in the white community.

"I've seen your work in Hourglass, your commitment, and your
work ethic," Mike ventured. "I've seen some of your newsletters.
They're good. The book club work wouldn't be that different. You
could work from home after your children leave for school."

"I've still got the Hourglass mailing list." I said with a laugh.
"It's a good place to start." Our plan began to take shape. Sometimes it seemed that all my organizations started from the mailing
list of the last one.

As we developed book club plans, I began to appreciate Mike's
leadership style. He listened. He was open to my ideas. "What
do you think?" was his signature phrase, and what I thought was
integrated into our work. We worked well as a team.

MIKE APPROACHED SHEILA and a number of other white
activists with the idea of a parallel organization of whites to collaborate with the League. This would eventually become the Motor
City Labor League (MCLL). This could be a home for the book
club we had been discussing. It would be my role to handle communications, order the books, and organize the meetings. Mike
suggested that he knew many people across the country who qualified as potential speakers, and he rattled off several books that we
could feature. The book club could bring tremendous strength to
our efforts. Mike's gift was that he made it sound so simple. I soon
learned that he was a great delegator.

Sheila took the reins of the organization and was joined by Frank Joyce, who headed People Against Racism. Both Sheila and Frank were veteran movement people, but Sheila was the functional leader of MCLL. Lynda, Sheila's housemate, was her staff person. I took responsibility for the book club. Early on, Sheila and Lynda were joined by Brian Flanigan, a young veteran home safely from the Vietnam War and hired on the line at Ford Rouge, only to be injured and disabled by falling equipment. Brian was a tireless worker, talented poet, and artist who later went on to become a journalist at the *Detroit Free Press*. It was Brian who created the graphics needed for the book club's invitational brochures.

In MCLL's all-white membership were aspiring intellectuals who were studying revolutionary thought and practice under the tutelage of the League of Revolutionary Black Workers. Membership was by invitation, and decisions were made by a process called democratic centralism, which means that members took part in policy discussions but decision-making was solely in the hands of the leadership.

Since I was already engaged full time in the book club effort, I was not directly involved in the foundational work of MCLL. After Mike and I had our original book club discussions, I took the lead in organizing the program. Generally, I worked alone, but major decisions were discussed with MCLL leadership at our weekend meetings. I consulted with Sheila on day-to-day issues that extended beyond my area of specific responsibility.

Over time, veteran activists in the organization began to see themselves as revolutionary intellectuals, but I didn't see myself that way. I thought of myself more as a facilitator, contributing what skills I had to those who would lead the black freedom movement. I listened, and I facilitated where I could. Whites were in a unique position. They had more flexibility in numerous ways than blacks. With this in mind, I often found myself willing and able to take a risk to accomplish a supportive task—my activist résumé was growing.

This type of organization was new to me, as well as a bit of a giant step from my early movement activities. All those experiences had taken place on my familiar Catholic turf. Cadre work, as we called it, was a bit of a reach at first because of my limited study of the revolutionary theories that were so vital to the vision of what we hoped to create. But with the book club as my lily pad, I was like a contented duck in my own small pond.

Education was critical to becoming a revolutionary in those early days, and MCLL members set out to develop an understanding of the world we lived in. From the start, the League sent representatives from their organization to conduct Sunday morning political education sessions for MCLL members. This was a different kind of Sunday program than I had known in the Catholic Church. Our "strictly work" educational sessions took place at the organization's new, unfurnished headquarters on East Grand Boulevard. No frills; no food. I attended the very first sessions with maybe eight to twelve others. Sometimes my son, Ken, would skip his weekend visits with his father to come with me. It gave him some space from the other kids, and he found it interesting to spend time at our headquarters.

These educational sessions exposed us to radical thinking and theories. We read works based upon Marx, Lenin, and Mao— sources of thought that influenced not only the League's revolutionary thinking but also the thinking of many radical black activists of the day. These theories provided an effective counter-narrative of empowerment to a community no longer willing to accept the white majority's promise to blacks of an American Dream that was never realized. Racism's deep, lasting toll had lingered long enough. The League and others were committed to finding a new way of seeing—and changing—the world.

We white revolutionaries were getting an education in how to see the world around us differently, grasping for the first time how everything was actually interconnected. This understanding completely changed my worldview. I saw the deeper issues of class and power, of the historical transformations that have led us to this place in time. I understood that history wasn't a given, that it was created through decisions, and that individuals have a role to play in making the world they want to live in. I came to learn that if you keep piling bricks on a board, it will eventually break, a cautionary tale often applicable to myself.

Organizations of the period were struggling to find their place in the wider effort. As our work developed, we came together from many perspectives. At one end of the spectrum were moderate but compassionate whites who had become politicized in the radical Catholic movement. The Ad-Hoc Action Group attracted intellectuals and professionals from both races in its targeted fight against police brutality. At the forefront was the black vanguard found in the Dodge Revolutionary Union Movement (DRUM) and the League of Revolutionary Black Workers, followed by the League's white support group, the Motor City Labor League. Some smaller groups like People Against Racism and the radical National Lawyers Guild were all in sync. All these individual pieces had the potential to coalesce into a significant people's front in our city.

None of it was perfect, but it was a broad coalition led by blacks. In addition, some of the most talented lawyers in the country were coming together around the action. This was an era and a place that was ripe for a societal shift. In his writing, Kieran Taylor called Detroit the "American Petrograd," the city in which workers and their allies would lead a socialist revolution.

Activists in Detroit had been motivated against racism for decades—struggling, taking chances. This current configuration was their best hope for significant change. We believed that after 1967 Detroit, the unity of blacks and whites was strong enough to lead to qualitative change. If vanguard blacks, the most oppressed, could win their freedom, the face of our nation would change.

All this change starts by people coming together to talk, to listen, and to learn. The goals for our book club forums were geared toward building a base of like-minded others, but they were also designed to develop a shared political perspective. To this end, we settled on a name, taken from an essay written by the "Black Manifesto" author, James Forman: The Control, Conflict, and Change (CCC) Book Club. It is amazing to recall that during our CCC Book Club forums, with hundreds of people attending, there were no arguments about platform, no protests of speakers, and no grandstanding. Our will to move blacks and whites forward together was our singular, overriding mission.

During this period, Mike's and my personal relationship was developing. Spending time together to get to know each other was challenging. Unlike most couples who casually date, eating out or going to a movie was impossible for us. While it was becoming more common for blacks and whites to work together in movement activities, an interracial couple out together socially was still not acceptable. There were a few hangouts near Wayne State, like Verne's or Cobb's Corner, that were more accommodating, but because of Mike's political standing, even those locations were off-limits to us. A member of the leadership of the League of Revolutionary Black Workers does not date a white woman in public.

Understanding that our situation was unusual and also that it was risky for both of us, I once quizzed Mike about what had first attracted him to me. The kids were at school and Mike had stopped at my house so I could type a document for him.

When I finished and handed it over to him, he said, "Hmmm . . . nice job," and he gave me a little peck on the cheek.

"Why do you find me so attractive," I asked teasingly.

"You work so hard and have so much responsibility—and you handle it so well," he said.

I was disappointed that he hadn't said something more personal. That's the same reason hundreds of people love me, I thought. I work hard. His answer wasn't very satisfying, but I have to admit, it fit my profile. Perhaps Khalil Gibran was right: "Work is love made visible."

THE CONTROL, CONFLICT, AND CHANGE BOOK CLUB

Political education is paramount to clarifying the problems we face in society today . . . Answers to today's social problems can only be found by a critical analysis of social forces at work in the world.
—CONTROL, CONFLICT, AND CHANGE:
A CONTEMPORARY EDUCATION
PROGRAM, DECEMBER 1970

WE WERE DOING THE RIGHT THING at the right time. White liberals and progressives were feeling an urgent need to participate at a new level in the struggle that could bring about change. These were Detroiters, folks committed to the cause of civil rights and antiwar, who were eager to work with blacks in a forum where they could make progress together. Detroiters are pragmatic and resilient. Detroiters never quit. It was time for blacks and whites to solve problems together, and we believed that Detroit was a city where that could happen.

There's something honest and down-to-earth about Detroit. It's a place of grit and determination—no pretensions, no whining. A working-class city that never tries to be anything but itself, Detroit gets in your blood, and you live with it every day. I saw people flocking to Detroit to make a revolution, and I believed that here, if anywhere, whites could follow black leadership. I wanted to be part of that, and I was willing to give of myself to make it happen.

Although I had no training or background for the role I would play in organizing the Control, Conflict, and Change Book Club, I'm a self-starter. I knew how to stay focused on a goal and leave no stone unturned. In a practical way, probably stemming from my experience raising my family, I had a pretty good grip on how to anticipate problems and not be distracted from my responsibilities. I had no hesitation that I could make a difference. And there was something about books that called to me. There was so much I didn't know about the world that I was longing to learn.

I wrote the text for the first CCC brochure. The theme was the importance of people of all colors and backgrounds struggling together for justice and respect as we entered the new decade. Mike selected our first book, *The Man Who Cried I Am* by John A. Williams—a novel based on the life and death of Richard Wright about covert actions of the FBI in the United States. Attorney Ken Cockrel and his law partner, Justin C. Ravitz, agreed to be the speakers for our first session, to be held at the Methodist church on Woodward Avenue in Highland Park.

For each CCC gathering, we started with a list of potential speakers. Then we determined who would be the best person to contact those speakers. For instance, Frank Joyce contacted antiwar speakers; someone from the League contacted radical blacks. Many of the speakers—like John Watson, John Williams, Ken Cockrel, and James Forman—were actually members of the League.

Most speakers from out of town made their own travel arrangements and covered their own expenses. Often I made the offer and speakers stayed with my family while they were in town. Their presence and interactions with us were enriching to my children. The kids had a great time when Gwen Patton, a black feminist from SNCC, stayed at our home. After conducting a session on the book *Sexual Politics* by Kate Millett, she cooked pig ears for the kids in our kitchen.

I sent out the brochure to our large mailing lists from Hourglass and Ad-Hoc. "Education is a tool that will unite us as one people in our common struggle against inhumanity," it read. The brochure had a tear-off portion on the back for the name and address of the respondent. One simply filled it in, stamped it, and mailed it back. It happened that the return portion had snippets of the program on the reverse side. As the multitude of responses came in, even our mailman, who had evidently read what program details he could see on the back of the tear-off, rang our doorbell and asked me if he could attend.

Feeling my way through the first steps of the plan, I ordered books from the publisher and bargained for the ability to pay forty-five days after receipt. Several cases of books were delivered by United Parcel Services and deposited in my dining room. These we would sell and mail to participants, allowing them one month's reading time prior to the book club meeting.

From among community leaders who were active and respected for their work in civil rights, we recruited and trained volunteers to facilitate the book discussions. Some were clerics, some professionals, some community activists. Most were white, but some were black. They were all excited, and no one turned us down. Each month, in a large session at my house, we trained the couple dozen discussion leaders by having a conversation about the essence and meaning of the book on the program. Folks who assumed these leadership roles in the CCC were drawn together like a team on a mission.

A check for $3.30 covered the cost of membership, the first book selection, and postage. I had a great deal of bookkeeping and organizing work to keep track of. Most of the time, I squeezed in reading the book—a chapter or two at a time—along the way. Gradually, I was forming a political perspective. We were educating ourselves and building a core of conscious citizens, many of whom would move on to more prominent roles in the movement.

Three hundred and fifty people showed up for our first CCC Book Club meeting. It seemed as if everybody involved in the Detroit-area civil rights movement attended, and the Highland Park church was bursting at its seams. The pastor from Central Methodist Church, a very large church on Woodward Avenue at

Grand Circus Park in downtown Detroit, was there and offered us the use of his church's large facility for upcoming meetings. We breathed a sigh of relief that we would have a larger space in the future. I was elated at how things were unfolding, and I doubled down on keeping up with the work involved.

We studied works such as *Soledad Brother* by George Jackson, an incarcerated black militant turned writer who was later killed by his prison guards. Jackson wrote about prison conditions in California. Margaret Burnham, his lawyer, came to speak with us. Another book on our agenda was George Rawick's *From Sundown to Sunup*, a research study on how enslaved Africans communicated with each other on and between plantations. We also read Pierre Vallières's *White Niggers of America*, on the efforts for secession by the French-speaking Parti Québécois in Quebec. The author traveled from Canada to be our speaker.

The book club was a huge success and became a flagship for the Motor City Labor League. More than three hundred people attended on a regular basis. I opened the public sessions and handled administrative announcements. Then the person in MCLL or the League, who was most closely related to the topic, introduced the speaker.

My children were involved in all of these activities and usually attended the large monthly sessions. My son Ken took the surviving photos of the CCC Book Club and its large crowds. During the sessions, my children sat at discussion tables or with the speakers at the front of the room. I have photos of Christine at four years old, interacting with a speaker, and of Carolyn with a small friend, standing to the side of another speaker's platform and listening to the main presentation.

When we had training sessions for volunteers in my home, I normally had a babysitter stay upstairs with the children, but they were welcome to sit in when they were interested. Throughout this period, they helped collate materials and interacted with the adults who stayed in or visited our home. During the large meetings in our house, Christine, small and fragile-looking, with a tentative approach to life, would lie across my lap and demand that

I rub her back while I sat cross-legged on the floor listening to the discussion. Michael sat in on the training sessions and even occasionally asked questions, trying to understand the material.

In our basement we had a mimeograph machine, which both Ken and Michael knew how to run. Ken, who was by now growing into a young man, was fine-featured, slight of build, and intense. He was bright and immensely talented, but quiet. He kept his thoughts and opinions to himself. Michael, while still so young, was all energy and purpose. His vision limitations had held him back in some ways, but it had also forced him to acutely refine his other senses. It seemed there was nothing Michael couldn't do, despite his vision impairment.

Prior to the training sessions and again before the meetings, I busily plucked away on the typewriter, drafting and refining materials onto mimeograph stencils. Reams of paper were cranked out on that machine in the basement. Once the printed material was ready, I'd lay out the stacks of pages and call the kids. One by one they'd walk around the dining room table, picking up one page per pile and assembling packets of resource information. Greg could never keep a straight face as we worked, finding all manner of teenage silliness to keep us in stitches. At the end of our assembly line, a selected child sat and stapled the packets together.

Ken was interested in photography. We had a darkroom just off our basement fashioned in an underground room that jutted beneath our front lawn. The kids had discovered the room shortly after we moved in. It appeared to have been built as an air-raid shelter and still held civil defense food supplies sealed in large tin containers from the Cold War era. This darkroom was where Ken developed the photos he took of our political activities. Overall, ours was a pretty sophisticated administrative operation.

The children were well behaved and attentive. Only once do I remember a problem that occurred before a session. It was early 1971. We were setting up to accommodate the large crowd, a frantic activity before each session. One team was hooking up microphones and the sound system. A recorder sat on a table in front of the speaker's lectern. Lights were being unpacked from suitcases at the back of the room.

Frank Joyce, a member of MCLL's general staff, was an antiwar activist who had snagged David Dellinger—one of the Chicago Seven—as a speaker while he'd been in town for the Winter Soldier hearings, an investigation of the conduct of the war in Vietnam, sponsored by Vietnam Veterans Against the War.

In the bustle of the setup, a loud, angry child's protest suddenly rang out from the anteroom. Checking quickly, I found seven-year-old Michael in a loud argument with a couple of laughing League members. As I rushed to the scene, I caught sight of a small arm sweeping across a conference table and a loud crash of books hitting the floor. "That's my space!" my child was protesting, his voice echoing throughout the room.

"What's going on?" I was embarrassed that I had a child out of control and upset that he had knocked the beginning of their book display to the floor, possibly damaging the books. One of the men was picking up books. "Not a problem," he said.

"They moved my calendars," Michael wailed. "I already sold two of them."

"You're selling something personal here?" I was surprised. "Why didn't you ask me first?"

"I made them," he explained forlornly. I caught the glimmer of a tear in the corner of one eye. "They're calendars. They only cost five cents, and they'll last forever. They're perpetual." He struggled with the last word.

"This isn't your space, Michael," I explained. "This is our community space. It's not for you to decide."

We talked. In the end, a plan to share the table space was worked out.

That night was representative of how most of the book club meetings went—with a few surprises. It took a while to get everyone checked in and directed to their tables. Leaders of MCLL and the League lingered at the front of the room. A liberation flag and a Vietnamese flag flanked the stage platform. I opened the session, welcomed everyone, and explained the format for the book discussion. Then I introduced Frank, who introduced the speaker.

Dave Dellinger ascended the steps to the platform. "Before I begin," he said, "we have another guest this evening who I would like you to meet." Mr. Dellinger welcomed to the stage Jane Fonda, peace activist and screen star, and she spoke for a few moments about the Winter Soldier project.

Then, Dellinger turned the discussion to the historical defeat of the French by the Vietnamese. He explained that the United States was attacking an agrarian society with B-52 bombers and powerful artillery. "These are farmers and their families, many living in jungle villages. Thousands of U.S. ground troops are deployed into villages. But the Vietnamese are already winning," he told us.

After his presentation, our trained leaders took over to discuss aspects of the presentation. At the end of the discussion, attendees were able to ask questions of the speakers. Afterward, copies of the book to be discussed at the following month's meeting were sold.

The CCC Book Club's success was uncanny. This was in the early 1970s, in the midst of civil unrest and a tightening of surveillance by the state. Our volunteers were a loose alliance of a wide variety of people who wanted to gain strength against the powers who wished to suppress our efforts. Respected white liberals, clerics, academics, professionals, and neighborhood organizers sat at tables and participated in discussions with black intellectuals, black power advocates, and members of the League of Revolutionary Black Workers. It was a unique mix of activists who were eager to take time out of their lives to participate in creating a better world. There was only one way our enemies could deal with us, and that was to infiltrate.

It was common knowledge that J. Edgar Hoover had developed an FBI counterintelligence program during the McCarthy period. First, it monitored communists. Later it expanded. By the mid-1950s until the late 1960s, the FBI was monitoring dissenters using tactics of espionage normally reserved for foreign enemies.

As discontent spread across the nation, local police departments established counterintelligence "Red Squads" to carry out the fight. When we held meetings at my house, two strange men were often parked out front. As people entered, they would often rhetorically inquire, "Who are the two guys sitting in the car out front?" We assumed that the guys were not only taking license plate numbers but listening in, too.

Using foresight during our planning period, I came up with the idea of an assigned seating system with table numbers to control circulation in our crowded room. Disruptive individuals or folks suspected of being "the police" were seated at one specific table, which we fondly called the "renegade table." That table discussion was led by our most advanced members who were prepared to deal with disruptive, self-aggrandizing, or backward folks who had closed minds or negative intentions. We never identified the provocateurs or agents who were intentionally trying to destroy our efforts. We just knew that they would be there.

Many years later, state police Red Squad files became available through the Freedom of Information Act. My files consisted mostly of Hourglass and Ad-Hoc activities and, of course, the CCC Book Club. The documents, in which the names of the police agents are redacted, confirm that the events were heavily infiltrated by the police. Names and license plate numbers of people attending meetings at our house were also recorded. There was even a memo, addressed to book club members and affixed with my forged signature, urging them to support the White Panthers, a radical white group in Ann Arbor, Michigan, with very different politics than what we espoused.

As I scanned the written reports from the infiltrators, I noted comments describing their difficulty circulating during our meetings because of the assigned table arrangements. This made me smile. The "renegade table" had been a good plan.

Mike began to spend more and more time at the house. His frequent presence meant that folks who wanted to meet with him could catch him at my place. Soon our home became a primary meeting spot for his entourage, and I realized much too late that the character of our living space had changed. It had a negative impact on my children. This became a significant issue, primarily for the girls, who felt that the intimacy of their home had been invaded. They lost their privacy, and the space no longer felt like their own. We stopped holding our family ritual on the second-floor landing each evening as new activities became part of our lives. Forums for personal expression between the kids and me were less frequent. Strangers who had no interest in my children were visiting the house at all hours of the day. The effects of this affront have followed my girls into adulthood.

One of these strangers was a person I'll call Charlie Williams. Charlie was a nuisance. When Mike was there, he would hang out from morning until night. He was one of those nonstop talkers who never seem to take a breath. His endless monologue droned on at our kitchen table until I pretty much showed him the door.

He seemed always to have a scheme. At one point, he wanted Mike to claim that he was his employer and then lay him off so he could get unemployment insurance. It was a typical Charlie plan—and one that could have resulted in a felony charge if Mike had followed through and been caught, which seemed to me the point of Charlie's shenanigans. Mike tolerated Charlie much longer than I. We disagreed on this. Mike traveled a lot and claimed that Charlie kept him awake with his incessant talking during long trips to New York, Chicago, or Gary, Indiana.

One day, as folks were leaving the house after a League meeting, I happened to notice Charlie talking with someone on the sidewalk. He set his briefcase on the grass apron. When I looked again, Charlie's car was pulling away. The briefcase sat unattended, right where he had placed it. Everyone else was gone. As Charlie's car pulled away, a police car immediately rounded the island. An officer got out and picked up the briefcase. I had no idea what was inside, but Charlie had been active in the League and had access to a lot of information from meetings and his time with Mike. I wondered: Was this intentional, perhaps even prearranged? I panicked.

Mike ran the League's printing business, which was called Black Star Publishing, and he was working that afternoon at the print shop. Money was tight, and there was no phone there. I didn't normally frequent the shop, but I felt it was urgent to let someone know what I had seen. I located my keys, got in the car, and drove to Black Star. When I got there, I saw the official posting on the shop's outside doors. "Property of the U.S. Government," plus a notice stating there were sixty days to appeal.

I knocked on the metal door, feeling some urgency. One of the workers let me in. Upon entering I noted that the presses were in full production mode. Mike was surprised to see me and motioned me into the office where I told him the "Charlie story."

"It's okay," he said in his usual calm manner. "I'll follow up. Don't worry. Now, you need to get back home."

That was the end of it. Mike and I had a standing agreement not to discuss his work. Charlie stopped coming around.

Mike hadn't told me that the shop was being closed for delinquent taxes. They simply didn't have the money. The printing equipment was soon confiscated, and Black Star ended its run. The police and government were hovering, always looking for opportunities to descend and crack down on activists. The endless pressure took its toll.

THE SUCCESS OF THE BOOK CLUB was deeply gratifying but also overwhelming. As the workload grew beyond what one person—or her family of child volunteers—could do, Mike sent help. Nancy Waggoner, a volunteer from VISTA, the domestic Peace Corps begun under President Kennedy, made herself available to assist with the paperwork. Nancy and I were both paid a nominal stipend from MCLL for our efforts—I believe it was $30 a week.

In addition, a couple of volunteer typists spent two or three days at the house after each meeting painstakingly transcribing tapes of the lengthy presentations, using an old-fashioned Dictaphone machine with foot pedals. Afterward, stencils of the presentations were taken to the basement and the cranking and collating began anew. Copies of the previous session's presentation were available at meetings, just in case someone had missed it.

I loved the work I was doing with the CCC Book Club. We were achieving big things: whites and blacks were working together to raise consciousness in the post–civil rights era with recognition that black self-determination wasn't an accommodation, it was a necessity. For me, the work possessed a social element and brought me into contact with people of all stripes. It gave me an opportunity to motivate people to contribute to the cause and to find solutions to problems.

On the one hand, I was learning so much. As my relationship with Mike deepened, I was getting brief glimpses into his life as a black man, making racism real to me on a personal level. In carrying out my work with the book club, I was learning new skills. I did a lot of short-term decision-making, as anyone would do in developing a business model. It was a huge endeavor; things were going well, and I redoubled my efforts.

On the other hand, the CCC Book Club was more than a full-time occupation. Even though I had Nancy to help me, the scope of work was endless. It was simply taking over my life. The reality was that the daily responsibility of this rapidly growing operation rested squarely on my shoulders. Tending to things—my work specifically related to the book club as well as my responsibilities on the leadership body of MCLL—required every moment of my day, leaving me with less and less time to deal with the needs of six children. Even my ability to leave my house became severely compromised. When I couldn't go to the MCLL, they started coming to me.

This meant daylong Sunday meetings being held in my home, robbing me and my children of even more time. The participants at these meetings often took advantage of my generosity. Food that I needed for my family would simply disappear. Messes would get made and were left for me to clean up. The work that was being required of me became even more overwhelming.

As time went on, I began to understand that, as a human being, I had limits. I also had a responsibility to my children. I loved the work, but the bricks I was stacking on my board were threatening to outweigh the capacity of the board to hold them.

My commitment to the organization was firm, but my commitment to my family had to be absolute. I had every reason to believe I'd find a new way to apply my zeal and skills toward the cause we all believed in.

My grandmother, Cathleen Boyle Shuell, circa 1945

Joann with her mother, Esther Jorn Reschke, 1939

Joann with her father, Barry Conway Reschke, 1940

Joann at seven years old, 1944

Joann at Our Lady of Mercy High, 1953

Activist Frank Ditto, Hourglass, 1968

U.S. Army, Detroit Rebellion, 1967

Cops on 12th Street, Detroit Rebellion, 1967

Joann, circa 1970

The house at 630 West Boston Boulevard, 1967

The six Castle children in Taylor, 1967.
Clockwise beginning top left, Michael, Jeff,
Greg, Christine, Ken, and Carolyn

Father William Cunningham,
1982

Anti-STRESS Coalition in D.C., 1971

Ad-Hoc Detroit News *protest, 1969*

Mike Hamlin, League of Revolutionary Black Workers, 1969

Dow Chemical protest, 1969

Detroit News *article that describes Joann's confrontation of Archbishop Dearden, 1968*

Ad-Hoc activists, 1969

Hundreds attend CCC Book Club discussions

Joann, cofounder and moderator, CCC Book Club, 1970–1972

Mike Hamlin, cofounder, CCC Book Club

Are you *grappling* with
Today's Social Issues
with a 1950
or 1960 Education?

control
conflict
change

A CONTEMPORARY EDUCATION PROGRAM

Control, Conflict, and Change (CCC) education brochure, 1970

Gwen Patton, civil rights activist

Legendary activist Ken Cockrel at CCC

Jim Forman speaks at CCC

Social justice pioneer Sheila Murphy,
CCC meeting

Book Club meeting full house

Dave Dellinger, antiwar activist, CCC speaker

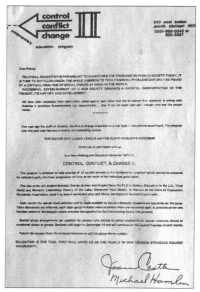

CCC II Book Club invitation, 1971

Frank Joyce, Founder, People Against Racism

Jane Fonda, CCC guest

Mike, Mike's mother, Maybelle Hamlin, Alex, Michael, and Christine, 1976

Family camping in Maine, 1973

All my children growing and thriving, Detroit, 1976

Extended family basketball team, 1976

Wedding celebration, Detroit's Greektown, 1975

Sailing on Lake Erie, 1989

Joann and Mike, soul mates forever

Joann's staff at Metropolitan Hospital, 1985

The Castle-Hamlin children, all grown up, 1993

Joann's parents, Barry and Esther Reschke, circa 1984

Castle-Hamlin blended extended family, 1999

Joann and sister, Karen, 2009

Joann and Mike, renewing their wedding vows, 2010

Granddaughter Ella,
Generation Next, 2016

Mike and Joann with son Alex, 1993

Viola remembered, Ann Arbor Women's March 2017

ANATOMY OF A MOVEMENT CRISIS

If you tell the truth, it becomes a part of your past.
If you tell a lie, it becomes a part of your future.
—ANONYMOUS

IN NOVEMBER 1972, an informant delivered a note to the FBI-backed, state police–run Red Squad about turmoil roiling the Motor City Labor League and the Control, Conflict, and Change Book Club. It spoke of a big split—"a major inner-conflict"—that pitted two factions against each other, naming me as the head of one and Sheila as the head of the other.

"People are awaiting a decision from Castle and her faction," the informant wrote. "The newly formed group may have a better cooperation with the church leadership in this area with less emphasis on division factors, such as the current accent being placed on black antagonists . . ."

For an informant, this unnamed person was remarkably *uninformed*—at least about the actual details.

I wasn't leading any faction. I was firmly rooted as an employee in the Metropolitan Hospital emergency room, using my left hand to organize the workers' union, while using my right hand to display enough respectability to keep my job. There was no returning to Catholic activism, nor was there any rejection of my belief in black self-determination or my belief in the need for black-led organizations. What the informant had gotten right was the bigger picture: the movement, the organizational efforts of activists, was beginning to tear itself apart. The cluelessness of the police informant provides a kind of bitter irony because, in the end, we played into their hands.

LOOKING BACK over those two years in MCLL, I can see how tumultuous and unforgiving the early 1970s were. The MCLL was growing, and there were lots of new people coming to Detroit to be part of the revolution they believed would begin here. A good number of them were professionals of some kind—lawyers, talented artists, educators, or people raised in the movement who understood the meaning behind revolutionary rhetoric. I was relatively new at this game. I didn't have a *lot* of experience, but I wasn't just along for the ride. I truly believed that we could play a role in changing society.

The churn of people also presented opportunities for those who didn't share our viewpoints or our goals. There was always the threat of the government's attempt to infiltrate and do damage to individuals and organizations. There were also opportunists who saw the chaos of the moment and took advantage of it for their own purposes. Late one night in the summer of 1971, I was warned that some people like this were coming to Detroit.

The phone rang at two a.m. For a few moments, I was confused about whether I was awake or asleep, but the persistent ring finally seized my attention. I stumbled out of bed and reached for the receiver.

"Hello?"

On the other end of the line was a prominent movement person who had spoken at the book club a few months back and had stayed in my home.

"Joann," the person said, "I have something to tell you. Can you hear me?"

"Yes, I'm here."

"There are some folks heading to Detroit, and they are up to no good," the person warned. "Be careful."

In the morning, I was still trying to convince myself that this call had really happened. But I soon forgot about it amid the demands of my busy life. I wish I hadn't.

About six months later, in early 1972, the success of our work was taking a substantial toll on my family and me. Isolated in my home, I had been spending long hours doing the book club's administrative work, and I was buckling under the stress. Also, I feared I was not giving my children the full attention they needed. Something had to give. So, in January 1972, I resigned from the leadership body of MCLL and proposed that the book club be moved from my home. Those in the MCLL promised that a new coordinator would take my place in June, and I began considering what my next steps would be as an organizer and an activist inside our organization.

My resignation was an acknowledgment—after much soul-searching—that I could no longer single-handedly mother six youngsters while continuing to devote the inordinate amount of time required to be in the leadership of the organization. But it also took me out of the heart of the work being done, as well as the decision-making process for moving forward.

Shortly after I resigned my position, I attended a late-night meeting at Sheila's apartment with some MCLL leaders and a handful of members of the League of Revolutionary Black Workers. My understanding was that we were there to discuss the direction of MCLL and our relationship to the League. I was somewhat baffled by the need for this seemingly clandestine late-night meeting but pleased that I had been invited. Since my resignation, I had felt as if I was losing my stream of continuity with the flow of communication and paddling like mad just to stay afloat. Sinking was not an option. I was looking forward to the meeting, but if I had had any clue about what I was walking into, and what had occurred to necessitate this meeting, I would have felt very, very differently.

When I arrived, I was surprised to find that neither Mike nor Ken was there. By this time, Mike and I were a couple, but we were not yet living together. Mike had been extremely busy lately, traveling nationally to lay the groundwork for the upcoming Black Workers Congress. Ken was deeply involved in his legal work, trailblazing some significant cases to benefit the black community. His credibility and his popularity were at an all-time high.

We gathered in Sheila's living room. It was very late at night. The lighting was dim and the atmosphere, because of the late hour, was conducive to slumber. Folding chairs were set about, sandwiched between the pieces of her living room furniture. It seemed as if it was going to be a long night—long meetings were not unusual— and my mind was drifting. The League people attending our meeting were, by and large, a handful of rank-and-file support staff, which surprised me. As usual, Shelia chaired the meeting.

Things proceeded routinely until I heard Sheila explaining, "We're going to be making some changes to the organizational structure. Warren, who has been working closely with me, will be taking over the educational component of MCLL's program and bringing it up-to-date."

Shocked and confused, I snapped to high alert. What had I missed? Searching for an explanation, I looked around. Everyone else seemed to be taking her words in stride. Warren was a recent transplant to the Motor City, so I couldn't understand his rapid rise to a leadership position. I didn't dare ask a question and disrupt the meeting, though. One just didn't do that in an organization like ours, which had strict codes of conduct and followed organizational deference. I was clearly out of touch with what was going on.

Sheila continued, "I will no longer be the liaison to the League; Warren will take over that responsibility." The levels of shock layered on as I grasped that something had gone very wrong, and I was just now discovering it. What I didn't realize at the time was that I was witnessing the irreversible rupture of our sister organizations.

Her surprises didn't stop there. Next, she announced Ken's plan to run for city council, along with Justin's bid for judge. The MCLL, she said, had agreed to provide support for their campaigns. There was no discussion. No one objected, and in my ignorance of what was going on, I initially believed that this was a joint decision of the two organizations.

There was yet another revelation: the MCLL's plans to open a Chrysler workers' resource center, which had been on the organization's drawing board, was put on hold. I was crushed. I had envisioned my post–book club future to be with the resource center, which had seemed to be a good fit with my desire to be of service to workers. I believed that revolutionaries should be working with the people on the ground, not in long meetings arguing over theory, as was becoming our habit.

As these MCLL changes rained down on me, it felt as if the organization's core philosophy and policies were being uprooted. I had been a member of this organization from its inception. I didn't understand why this was happening, but in the context of what appeared to be a done deal, I was reluctant to voice my fears. Sheila never left anything to chance. The proposed changes would turn us into a campaign-based support group.

I had to acknowledge that, among other losses, I was also reeling from the unanticipated loss of my relationship with Sheila. I'd been blindsided by her decision to run MCLL with Warren. To me, the decision to back Ken's campaign underscored the unpredictable alchemy of personal and sexual relationships. In the heat of personal versus political battles, allegiances can shift instantaneously, and relationships can be sacrificed on the altar of personal ambition.

PRIOR TO THAT LATE-NIGHT MEETING, I knew that Sheila and Mike had been getting together weekly to coordinate MCLL's actions and direction as it related to the League's wider efforts. But I didn't know that Sheila had approached Mike about throwing the support of the League behind Ken Cockrel's plan to run for Detroit City Council. I learned that Mike had steadfastly resisted. He had told Shelia that the League would never agree to do that because it was against the League's strategic goals, but she kept coming back. Finally, Mike took Shelia's request to the leadership, and they turned it down. She continued to persist, however, until, finally exasperated, Mike told her, "Just do whatever you want to do." And so she did: she supported Justin Ravtiz's run for judge, then backed Ken's run for city council.

UNTIL THAT period in our movement history, MCLL had always taken a position against electoral politics. We professed and acted in concert with the belief that change comes up from the grassroots. I was certain that these new initiatives would turn our organization upside down and force us to place our trust in the Detroit City Council—unpredictable, at best.

Mike didn't talk to me about his political work. It was only after the fact that I learned that there was a pending split in the League. Officially, Ken Cockrel, John Watson, and Mike would move their work into the Black Workers Congress. But in actuality, Ken was busy with his legal practice, and John left town. Mike alone would move into the BWC. The League's leadership structure was drifting apart.

These competing undercurrents strengthened the hand of those pushing the move toward electoral politics. When the League itself refused to throw its support behind Ken, Sheila organized a coalition of League and MCLL supporters for this purpose. The people at the meeting, some old comrades and some new—like Warren—were poised to become the foundation of Ken's and Justin's political campaigns.

Warren and his wife had been in town for only a few months, but I'd already taken a dislike to his arrogance. Likewise, Warren held a differing view on politics than that espoused by the League and MCLL. With him now in control of our educational programs, I worried that the result would be an abrupt change in strategies for our future work. After the disturbing late-night meeting, I tried to make sense of my thoughts. My book club work was largely a solitary endeavor. In the absence of any other people to talk to, I started writing. The unexpected result turned into a position paper—my first mistake.

We were deadly serious about our organization's use of a historic "democratic centralism" model as our blueprint for revolution, where leadership makes its final decisions only after listening to everyone. But in revolutionary conditions, things happen fast. Un-expected crises demand calculated risks and unapologetic action. Without these qualities, I agreed that organizations can never harness the momentum necessary to create and sustain institutional and societal change.

Our organizational structure was very rigid—out of necessity. There were threats all around us. The prospects of arrest, or jail time, or death were not abstracts in our world. Discipline, then, becomes a safety guard against threats. Strong leadership needs to make decisions that those committed to the cause will follow. But I believed that such decisions had to reflect the fundamental mission of the organization.

In my distress, I felt compelled to express my concerns, and I began to question the decisions of our leadership. The words flowed onto the paper: "Where was the democracy in our democratic centralism? Why were our decisions made in private? Why am I learning about these essential changes in a public meeting with outsiders' present?" Everything was happening so fast; I couldn't process what was going on.

Then I made my second mistake. I was deeply opposed to the attempt to make MCLL an electoral politics support group, and I began saying so. My first breach was with Sue, a woman who had volunteered to type the book club speaker presentations on the Dictaphone. This woman was an insider, recently assigned to the general staff of MCLL. I liked her, and she brought her child with her when she came to work. We had things in common. Or at least I thought we did. I had no idea that she was in a relationship with Warren.

My second breach was with a member of the MCLL general staff who was also a minister. He stopped in to pick up a book one afternoon. Because of the recent developments, I missed being on the staff of MCLL even more now. I was overwrought and desperate for information. Like a retired captain without a ship to sail, I was no longer at the wheel and had lost control. It's hard to give up control when you have such impassioned feelings about the direction in which your ship is headed.

These disruptions may not seem like big mistakes outside of the context of that time. But in this situation, my acts of questioning how decisions were being made amounted to nothing short of insubordination. Word got back to Sheila quickly. I was summoned to appear before what felt like a tribunal, one that would make recommendations on how my rebellion should be handled.

In the committee meeting—I'll call it a hearing—there was no discussion of my position paper that addressed how the MCLL had always opposed electoral politics. Instead, the meeting quickly escalated into an itemized assault on my character. I was unprepared. No one had ever treated me with such disrespect. The words flung at me stung like acid: I was "ultra-democratic, a black sycophant, patronizing, and delusional." Also, I lacked "organizing experience and was always moaning about needing help."

One of my accusers, all of whom were men, stated, "Everyone knows that if Sheila had not held it together all this time, the book club would have been an ultra-democratic fiasco."

Ultra-democratic fiasco? I had built the book club from scratch. I had created the infrastructure—the processes to implement the concept, to coordinate the tasks, to put people in place to get it done. Hundreds of people attended each session. The book club was a huge success with both local and national implications. Requests for information, materials, and aids to develop similar programs had come from across the country. Through personal appeals, over the past year I had raised $4,000—a large sum at the time—$3,000 of which had come in during the preceding two months to keep the education program functioning. The finances were in order, bookkeeping and materials up to date, and everything was paid in full. The concept was working beautifully.

It was beyond my capacity to think of any defense that made sense in this situation. It felt like an inquisition without the crucifix. Everyone present was asked to answer yes or no to whether sycophancy and lack of political organizing constituted the book club experience. The men agreed. I sat silent, reliving my old fears of being labeled a hysterical woman.

I had some charges, too. These men were supposed to be the book club's oversight committee. They had never proposed a meeting to discuss or solve these so-called issues nor had they done anything to help. If there was dissatisfaction with my work, no one had ever expressed it to me.

Finally, I spoke: "I need some time to get my perspective back. I'm asking for a six-month leave."

"Impossible," someone sneered. The others agreed.

"Why?" I asked. "Everyone knows the situation I'm in. I've worked so hard. I've given so much. I'm neglecting my family." Even as I heard myself appealing for understanding or mercy, inside my head and my gut, I tried to reason: How had I let myself be reduced to pleading like a beggar? What did this character assassination have to do with my CCC Book Club work? Yes, I made a serious misjudgment when I committed my thoughts to paper and spoke indiscriminately. But on the scale of justice, how do these misguided actions balance against my proven ongoing contributions? So help me out here. I'm a friend, not a foe.

"I need to get things in my home under control, and then I'll be back," I ventured, trying to rise up from my proverbial knees. "I'm committed to doing this work."

"We can't just have people coming and going," said one of the men, a lawyer. "It would set a precedent."

"But others—" I began, thinking of a person who was now "on leave."

"MCLL is at a critical stage," one of the men said, cutting me off, "and you would not be able to make up the loss of political development."

I regained a modicum of self-possession and countered: "I presume, from that type of logic, we'll never again be able to have an expansion of the membership." I was exploding inside, but I didn't dare say anything to make the situation worse. I was afraid of being judged irrational. I felt like a woman facing a firing squad consisting of three men who were reveling in their gender roles.

The all-male committee decided that a new book club coordinator would take over in the middle of March. I would train that person and then the office would be moved. I was asked to give a two-week notice of separation from the organization.

I was devastated, and my thoughts were swirling. How could this be happening? I knew that I had handled the meeting badly. I was overcome with remorse about not defending myself. Had I *no* self-respect?

Then I realized that the monthly book club meeting was to take place in a couple of days. I moderated those meetings and was the face of MCLL in that role. How could I possibly manage that task now? I recalled with some irony that just a few months earlier, the MCLL had presented me with a plaque in appreciation of my work. I was so touched by the gesture. It read: "A journey of a thousand miles begins with a single step."

The next time Mike stopped by the house I vented and used him as a sounding board. Mike listened but let me grapple with my thoughts. He didn't tell me what to do, except when I suggested that I wanted to announce my departure from the podium at the upcoming meeting.

"These people are important to me," I told him. "Many of them helped me create the momentum for our success. We worked so hard and so well together. I don't want to just disappear."

I paced around the kitchen "How can they just throw me out?" I wailed. "At least I want to say thank you and good-bye to all the book club members I've worked so closely with. They have always supported me!"

I was so proud of what my efforts had brought about. I simply couldn't square the book club's indisputable success with my unceremonious dismissal. I roared: "I just raised four thousand dollars, for God's sake!"

Mike, with great calm, looked at me and said, "Let it go."

"I'm not ready to let it go," I shot back. "I love this work. I'm good at it!" I stopped to take a breath, and my emotions welled up again. There were tears in my eyes. "What about the kids? They're so invested. How do I explain this to them?"

"Sometimes you just have to let things go," Mike answered. He drew me in and hugged me tightly, whispering in my ear,

"I'm here for you." Then he quietly left out the back door.

In my heart, I knew that Mike's counsel was right. I shouldn't announce my departure to the public. But I was hurting, and I wanted to hold on to all my friends and cohorts who would be in the room. I felt completely alone, and Mike had just walked out the door. Something in me sensed that Mike was distracted by some deeper pain of his own.

A few days later, on the second Tuesday in March 1972, I stood at the MCLL podium, looking at the sea of faces in front of me. I still hadn't been able to banish my need to say something— anything. I felt dizzy and distressed. There was a pain in my gut and pressure in my chest. Those physical sensations were what I remembered.

The details of what actually happened, however, evaporated from my memory the instant I left the podium and walked out of the building. For decades, I believed that I had made the routine announcements and appropriate introductions and said nothing at all about that Tuesday being my final CCC Book Club meeting. It took a visit to our book club materials archive at Wayne State University forty years later, as well as some conversations long put off, before I was able to liberate from my subconscious the deeply buried memories of that night.

In reality, I did say something, probably something akin to what the informants who attended the meeting reported to the police. According to the Red Squad documents in my file, two different infiltrators wrote identical descriptions: "Joann Carole Castle resigned at this meeting. She stated that her reasons for resigning were personal and because of the confusion within the organization. She then introduced the new CCC director . . ."

After my departure, all hell broke loose. The final breaking point had been reached. Ken Cockrel took the microphone and, using his oratorical gifts, began denigrating me while making sure Sheila was protected against any questions raised by my unceremonious departure. Mike, who was in attendance, saw what was about to occur. He stood and shouted, "Ken is a stalking horse for Sheila!" At this point, Sheila took to the microphone and labeled the whole problem one of "sexual politics." Eventually, the program began.

In retrospect, I suspect Sheila was trying to downplay the situation. When she spoke of "sexual politics," she meant that we women follow the politics of our dominant men. Although she was referring to me, the pattern extended to Ken and her, and to a number of others as well. Sheila was in a relationship with Ken; I was in a relationship with Mike; Warren was in a relationship with Sue, the woman with whom I had shared my concerns about the organization. All three couples would eventually marry.

Kate Millett wrote a book in 1969 titled *Sexual Politics*, claiming that sexual relationships have a frequently neglected political aspect. The role that patriarchy plays in sexual relationships has a long history in Western society and extends into our political life. We were young and passionate about our work and our politics. It should have been expected that the stress of being in the movement and the raw emotion of the struggle would draw people into sexual liaisons.

When I arrived home, I was completely discombobulated. I couldn't sleep. I couldn't think. I didn't understand. I told myself that all of the folks in the MCLL knew what had happened. Surely someone would call me to say they agreed with me. But no one called; no one visited. The paperwork says I wrote a letter of resignation. I couldn't locate a copy.

A few days later, while I was picking up the kids from school, MCLL members entered my home. They must have brought a truck. They took all my file cabinets, even those containing my personal papers, family medical records, my bills—everything. I felt invaded.

Then Sheila came with Warren. They said they came for the mimeograph machine in our basement. I had no problem with that—it belonged to the organization. Before they finally left, we argued in the front hallway. Some of my children were present and watched this spectacle. As Sheila turned to leave, she lifted her hand and shouted, "I will destroy you in this city!" These were revolutionary times. You were either in, or you were out.

The fallout is my interpretation of events and, as Sheila recently told me, we all have our own interpretation of what happened. I have no idea how the very public splintering of the leadership of the MCLL and the League may have affected the evening's book club program. But I do know that an enormous price was paid—on all sides—by our collective political divorce. Ken and Mike and Sheila and I would never be the same.

IT WAS YEARS LATER when I remembered the late-night phone call about new folks coming to Detroit. Warren gained a lot of power and influence in MCLL and played a pivotal role in the radical changes taking place in the organization. He was brilliant and no doubt the perfect counterpoint for Shelia's efforts on behalf of Ken's campaign.

But this was only one piece of a larger picture. In assessing the downfall of the two organizations, it's hard to know the primary cause of MCLL's dissolution because so many dynamics were at play. The decline of the League and the end of our sister organization relationship cut us off at our roots. Our Red Squad files confirm that outsiders with adverse intent were in our meetings, in our planning committees, and in our homes. And when we were most vulnerable, personal ambitions—which always influence the dynamics of organizations—seemed to contradict or override our collective passion for our cause. Our ignorance of the complexity of human behavior both inside and outside our organizations blinded us to the inevitable power that was at play.

As Ken's and Sheila's political stars began to rise, the activist organizations they spearheaded began to unravel. MCLL's leadership had first fractured over the question of advancing electoral politics, and it later crumbled further along sectarian lines, soon fading entirely from its once indisputable heights. Meanwhile, just nine months after my exit, Justin Ravitz got elected as a judge with the support of former MCLL and League members. A few years later, Ken would be elected a city councilman.

Ken continued to be at odds with other council members, and, ultimately, he concluded that he couldn't get anything done in the forum. He was contemplating a run for mayor of Detroit when he was stricken with a fatal heart attack at age fifty. After Ken's death, Sheila would keep their dream alive, going on herself to win a seat on the city council and to become a formidable political force in Detroit, a position she retains to this day.

LEAVING THE MOTOR CITY LABOR LEAGUE was traumatic for me. I lost my work, my foundation, and my friends. Had I been a little wiser and not so blinded by my fervor for what we were accomplishing, I would never have let it hurt me so much. Why had it taken forty years to see what a naive idealist I was?

Working effectively with others requires trust, and I've learned over the years that I would rather trust than not, though there are two things to consider: On the one hand, my trust of others is interwoven with my capacity for compassion. This is and always has been the foundation for all my social justice work. On the other hand, my trust of others makes me vulnerable, not a good trait for the combat of the movement. Combat demands that you be on guard, and in this case, I wasn't.

These painful memories took me deep into my psyche. For all my self-proclaimed worldliness, looking back, I marvel at my profound naïveté. I was deeply hurt because I gave too much and didn't remotely know how to protect myself or my family. I never expected that revolutionaries would harm someone who labored for their success. It was on this battleground where I learned that for an activist, *too much is still never enough.* You must remain conscious no matter how tempted you are to go back to sleep. You must protect yourself because that's the surest way to protect others and your cause. That's what "being woke," as the young activists intone today, really means.

Yet through all the ups and downs, the value of the book club experience was undeniable. Though short-lived, the book club remained true to its mission and advanced its greater educational goals. Whether thinking about the CCC during its time or considering what role a reinvented CCC could play in the present era, it reminds us that there is an obligation for whites of conscience to educate and organize other whites about the realities of class and race in our society. The CCC Book Club model was on to something important that can continue to take society forward: education, collaboration, and coalition building between blacks and whites. We *were* an imminent threat to the status quo.

REVOLUTION DISSOLUTION

Information received from the above-mentioned source
[name redacted] is that James Forman n/m 10-4-28
is now living at the residence of Joann Castle . . .
—SPECIAL INVESTIGATION UNIT,
DATED 5-30-72

IT WAS AUGUST 1971. I sat in the front seat of my car, watching the travelers come and go. Close by and overhead, I could hear the sounds of jets roaring into and out of the sky, bringing people to and from Detroit. Jim Forman was coming to town to lay the foundation for a national organization, the Black Workers Congress. Mike had gone to retrieve our passenger.

When Mike asked me if Jim could stay at our house when he visited Detroit, it made sense; 630 West Boston Boulevard had long been accepted as a safe haven for movement people when they came to town. Jim was a deeply influential and well-connected black power activist far beyond his foundational work around the "Black Manifesto," which he had authored. He was a significant figure in the early days of the Student Nonviolent Coordinating Committee and a comrade of national black power leaders like Stokely Carmichael and H. Rap Brown. Providing Jim with a place to stay, where he could have easy access to conversations with Mike, seemed like a good idea.

I watched Jim as he and Mike walked to the car. Jim was older than us, perhaps near fifty, bearded, and graying. *He's tired,* I thought. Jim moved sluggishly, as if the weight of the world were on his shoulders. He sat in the backseat of the car, and as we drove I kept meeting his eyes as I looked in the rearview mirror, so I knew that he was watching me just as I was watching him. Once he was at the house, he was cordial, but he was busy with work and often out at meetings.

During his time with us, he asked if I would help him retrieve from a city in Canada a package that was intended for the Black Workers Congress. The package contained money donated to their organizing work. The arrangement was that I would meet a known individual who would hand the package to me in the ladies' room of a specific location, and I would bring the package back to Detroit. It would be a day trip—fast and simple enough—and I had to admit that the prospect of this trip fed my adventurous spirit. It was something that I could do, to pass, so to speak, without being discovered, and it was an opportunity to feel as if I could offer some value to the cause in the wake of my deeply painful split with MCLL. I agreed that, as a white woman, I was the most logical choice to pull off this mission without raising suspicion.

A friend of mine had a sister who lived with her husband and family in Windsor, just across the Canadian border from Detroit. I had met them at a Detroit cultural event a few years before, so we were acquainted. I arranged to have dinner with her family. I told them I was visiting friends in Quebec and asked if I could leave my car in front of their house to save the cost of parking at the airport. In the morning, my friend's sister drove me to the airport before she went to work.

At the airport in Windsor, I bought a plane ticket under an assumed name—you could do that back then—and arrived at my destination in the early afternoon. I picked up a French-language newspaper, thinking that it would make me look more local. I carried it under my arm as I waited for a bus to take me to the designated meeting place. I noted with wonder that the view of the river and the busy logging boats in the gorge below the bus stop was the same scene that was on the Canadian bill I had used to buy the paper.

A man spoke to me casually in French, *"Bonjour, madame. Où allez-vous cette belle après-midi?"*

"No speak French," I nervously offered. He gestured to my French-language newspaper. I blushed; my heartbeat quickened. Was I being followed?

I arrived at the designated place and was relieved to see my contact. We entered adjacent toilet stalls, and she passed the package under the partition. I placed it in my boot. I then left and headed back to the airport by bus. Things were going according to plan.

As I walked, however, I could feel the envelope moving upward in my boot, and when I was standing in the aisle of the bus trying to balance against its stops and starts, the bulky envelope was creeping into view. It occurred to me that it was obvious that I was hiding something in my boot. I'm sure my demeanor suggested my discomfort. When I finally got a seat, I tried to shift the package to a safer position without being noticed. Suddenly, I was growing uneasy.

At the airport, there were weather concerns, but the plane took off toward its destination. A short time later, though, the pilot gave us some bad news: the Windsor airport was closed, completely socked in by fog. We would land in Toronto and be taken to a hotel. As we landed, they called people by name for transport to our accommodations. I almost missed my assumed name while I was deep in thought about not being home that night for the children. What would they be told about where I went, and how could I let folks know what had happened to me?

By the time I got to my hotel, it was getting dark. Once in my room, my stomach reminded me that I needed something to eat. No vouchers in those days; you were on your own. In fact, the hotel accommodations were minimal, with only the bare necessities, and the neighborhood was anything but tourist friendly. I had to make a decision: Was it more dangerous to carry the package on me or to leave it in the room. I decided to carry it but in a more secure location. I placed it under my clothing.

On the street again, I noted that the weather was deteriorating. It was damp and misty. I shivered and wrapped my light jacket tighter as I searched for a nearby eatery. Once I found a spot, I ordered and ate quickly. It was fully dark when I left the restaurant. Things looked different than they had just thirty minutes before. The sidewalks were deserted. The dim streetlights seemed to glow a ghastly green and cast deep shadows around the unfamiliar structures. I was in a state of heightened awareness, and every small sound seemed to scream with danger. I began to think that someone was following me.

I stepped up my pace and changed my path. It was late, and a woman alone after dark is always a target for robbery or assault. It's hard to look as if you know where you're going in a strange city when you don't. Once I finally reached my hotel, I slept little, if at all, and got up early to get ready to leave. An airport van was waiting for us at the hotel door.

Upon arriving at the airport, we were informed that the fog had not lifted and that the airport remained closed. We would be transported to the Windsor airport by bus. My short sortie was turning into a long, complicated mission. I was eager to call home but uncomfortable making a call since there was always a chance our phone was bugged. We arrived in Windsor that afternoon. I hailed a cab, but as we tried to leave the airport, we were stopped at the exit by a police roadblock.

I calmed myself and explained that I was visiting family and on my way home. I was permitted through. I was, thankfully, able to retrieve my car without needing to provide any explanation. Only one more hurdle remained: the border. I was sweating profusely beneath my calm exterior as I approached the tunnel border crossing. I showed the border agents my driver's license as identification. They waived me through. Twenty minutes later, I walked into the warmth and safety of my home with the package intact.

As I reflect now on this experience, I say to myself: What were you thinking? Was it the desire for approval after my public pillorying with the MCLL? Or my unspoken radical's oath to support "power to the people" by any means necessary? Or was it simple ignorance and pure naïveté? I marvel that I didn't exhibit better judgment or instinctive self-preservation when faced with Jim's request. What if I had failed? While I felt the mission was noble and important because the funds would go to support work that I believed in, I was overeager to be of service. Activists must always think carefully about accepting risks. This lesson came through loud and clear to me later as I examined my behavior. When I was approached again about bringing contraband into the States, I declined.

At the time, it seemed as if I was plummeting from one poor choice to the next. I needed some time and space to heal. Mike and I were both deeply affected by our separation from our organizations, which had been so much a part of ourselves. I was still grappling with my MCLL wounding. The split in the League destroyed Mike's vision of what that group could become. Mike had a grand vision of a mass organization led by a cadre dedicated to social and political revolution in the United States. Goals included addressing the concerns of the black community and confronting the institutions that helped maintain exploitation and oppression.

BY THE SPRING OF 1972, Jim and his family had moved in. Our big household had expanded to include Jim Forman and his wife, Dinky, and their beautiful cherub-faced kids, Lumumba and Chaka, ages four and two. These curly-headed, brown-eyed children were a joy to behold. Chaka was still an innocent child, and Lumumba was bright, clever, curious, and devious.

I had expected Jim to have a black family and was surprised to see that Dinky was a white woman. I was just as surprised at how much younger she was than Jim, who was in his mid-forties but appeared much older. But I didn't question their relationship, and Dinky and I never discussed it. In the context of my life and my family's personal experiences, a mixed-race couple was not that unusual.

My kids were now doing well in school and seemed comfortable with people in our home. We openly communicated, laughed, and pitched in together to make things work. At the end of each busy day, we all sat down to a community meal in our spacious dining room. Although I learned later that some of my children had issues as they matured, at that time everything seemed to be going well, and our family life, despite its deviations from the norm, appeared strong.

Having people in the house eased the burden of meal preparation and child care. And Jim and Dinky always paid their way, which was a huge help to me in meeting expenses. I tallied up all the bills at the end of each month and divided them by the number of people living in the house. Everyone paid their fair share. I was finally able to catch up on the high utility bills in our drafty old house.

From the very beginning, Jim tended to keep to himself. He was getting older, and maybe the sheer number of us in the home was more than he'd bargained for. My kids, except for Greg, who played chess with him, thought he was unfriendly. I knew that Jim had an outstanding and courageous history in the fight for civil rights. He was, without doubt, a brilliant strategist.

Mike was busy with organizing activities, and Jim was traveling. Dinky and I carried the main responsibilities for the household. We shopped for food together at Eastern Market, and she mapped out the cooking assignments. The plan was serving us well, but the economy was changing and our needs were outstripping our finances. As a single mother, I continued to be the primary provider for my children.

The U.S. economy had been growing during the late 1960s and into early 1972, which aided President Nixon's reelection campaign and contributed to his victory. Nixon also promised to wind down the war in Vietnam. He failed his campaign promises on all counts. Known for his "dirty tricks," Nixon partnered with the FBI and the CIA to engage in undercover operations against activists and expanded the Vietnam War into Cambodia. He was charged with criminal behavior during the Watergate scandal and resigned. His failed policies spawned the onset of the great 1970s inflation, which eroded my ability to meet my bills and ended in the recession of 1973–75.

I've always been frugal, and I noted every penny that flowed through my fingers. The divorce left me at a financial disadvantage. The child support was totally inadequate, and I received no alimony. I had no medical insurance and no savings. I was struggling to keep us afloat. We needed financial stability, so I began to look for employment to supplement our income. I remained committed to activism as the foundation of my life, but I was also entering a new phase when family concerns and a need to change direction became paramount. My passion for social change was redirected from movement work to community work.

For these reasons, Metropolitan Hospital was at the top of my list of potential employers. The hospital had a union, and employees received benefits, including health care. It was located in the heart of the district where the 1967 rebellion started, less than a mile from our home. That short drive to a neighborhood hospital opened a door for me to rededicate my life to helping others. I was hired on the spot to work as a receptionist in the emergency room. I was thirty-five years old, and Metropolitan Hospital would be my new activist platform.

Politically, these were still tumultuous times. Many political people falling afoul of the law were being killed or jailed. The Black Panthers were flexing their muscles in Detroit. They began practicing military-type drills on the quiet street behind us, in full view of the upstairs windows of Jim and Dinky's room. Jim had had a bad experience with the Panthers just before coming to Detroit, and their activities in our neighborhood were making him feel paranoid. Somehow he felt that these drills were intended to be some threat toward him.

One day, the FBI came to our door asking for Mike. I did my best to behave like a housewife. The one speaking flashed his badge. "We're looking for a Michael Hamlin."

"No, not here," I answered above the din. The dog was wildly barking in our vestibule, and I held the screen door closed with my hand, knowing that our little dog, Snoopy, would cheerfully let them in if the decision were his. Don told me later the operatives also visited him. I have no idea what he said to them, but they never came back.

Work in the emergency room was absorbing and fascinating, as well as physically and mentally draining. Sometimes when I came home, Jim would get on my nerves. He would be walking around the house, his writing in his hands, expounding on his latest theories and linking himself to Frantz Fanon, the great Martinique-born psychiatrist and revolutionary, known for his work on the psychopathology of colonization.

While I understood the importance of Jim's scholarly work, my life at the moment stood in stark contrast. My day consisted of an exhausting struggle to get myself to work, to see that my kids were cared for, to assure that food was on the table, and then to get everyone to bed before the cycle started all over again. We lived on different planes of reality. By contrast, I thought my relations with Dinky were intact.

In the summer of 1972, Dinky went on a summer road trip with her children, and she generously took Ken and Carolyn along. Jim was out of town most of the time, which meant Mike was on his own with the children. One Monday evening, I pulled into the driveway at five fifteen, exhausted. Mondays were always crazy in the ER. It was a predictable pattern. It seems that everyone just ignores their health on weekends and then decides it's an emergency on Monday.

Both our front and back doors were wide open, as usual. I loved the freedom of movement we chose for ourselves. I waved to the kids who were in the backyard.

"Dinner should be ready soon," I called as the screen slammed behind me, rousing Snoopy, who gazed accusingly at me.

Mike was in the kitchen looking solemn. "Call the kids, it's almost ready," he said.

I shed my uniform and hustled to get the table set. No one was ever late to a dinner call. If you dallied, you just might lose your share to someone who had responded more promptly.

"Where's Mike?" I inquired a short time later when he didn't appear at the table.

"He went out the front door a few minutes ago," Jeff noted.

"I'm sure he'll be right back," I said. "Go ahead, get started."

I returned to the refrigerator for a pitcher of fresh-squeezed lemonade, one of Mike's specialties. Mike hadn't looked good when I came in. I should have asked about his day. As the meal progressed and he didn't appear, I got worried. Something was wrong.

The kids ate with their usual rumpus, a combination of play and sibling rivalry, not always ending with grace. I gathered from the chatter that this had not been a good day and Mike was disturbed with their behavior. As everyone noisily rinsed and stacked their dishes in the sink and returned to their activities, Jeff appeared in the doorway.

"Mike's sitting on the island behind the trees," he said.

I took a deep breath and headed that way.

Mike's back was to me, his arms tightly hugging his legs, as if to comfort his soul. I touched him carefully. He began to cry and pulled slightly away. "I don't know if I can do this. I need time to think."

I slid down next to him, crossing my legs and pulling him close, his head against my chest. His breathing was warm and close to my heart, his face moist in my embrace.

"The kids"—he began and then hesitated—"they're rejecting me. I don't know if I can do this."

"Tell me how I can help?"

"You can't help. I need time to work this through." He freed himself from my arms. "Go back in the house and let me think."

I felt bad. I wanted to comfort him—it mattered to me that he was hurting. But out of respect, I left him alone.

I spent a sleepless night watching the headlights of the cars on Second Avenue flash across the bedroom ceiling. I watched the shades of the night sky turn from dark to dawn, listening for his sound, longing to have him close. He had to make his choice. I had no choice to make; the children were part of me.

Morning came, and I had to go to work. Responsibilities continue, no matter what crises befall us.

Jeff was in the kitchen early, his young face distressed, obviously suffering from some sleeplessness himself. "Mike slept in the car last night. Mom, I'm sorry if I did anything. I don't want him to leave." His emotion startled me as I tried to digest his story, my own mood was already precarious. "Please don't let him leave," he added.

I was torn, should I go out to the car or not? I slowly, deliberately dressed for work. Be natural, I thought, let it flow. But when I approached the car, it was empty.

Somehow, I made it through the day, assisting the patients who came in, filling out paperwork, making phone calls as required. I was smiling, going through the motions, but my mind elsewhere. I left as soon as my shift was over.

Mike was sitting in the kitchen when I arrived. He stood as I entered, his arms reaching out to me. "I'm here for you," he said. I stepped into his embrace and drew comfort from his closeness.

"What happened?" I asked.

"It wasn't anything specific. Sometimes it's all just a little overwhelming," he mused. I knew that feeling.

Although Mike had been married twice, he had no children, and his experience in managing kids was limited. The everyday, all-day requirements of children must have been a stretch for both them and him. Mike and I knew that we needed to be conscious of whether our relationship was helping or harming the children, but sometimes it was hard to judge. Mike had been raised as part of a large extended family just like ours. I often spent time with Mike's family on weekends when Don had the kids. But my children didn't share those weekends with us. Having a man in the house seemed acceptable to the boys. But the girls were more withdrawn and cautious about the interracial dynamics of our lives and the presence of adult men of color in our household. In the context of our culture, these undercurrents had to be considered whether we agreed with the societal propaganda or not.

During this time, Mike was often on the road for the BWC, attending conferences, speaking, organizing nationally to unite groups connected to Jim across the country into a mass working-class organization led by Marxists. Jim was the founder of the organization and still struggling to call the shots.

One day, as I was doing dinner duty, Jim entered the kitchen from the backstairs.

"Mike is going to be transferred," he announced somewhat gleefully, "to Cincinnati to establish a new base for the Congress." I was aghast, standing at the sink preparing a casserole.

"You'll still be able to see him," he added, casually informing me of a decision that was going to turn my life upside down. "You can meet in Toledo."

Politically, I understood the premise of democratic centralism. Nevertheless, I was stunned. Leaders of political organizations sometimes make necessary strategic decisions that outweigh personal desires. But I was devastated by this news. Why wasn't Mike telling me this?

I tried to make sense of this development. I had to admit that I always knew that Mike might be called away by his national work. It was a risk that came with being involved with him. As one might expect, I had a few questions for Mike when he came home that evening.

Mike worked long hours, and I was often asleep when he arrived home. But that night I was awake, and I waited until he got into bed before I brought up my conversation with Jim.

"Have a good day?" I asked, controlling my urge to dump everything.

"Busy," he responded—nothing more.

"Jim talked with me today." I tentatively searched for a footing to open this discussion.

"About what?"

"About your being transferred to Cincinnati." I hesitated, but he didn't pick up the thread. I sat up to see him better. "Why didn't you tell me about this?" I said accusingly. "We agreed not to talk about your organizational work, and I accept that, but if you're disappearing out of my life, I'd like some notice." Then I added, "From *you*—not from Jim."

"Yes, Jim mentioned this to me," he said. "I haven't made up my mind how to respond. This is totally Jim's idea. I'm the chairman of the Congress. He has no authority to send me out of town, but I think he believes that League people in Detroit would listen to him if I wasn't around. That's how this all started . . . Don't worry," he told me, "I'll take care of it."

Mike did not go to Cincinnati, and Jim never mentioned the possibility to me again.

By 1973, the deterioration of the Black Workers Congress was well under way. Jim's plans for the Congress had not unfolded as he envisioned. After Watergate, the country was in chaos. Nixon's alliance with J. Edgar Hoover's **COINTELPRO** surveillance and destruction programs was responsible for effectively infiltrating and wrecking movement organizations. Political movement groups all over the country were in decline.

The demise of the BWC was confusing and painful. Sectarian logic was prevailing. Everyone was suspicious of someone else, and people were being purged from the organization. Jim was getting paranoid and erratic. He kept seeking new blood, new young people to carry out the work. First, he expanded membership to white working people. I attended a couple of meetings that included whites who were working closely with the nationally based Congress. At one meeting, which was led by two members from out of town, tempers raged and the gathering ended with the outsiders, from New York, I believe, purging all the local people in the room from the organization. In this environment of disintegration of the movement, chaos ruled.

Shortly after these purges, I began to find strangers in the house when I came home from work. Jim would say they were there to help expand the ranks. I didn't know how long folks had been coming to the house or what they had been doing while I was at work. I began to feel uneasy. I was worried that Jim's actions could be compromising the safety of my family because I wasn't home to protect them from intruders.

One evening after work, I walked into our library and found

a young man whom I didn't know riffling through papers in my desk drawer.

"What do you think you are doing?" He froze. There was another young man in the room as well, and he turned toward me when I entered. My temperature was rising, my heart beating hard. "Who *are* you?" I demanded.

"I-I'm working with Jim," he stammered.

"Get out! Get out now, and don't come back!"

I didn't recognize the power of the voice that came out of my mouth. I was literally spitting mad. The men moved slowly toward the front door, walking backward, their hands in the air, as if they expected an attack and were signaling they wouldn't hit back.

Jim entered the hallway behind me. "What's going on out here?"

"They were going through papers on my desk," I said. "Do you have any idea who they are?" I watched their hasty retreat down the front walk. "Why were they going through my papers?"

Jim was taken aback by my reaction. Shaking his head, his shoulders sagging in a defeated gesture, he offered meekly, "We need new young people to carry on the work."

"I won't have strangers in here when I'm not home. This is my house. I make the rules!" I felt Jim had crossed the line, and my mother-bear persona emerged in the face of this violation of my personal space. In that moment, I wasn't thinking about Jim Forman's family; I was thinking about mine. I felt threatened. I'd had it.

"I want you out of here tomorrow," I said as calmly as possible.

Later that evening, I told Mike what happened.

"There's a lot going on," he said quietly. "I can't talk about it now."

I didn't press him, but I still felt threatened, compromised, vulnerable. Eventually, I slept.

I don't know what Jim told Dinky about the reason for their abrupt departure. As I dressed for work early the next morning, I could hear her in the upstairs hallway. She was shouting, accusing. I tried to approach her to explain what had happened, but she was too upset. Mike was still asleep, and I needed to leave for work. This would have to wait.

When I got home, the Formans were gone.

I don't know why I expected that Jim would go and Dinky and the children would stay—I simply hadn't thought that far ahead. I cared deeply for Dinky and valued her as a friend. Things had escalated beyond reason. How did we get to where we found ourselves? Everything was spinning out of control; everything I had worked for was disintegrating. I didn't know where to go from there.

Jim had a long history in the struggle before I met him in the early 1970s. No doubt it had been a very stressful struggle. Political struggle can be a carnivorous beast, and legendary struggle often took a legendary toll. Jim himself used to repeat the phrase "stress effects" when movement people started acting crazy. I tried to allow for this disconcerting truth in my interactions with others, especially Jim.

During the nearly two years that Jim lived with us, I noticed that he always seemed to be alone in his efforts: planning, fund-raising for the cause, or writing his books. I learned later that Jim was never accepted by people in the League, never really able to integrate with the rank-and-file efforts in Detroit. He was out of step with the changing times. Although Jim saw himself as a visionary, he had no experience in working with militant factory workers. After a life of devotion to the cause, "stress effects" took their toll on Jim.

A few years later, I heard that Dinky had left him, taking their sons with her. I knew that Dinky's mother was a writer, and once I had heard her mention that she was related to Winston Churchill through a family marriage. But the household was always so busy, I didn't take the time to inquire further about Dinky's family. It was many years later when I realized that Dinky was the daughter of the famed British-born activist and journalist Jessica Mitford, one of the Mitford sisters.

About the time of the Formans' departure, my relationship with Mike was going through its own turmoil as we struggled to figure out how our life together—as a family—would, or could, work. Mike paid the price for his political activities. He had to quit his position at the *News* or be fired when he called in sick and was then seen by management actively leading a demonstration on TV related to the Black Manifesto. He lost his job six months before his pension kicked in. He was driving a school bus and continuing his political activities when I met him.

Mike was good to me and had always wanted children. He joyfully bantered with my four boys, using humor to get them to open up and talk about their lives, and he taught them how to recognize danger on the streets. He and the boys easily bonded.

Once I took the job at the hospital, Mike was the one who picked Michael up when his angry outbursts got him ejected from his classroom at Friends School. Mike was the one who went to the junkyard with Ken, looking for parts to piece together our Volkswagen and keep it running. It was Mike who drove Greg and his girl to the junior prom in our car with the hole in the floorboard. Mike was constantly chatting with my children about their futures, encouraging them to get good marks in school and informing them that they *were going* to college, a place I knew nothing about.

This was not the norm back in the 1970s, not by a long shot. Mike's willingness to take on a substantial part of the child rearing was not only a tremendous help but also an act far ahead of its time. Still, we faced challenges.

THE CHILDREN weren't the only members of my family who had to make adjustments to our relationship. At one point Mike and I were returning from a getaway to Mexico. On the way back I began having sharp pains in my abdomen. The troublesome pain turned out to be a gallbladder attack apparently brought on by spicy food. After a visit to the doctor, I was scheduled for surgery.

My mother learned of my illness through my sister and visited me once while I waited for the date of my surgery. I hadn't seen much of Mother and Dad. They had stopped by on one occasion some months before, but when they glimpsed the activity in our house and Mike's Chairman Mao poster in our dining room, they excused themselves and left abruptly.

Mother had told me that she would not come to Harper Hospital because she was afraid to drive in that area of the city. She arrived, however, on the morning of my surgery, just as the orderly was pushing my stretcher out of my room and to the surgical theater. Mike was kissing me on the forehead and holding my hand when I saw her standing in the hallway. It startled me because I hadn't expected her, and I knew that she was shocked. I realized it must have been difficult for her to make her way to the hospital, and I was touched that she had found the courage to come.

In that instant Mother learned that what she had feared most had come to pass: her daughter was in a relationship with a black man. The dismay on her face was apparent. There was no time to think as they wheeled me away; I was already getting groggy. The surgery was complicated, and though I was in the hospital for ten days, she didn't return.

Some weeks later my mother and I sat in my kitchen. It was April. There was a promise of spring in the air, and the window was slightly open. It was the first time I had seen or heard from her since my surgery. Mother sat uncomfortably in her chair as I served tea.

"I knew you were seeing someone because the last time I came over there were men's clothes on your bed." She fidgeted in her chair, no longer able to contain her emotions. "How could you do this to me?" The words burst tearfully from her throat. Her hands flittered, and her expression was one of agonizing pain.

"Every time I see a white woman with a black man, I think it is because she couldn't get one of her own kind. You can! You can!" she shrieked. She covered her face, trying to hide from reality.

I made a special effort to be gentle with her, but she was not receptive. In one sweeping gesture, Mother tearfully scooped up her sweater and purse and, without looking back, left the house.

Toward the end of that summer, I heard from her again. She called to say she would like to see me.

"Mother, I'd like you to meet Mike," I told her over the phone. "I think you'll feel differently if you could just get to know him."

"I won't come to your house," she quickly said.

"Then you name the place."

She hesitated. "Can we meet at Belle Isle?"

It was a good omen. My mother loved the outdoors as much as I did, and she spoke the name of the island tenderly. We shared good memories of the place.

We were to meet at the head of the island park, which lies in the Detroit River not far from the city's center. At this particular spot, the island is open to the vast sky and swept by the predominant west wind. The unencumbered view overlooks the city skyline, the city I love so much. This was a place I had often visited as a child with my mother, her sisters, and my cousins on those traditional Wednesday get-togethers. Grandma's spirit lingers there.

That day, the summer sky was a brilliant blue and the sun pleasantly shining. A gentle breeze was blowing as I walked across the grass from which I had once plucked dandelions for my grandmother to make wine. I saw Mother sitting at a picnic table, looking small and fragile. It was another of life's significant moments that lives on as a vivid picture in my mind. I can still feel, touch, see, and smell the savory etchings of that moment. I was wearing a yellow T-shirt with multicolored stitching and a full skirt, my favorite, was blowing softly in the wind.

I was filled with emotion seeing her there, alone in the broad landscape. My arms and my heart ached for her love and support. She was the one responsible for my life on earth. She looked suddenly older to me, and I understood it had taken some courage for her to come.

I tried. She tried. But our conversation was brief, vague, filled with empty words that refused to fit the occasion.

Mike and I had arranged to come in separate cars. About a half hour into my time with my mother, I saw him walking across the grass. "Mother, Mike is here." I didn't want him to catch her unaware.

She stood up, took a deep breath, and walked toward him. "Hello," she said, her eyes meeting his only briefly. "I'm afraid I must leave now. It was nice to meet you."

And then she was gone.

I don't know what I had expected. It was a start, I suppose. Suddenly, though, I was overcome with a feeling that, despite the hopes I dared to have, I remained rootless, abandoned. Mike took me in his arms. "It's going to be okay," he whispered. "You're strong." I cried.

Up until her death, Mother continued to deny my relationship with Mike to her family and friends. Even her two sisters, with whom she was so close, were never to know. Following our afternoon on Belle Isle, my father announced that they had written me out of their will.

The break with my family affected me deeply because I believed that children have an obligation to honor their parents. One's existence in the world affirms the connection between parent and child. It was hard to accept that the source of my parents' rejection was their prejudiced feelings, but when I was growing up, white prejudice against blacks and foreigners was the norm. My parents held tight to their beliefs while I rejected them.

Because my parents had never been an integral part of my children's lives, their absence wasn't disruptive. Except for Carolyn, who had received some attention from my mother, grandparents were people who came into view on special occasions. My mother and dad never supported me when Don and I divorced. They just went on living their own lives, as usual. My heart was hurt when my parents disowned me, but I wouldn't, couldn't bend. Early in their lives, my parents made a decision to ignore the world around them. By contrast, I was totally committed to participating in the world and making it a better place. I would carry on because I knew I had to. *This is who I am.*

BY THE FALL OF 1973, the bulk of our radical movement work was over. This was not unique to Detroit. The disintegration of the left was under way across the country. We were splintered by sectarianism, lack of a unified goal, and infiltration by government agents and provocateurs. In addition, rising inflation and a slowdown in the economy thrust upon us the need to find paying work in order to survive. It was time to redirect our efforts and reinvent ourselves. Other comrades in the struggle were doing the same.

Conditions in the black communities had become deplorable. Since the rebellion in 1967, a primarily white police force was attempting to wrest control by brute force, while at the same time hard drugs, another means of controlling a population, began flooding into the black community. This ushered in a period of gang violence. "Drug war" racism was the new face of Jim Crow in America. Trapped by hopelessness, many people succumbed to illegal narcotics in a desperate attempt to escape the dogged struggle of their day-to-day lives. It was a lucrative business for the drug dealers. The situation was especially tragic for the young, who were often devoid of hope and saw no viable way out.

The character of our own neighborhood was changing. The emergency room where I worked continued to provide a window on what was happening in our vicinity. With drugs and gangs came shootings and fire bombings, as angry young men expressed their rage at their fate and took it out on one another. I came in contact with victims and perpetrators, as well as the cops who pursued them. My own children became fearful of the streets.

The change in our lives was perceptible. Casual work in the community ceased as we assessed what came next. Mike's prospects for sweeping change through coordinated movement activities gave way to a dream of helping people one at a time. He set his sights on getting an advanced college degree. I still had my job at the hospital where I felt I was doing meaningful work and had some influence through my union activities.

Mike applied for admission to Wayne State University shortly after the Black Workers Congress folded. His application was denied, which suggested that the college was not convinced he could manage the work, but we knew better. They were aware of Mike's radical history, and they didn't want any trouble. He was a thirty-five-year-old man who had been a journalist, a sergeant in the army, and then leader of a national organization. Mike would not be deterred. He went to classes at Wayne's Weekend College for a year, earned all A's, and then applied again to the

School of Social Work. This time, he got in with help from a new professor who had been in the BWC.

The world was changing, and we were changing with it. We reinvented ourselves and continued our activist work. The alternative—to stay stuck in the past—wasn't an option. Once the resolve of an activist is hardened into steel by the flames of a movement, the attitude becomes inseparable from the person. But evolving and changing, rising to new challenges and facing different circumstances, is also part of an activist's life journey. The movement was splintered and fraying, but that didn't mean our work was meaningless, or that the movement was dead. Quite the opposite. Society was demonstrably pushed forward by the efforts of so many during those days.

Yet a new era was on the horizon. The circumstances around us were changing, and we had to change with them. The roles I—and everyone else—had played during those days in the movement were no longer feasible. A new chapter in my life, and in the life of my family, was about to begin. There was still so much work to do. And all I had to do was turn the page.

PART **FOUR**

Leap, and the Net Will Appear

An Unlikely Love Story

I learned that courage was not the absence of fear,
but the triumph over it.
—Nelson Mandela

Today, conversations about the importance of cultural diversity in our education and employment sectors are commonplace. No one can seriously question how essential it is, if we are going to survive as a society. But in the 1970s, my family was a real-life case study in making diversity work in a very personal way. This in-the-trenches home training occurred at a level that most folks will never experience. Immersed in the day-to-day struggles of work and family life—and "stayin' alive" as John Travolta might say—it was not always easy to see our experience through this wider lens.

Culture is the culmination of our collective history and experience, our customs and beliefs. It not only defines our way of life but also provides the framework for our way of thinking as it is passed from one generation to another. Culture has deep roots and social, political, and economic implications. In essence, it is how we identify who we are and is the foundation upon which we construct our social relationships. The culture we come from often dictates our access to resources, our economic well-being, and how much leverage we have in decisions about our lives.

We are all products of our cultures. The clash between black and white cultures in the United States—as one-sided as it has been—has a long-disowned history. Often my closest friends and extended family made their own psychological projections about our blended family based on TV shows or biased news. But it is clear that they had no clue about the actual complexity of our lives. Indeed, there have been times when I am certain that we did not even understand ourselves.

Two distinguishing features of black culture are the interdependence of family members and the easy incorporation of extended family members who are not blood relations. Given the widespread restraints on black males in our society, the women play a strong role in the family, sharing what they have.

"Sharing scarcity is the bedrock of black culture," Mike explained to me at one point. Black families abundantly share food, folklore, insightful humor, and often general commiseration. These life-sustaining characteristics have been reinforced by generations of discrimination, poverty, and pain, and have functioned as survival techniques since the time of slavery. These traits serve to bond black communities together to protect the members against outsiders.

Whites often fail to realize that blacks and other minorities in America are forced to put aside their culture, shared history, food habits, and often their familiar language and idioms when they leave home in the morning to run errands, to attend school, to travel to work, and so on. In order to succeed by the rules and behaviors demanded by the dominant white society, they have no choice but to deny their culture and adopt white behaviors. Whites underestimate the overwhelming nature of racism embedded in the fabric of everyday social relations.

Another factor in our cultural divide is the primal defense response driven by centuries of racism when identity and experience as a people are confronted by a power that threatens to upend the way in which one is living, laying one bare to uncontrollable circumstances. Distrust by blacks of whites has a historical base that whites must accommodate in our mutual conversations.

Trust takes time and a demonstration of worthiness, as it would from anyone in another culture.

In hindsight, while operating in a world that provided no role models for our family's biracial reality, I mistakenly subjected my children to the idea that we could span the cultural divide by ignoring it and pretending that everything was normal. My children were having a level of experience that was unfathomable to me at the time. I doubt that I could have found the words to explain their everyday lived reality.

Today, I am all ears when I listen to my grown son, Michael, explain the history of prejudice in the United States to his young children as they all come to visit Grandma from France each summer. Michael's children were born and continue to live in Paris. Listening to some of these conversations and their questions about race and class, I sometimes believe my ten- and twelve-year-old grandchildren see us more clearly than we see ourselves. I also believe that Michael has learned something that I didn't understand at the time he was growing up. Prejudice and cultural diversity are topics that are often difficult for adults to grasp, but children have no framework for understanding unless we explain. That's why it's so important that we talk with them.

In early 1974, I learned that I was pregnant with Mike's child. We knew that others would judge us, but there was a certain satisfaction during this period in being bold in our love. Again, we were very shortsighted regarding the complications that would befall the kids in their social relationships as they embarked on the public expression of their mother's black partner and their mixed-race youngest sibling.

Mike loved kids, but despite two pregnancies in his earlier marriages, neither child survived to live birth. I was hesitant about the responsibilities of having another child and reluctant to marry again. But I loved Mike and understood his deep desire to have a child of his own. Mike promised that if we had this child, he would raise him—or her. Mike would remain true to this promise, taking on big parts of those challenging early days of any baby's life.

Our son, Alexander, was born in September 1974. I realized from the very day of his birth that we were facing a new cultural experience. Alex was born during the night. The next morning, after a new shift had taken over, a smiling nurse wheeled his small bassinet into my room, stopped short, and turned around.

"Oh no," I heard her whisper to another nurse in the hall-way, "We've got a baby mix-up. This is a black baby," she said in horror, and quickly left, wheeling Alex's bassinet back out of the room.

Five minutes later, the nurse returned, looking chagrined. "Good morning, Mother," she sweetly announced, and placed Alexander in my arms.

The joy I felt holding the innocent new life who had grown in my body and been nourished by my blood was a spiritual experience. I looked at his perfect fingers and toes, and the telltale dark markings on his fingernails, an indication of his African American heritage. I felt his calmness. It was such a miracle to see the reflection of both his father and me in his little body. I knew his life would be different from the lives of my other children. He would belong to two races and two cultures. He would be accepted one day and scorned the next for something beyond his control. I knew that as he grew up, he would necessarily struggle to find his place both physically and psychologically in a country that is obsessed with race. It would predetermine some of his choices and perhaps complicate the life of the person he would eventually marry.

WHEN ALEXANDER WAS BORN, I was still struggling to put the events of the last several months in perspective, and I welcomed the opportunity for a fresh start after things had gone so badly. Our baby was conceived during the anguish of watching our movement work fall apart, and he brought new joy into our relationship. I was hopeful that our post-movement life would offer me a chance to spend more time with all of my children. As I thought about our future, I reconsidered the idea of marriage. We had been together now for three years. Maybe it was time to cement our relationship.

Mike and I married on September 10, 1975, one year after our son was born. It was a group marriage in the Detroit City-County Building. To my understanding, our group ceremony was the last of its kind in Detroit. At first, our loving relationship was enough. But as I refocused on family, I realized that our marriage could some-day be important to the children. At the time we were married, interracial marriage was still illegal in thirteen states, although the Supreme Court had struck down the practice as unconstitutional in *Loving v. Virginia* eight years before.

We were one of eight couples gathered around a large confer-ence table in the judge's chambers

"Now is the time to present the rings," the judge announced, before adding, "if you have one."

My sister, who steadfastly supported us, was there. My son Ken took pictures. Alex, our one-year-old, was in our arms. The other children were in school. After the ceremony, we all walked in the warm, sweet sunshine a few blocks to Greektown, where we dis-covered a little restaurant already open for lunch at eleven in the morning. There we celebrated over an early meal, and toasted our future together with a bottle of wine.

Our marriage added a new dimension to our lives as we set-tled in for the long haul with a focus on family and on careers that would provide both purpose and stability. At the time, I was at peace with the world. But now, as I look back, I see how, by concentrating on the demands of the moment, I missed the big picture: we had created a very complex situation for the children to navigate.

The children were growing up, and it was time to ensure they developed skills that would get them to where they wished to be in their adult lives. Having moved from high school directly into motherhood, I was not equipped to guide them, but Mike had vision and experience in working with teens in just this way. With my blessing, Mike took on the role of coach, and he encouraged each of the children to pursue a college education.

Even though Mike was by then well established in our family, the transition from "Mom as manager" to "Mike as official second in command" was a challenge for all concerned. In some ways, I was sympathetic. To be truthful, it hadn't been that many years since their father left. Adding to the confusion, some of Mike's mannerisms were tied to the cultural aspects of his personality and were different from what the children were used to. He was also not the neatest person on earth. Both his personal manner and his lifestyle contributed a bit of chaos to our previously predictable family. The reaction wasn't uniform. I saw no resistance from the boys. However, the girls perceived that our family had been invaded, not only by Mike but by his entourage, who pursued his advice and counsel.

In addition, the children's friends were understandably confused by the interracial changes in our family, the never-ending political discussions, and the coming and going of strangers in our home. It had to be difficult for an outsider to fathom what manner of place our home was.

Carolyn withdrew at times and didn't want to share her feelings. In fact, for a couple of years, she literally wouldn't speak to us at all. In her heart, all she ever wanted was a chance to be like other young girls her age. "Normal," she called it. But our family wasn't normal. Carolyn seldom had friends over because they would see how different we were. Struggling with her vision was difficult enough, but according to Carolyn—even today—we made it impossible for her to find her rightful place in life.

Whatever issues they may have had with the adults of the household, the children fully accepted and embraced Alex as their baby brother. Sometimes, I thought his feet would never touch the ground. Because of Mike's and my relationship and his status in the movement, our baby captivated the attention of activist friends as well as Mike's family, and they all gave us love and support. Mike was very protective of his relationship with his blood child, who looks like a lighter-skinned carbon copy of him.

My brown-eyed, brown-skinned child was born with a gentleness about him that he carries with him still. Nevertheless, he was an active child, and, on my days off, I was destined to be a thirty-nine-year-old mother to a fast-moving, curious toddler.

Alex's hair was one of many new experiences for me. I had given more than my share of haircuts and had established a routine. Everyone lined up on the front porch to take a turn on the kitchen stool, draped with a plastic cape. Snipping away with my scissors and wielding my trimmer, I worked my way down the line. But Alex's tight little curls were more of a challenge and seemed to require an artist's hand. No matter what I tried, he looked neglected. I was incapable of mastering his locks until Mike's mother showed me how to braid his hair and snip off the ends.

Today, there are other biracial kids in our family. Greg, Jeff, and Christine all chose black partners and have biracial children. Since Mike had a white grandfather (the slave owner's son), Alex is light skinned; he has married a white woman whose family seems comfortable with the mix. As a family, we are on our way to populating a lineage of multihued people who are steeped in black culture and educated in black history.

GENERALLY, WE WERE WELL ACCEPTED, and we traveled far and wide as a family during those years. Only occasionally did we encounter untenable situations. One of those incidents occurred in the Detroit suburbs, an area that often gives me pause.

One evening in late December, we were kibitzing at the dinner table, having a jovial conversation, when Jeff interrupted. "Hey, have you heard that it's going to snow five inches tonight? Maybe we'll have a white Christmas."

Ever the mom, my immediate reaction was, "Who's got boots?"

"Remember those old boots I was wearing last winter," said Michael, who was nine years old at the time.

"The zipper broke and we threw them away."

Michael generally inherited his clothes from Jeff. But Jeff was eleven now and growing like a weed. His boots from last winter would never fit Michael.

"My old boots are way too big for you. You'd fall on your face." Jeff's chair scraped against the floor as he shoved it back then stood and demonstrated Michael's predicted fate. Gales of laughter rang out all around the table.

"Dinner's pretty much over," Mike said. "You all help with the dishes, and I'll run Michael up to Oakland Mall and take care of this."

Shopping options were limited in Detroit, as they often are in urban areas. Oakland Mall, about a thirty-minute drive north of our home, was located in the white suburb of Madison Heights. We shopped there often, since Sears had closed in Highland Park. Moments later, I heard the back door shut and the car pull out of the driveway. They returned two hours later.

"How'd it go? Get boots?" I inquired, my back to the door as I stood at the kitchen counter preparing the next day's lunches. When I turned around, I was shocked to see my nine-year-old son's troubled face.

"The security police followed us," he said. "We were walking back to the car, and they slowly drove next to us the whole time, shining their spotlight in our faces. It was scary," he said, then he trudged up the backstairs to his room, dragging along a package that contained his new boots.

"Michael, let's talk," I called after him.

"Mike and I already talked. I'm okay."

Harassment by law officers was particularly frightening. As a black man, Mike was in a peculiar position when he, the stepfather, accompanied his white children out and about without me. I knew he would protect the kids with his life. I also knew being profiled was potentially dangerous. When this happened, everyone involved had to proceed with caution. Unfortunately, in our world—then and now—a black man with a white child triggers an immediate alarm.

AS OUR OWN FAMILY DYNAMIC GREW AND MATURED, Mike began encouraging me to reunite with my relatives. My sister had been supportive when I reached out to her. But with my ties to my parents broken, I didn't know how to connect with my extended family. I missed my aunts, my mother's sisters. My mother knew of Alexander, but she never told her sisters about my seventh child. It would be years before I saw them again.

I had also lost contact with my many cousins when I was involved in movement activities. As my focus shifted back to a more "normal" life, my sister convinced me to attend a family Christmas Eve event at one cousin's house. I took the older children but left Alex with Mike. I was to find that I no longer had anything in common with my birth family. I was uncomfortable and so were they.

My mother's sisters, their husbands, and their kids had gathered at my aunt Anna's son's house. I desperately wanted to be part of the family—a family, any family—where I was accepted. My mother and dad were there, interacting with my cousins, whom they appeared to know better than they knew me. I sat awkwardly and watched. No one made a move to talk with me. My children mostly interacted with one another. My cousin's husband—the cop—was there. I remembered the day after the riot when he had come to our home and told me to get out of Detroit. I wondered if he had told his wife how I was living. From their point of view, my life would have been unfathomable.

I don't know if anyone was aware I had remarried or that I had a biracial child. I felt as if my presence was a pall on what might have otherwise been a joyous evening. The party was in the basement, and eventually I went upstairs to the kitchen to get some water and take a few deep breaths. There I ran into Dick, the youngest of Anna's boys. He sat down at the kitchen table across from me.

"I know about your new marriage," he said. "Karen told me. I want you to know that no matter what the others say, you're all right with me."

"Thank you for saying that, Dick," I said. "It's very uncomfortable to be here, not knowing what is on anyone's mind. Right now, I'm sorry I came."

"You can come to my house, anytime, and you'll be welcome," Dick said.

His words notwithstanding, my experience with the rest of my family left me feeling isolated and wanting. The family that I ended up fully joining was Mike's. His family accepted me as one of their own from the start, and they still do.

Not long after Mike and I became involved, his father died. I joined him at the wake. As I walked into the funeral parlor, Mike's mother reached out to take me by the hand, bringing me into the circle of family, despite my being the only white person in the room. I was someone she hardly knew; she understood only that Mike had chosen me. A calm and warmth always surrounded her. I greatly admired and dearly loved this strong, down-to-earth Southern woman whom everyone called G, for Grandma.

Over the years, my boys loved visiting Grandma G's home, which seemed always to be filled with loving family, laughter, and the delicious scents of Southern home cooking, from collard greens to custard pies. What a contrast to the visits with my family, where everyone sat stiffly on chairs and spoke one at a time, where children were expected to be seen and not heard and there was not a toy in sight.

Mike's mother's home was like a loving nest where family members, grandchildren, and friends laughed and played together in that tiny living room with the TV blaring. Babies and toys littered the floor, adults engaged with the little ones, and strangers were welcomed as easily as friends. The cultural differences between his family and mine were astounding.

Mike was very close to his family. His sister also had seven children near in age to ours. When we got together, we had fourteen—count 'em, fourteen—kids, plus Mike's sister, Eddie Mae; Grandma G; Mike; and me. The children greatly enjoyed hanging out with their cousins. The gaiety manifested itself in many picnics at Belle Isle, resulting in delightful cross-cultural learning experiences.

We had many wonderful times with Mike's mother, who was an elegant and loving woman, genuinely treasured by all who knew her. We often took her on vacation with us, which made our blended family even more outstanding on the landscape. We went to Niagara Falls together, along with Michael, Christine, and Alex. In later years, Grandma G joined us for weeks in Michigan's north country, along with Alex, and Greg's biracial daughter.

Living in Detroit's central city, our family had limited contact with racists. People in the Detroit movement were always supportive. Mike was respected and known for his work in the community, and when we attended movement events, the news media always called him by name. Mike, a leader with presence, carried himself with bearing and dignity. Over the years, my children picked up many black cultural mannerisms, which helped them fit in with an urban crowd, even as it complicated their ability to find peer groups in college.

When we traveled as a family, however, people looked and often talked among themselves. The stares and whispers made me uncomfortable; on a few occasions, they felt threatening. Things are better now than they were when the children were young. In recent years, when Mike and I traveled alone, we were often surprised when strangers approached us to ask if we were married and then to marvel at our many decades together. On the other hand, just a few years ago, I watched a woman who had been staring at us while we ate at a restaurant in Macomb County, Michigan, leave the restaurant and walk over to check the license plate of our car. I guess she thought we were from Mars.

We stood out when we traveled to places where there were few blacks.

In 1978, we decided to go on a camping adventure to Acadia National Park, on Maine's northeast coast. I'd always wanted to see Cape Cod, a sandy peninsula in southeastern Massachusetts known for its beaches, so we built a stop first at the Cape into our travel plans. Longing for surf and sand, we headed north to the coast. It was late in the evening and quite dark as we passed around the city of Boston. Realizing we wouldn't make our destination before it got dark, we stopped at a Howard Johnson's to feed the children before they fell asleep in the back of the car.

After we finished our meal, Mike took the children who were with us—Jeff, Michael, Christine, and Alex—to the car while I stopped at the restroom. I noticed two state troopers having a meal as I passed their table on my way out. I guess we knew that there had been race riots in Boston when whites had attempted to stop blacks from using the city's public beaches. But a race riot was the furthest thing from our minds that night. I made it to the car a few moments later, got the children bedded down in the back, and we entered the freeway heading north.

A few miles down the road, Mike said nervously, "We're being followed."

I checked the side-view mirror and saw the police car. No flashing lights, it was just keeping pace a short distance behind our Volkswagen van.

"I'm just going to act like nothing is happening and slowly proceed," Mike said. "The cops often pace me when I'm on a highway driving out of town."

"I walked by some state troopers at a table when I was leaving the restaurant. I wasn't aware they were watching us," I said.

"Yes, I saw them, too."

We drove for another five miles or so, deliberately trying to calm ourselves. We said nothing to the children, who were being lulled to sleep by the motion of the car. Then the lights came on, and Mike pulled over. He slowly rolled down the window.

"Just stay down," I told the children. "We'll be on our way in a minute or two."

"Driver's license," the cop gruffly said when he reached Mike's window. I was struck by his unfamiliar Boston accent.

Mike said nothing. He complied and pulled out his wallet, then handed over his license.

"Where you headed?" the cop asked, his flashlight bobbing from Mike's license to our faces and then to the frightened children in the back.

"We're on our way to Maine for a vacation." It was quiet for a moment, and then Mike asked, "Do you mind telling me why I was stopped?"

"We're looking for a stolen car, looks just like this one," the cop said with a sneer.

I tried not to laugh. Like this one? Our Volkswagen van, which we bought at the junkyard and our oldest, Ken, got running for us. Really?

Finally, the cop decided he'd had enough of us. "You just head straight out of town," he said. "You hear me? Get back on that highway and keep on going. We don't want you around here."

No problem with that. We were on our way to more friendly territory.

It was often hard to know what to expect when we traveled together. These sorts of experiences continued to occur even during the "more tolerant" years that followed. Once, Mike—by himself—took two light-skinned granddaughters under ten on a plane to California's Disneyland for a week. The three stayed in hotels and motels, and no one ever questioned him. Yet on an anniversary trip that Mike and I took to Arizona, a clerk at the tourist bureau refused to wait on us, and his supervisor eventually had to take over. It all depends on the territory.

Even more recently, I was driving with one of Christine's biracial children, a child of seven, asleep in the backseat of my car. I had a note, signed by Chris, that gave me permission to take my granddaughter to Canada. But this wasn't good enough for the custom's officer, who claimed anyone could have written the note.

"She doesn't look like your granddaughter. Wake her up for me, please."

I did as I was told.

"Who is this?" he asked her, pointing to me.

She replied, "Grandma."

"Do you know your mommy's phone number?"

She nodded.

"Can you tell it to me?"

She told him her phone number. He called and got verbal permission from my daughter. We were finally allowed to cross the border into Canada.

THERE ARE A LOT OF LITTLE THINGS in our everyday behavior patterns that stem from our childhood experiences. Certainly, I carry this sort of baggage. Mike did, too. But his baggage was a bit different from mine.

I watched Mike interact with the children, and I watched his mother raise his sister's girls. Mike's ways and those of his mother seemed very similar to each other, but their style and their rhetoric, emanating from their Southern roots, were not at all familiar to me.

Mike's early memories were of working in the cotton fields on the sharecropper's farm in Mississippi where they lived. He picked a young boy's share of cotton, but his main job was to care for his baby sister. At an early age, Mike worked in the plantation house with his mother. He was such a good worker that the owner's wife wanted to keep him as her houseboy, but his mother wouldn't let that happen. Given the disparities in our upbringings, how could one expect that his approach to raising children would be similar to mine?

Mike described two occasions when he was a child and a lynch mob on someone's trail stopped at their shack to seek information and water their horses. He understood danger, and he understood black folks' place in that brutally racist Southern society. His father drank, philandered, and beat his mother; his mother, in her strength, held the family together. Mike resolved to protect his mother, and, by extension, this early experience made him a good partner for me. He was respectful and accepted my demands to have control over decisions in my own life.

When Mike was nine, after only two years attending a one-room schoolhouse, he and his sister moved from the sharecropper's plantation into Canton, Mississippi, to stay with their grandmother, Mama Mag. With her two children safe in town, Mike's mother went north to be with his father in Kansas City and then to Detroit. When Mike turned twelve, he, his grandmother, and his sister took the train north to join his parents. They settled in Ecorse, downriver of Detroit to the west.

With the highest level of determination to learn, Mike began two years of study in an all-black elementary school; he then moved on to an integrated junior high school in Ecorse. Ecorse High was on the white side of the railroad tracks that divided the town. Mike's home and family were on the black side.

In school, Mike was an excellent student who shared the academic center stage. He developed friendships with his peers, including several top white female classmates. He was popular at Ecorse High—not only was he an outstanding student, he was also the star quarterback, a position of responsibility not normally offered to young black men at the time. In addition, he played first-rate varsity basketball and tennis. Mike often traveled on the school bus to intramural sports events with his team. His exposure across all these venues allowed him to taste what life was like for whites. This was when he began to understand what life could be like for a black man who was free from the chains of racial discrimination.

Mike was clear about his goals in life long before he completed high school. In his school yearbook he wrote: "My one ambition is to contribute something to the world." He wanted to help black people whom he saw suffering.

When Mike graduated, he applied to and was accepted at the University of Michigan, where he attended a premed program for two and a half years before dropping out due to financial concerns. Unable to get a job except in a car wash, he joined the army.

When Mike was in Korea, he experienced the global nature of racism that made him a very willing and eager student of some of the headier sociopolitical philosophies of the era. He came home from Korea angry about U.S. aggression in the Third World and the brutal racist treatment of poor peasants by American forces that he witnessed. While he was in Korea, word reached him about Emmett Till, Montgomery, Little Rock, and more. He came home ready to fight against racism and to "contribute something to the world."

I was fully involved in the antiracism movement and a mother of six when I met Mike. I was also recently divorced. He accepted me as I was, integrated me into his life, taught me about racism from his point of view, trained me how to read a newspaper with a critical eye, shared his love of books and jazz, and introduced me to his culture and family.

Mike and I shared an unlikely love story. Interracial love is founded on the acceptance of differences and the discovery of common ground that surpasses the limits of skin color. Success is a long shot because of the vast disparities in culture and experience. It took me a while to understand what made me feel so safe, so understood in Mike's presence. Over time, I came to realize that we held either end of a common thread—compassion. We are forever bonded by our commitment to alleviate suffering and expand the reaches of our humanity.

The whole notion of being with someone who "got" me, even before I "got" myself, brought a new dimension to my life. That perception, the experience of being "seen" when you're not convinced that you have value, is the first step toward fulfilling our potential for what it means to be fully human in a relationship. How could this happen when we were so different?

On the surface, Mike's and my relationship seemed unlikely, and, among our critics, it raised inevitable questions about our motivations. Yet for all our differences, meeting Mike was like coming *home*, in the broadest and deepest sense of the word. I had the sense in this topsy-turvy world that Mike was my "break-apart," which means, in mythic terms, that we were two parts of one organism that broke apart and then found each other again.

Years ago, Mike and I took a train trip to the Grand Canyon, where we celebrated our twenty-fifth wedding anniversary. The trip was a retirement gift from his coworkers and his union cohorts, when he was forced to leave his job for medical reasons. We stopped off in Sedona, Arizona—red-rock country—and in our travels ran into a vortex guide who coached people to have visions. Vortexes are heightened fields of spiraling cosmic energy. Just outside Sedona, this energy is near the surface of the earth, and it can be experienced in deep meditation and is considered to have healing properties.

As we inquired about the guide's mystical calling, the man told us he'd had a vision, when he'd glimpsed us coming toward him, that Mike and I had shared three lives together. That explains how I feel.

We were determined to live our lives to the fullest, without re-gard for the consequences. In his life, Mike surpassed any threat or fear. He was impervious to external concerns expressed by other people. This is one of the reasons he could chuckle even when faced with adversity. He was lifted to this height as part of his rage against racism in this country.

"Racists are cowards who attack in groups or mobs. I would die before giving you up against some racist threat," he told me. His words left me feeling secure and loved.

Mike was a man of broad experience and a brilliant thinker. Yet he always considered my point of view and supported my intellec-tual growth and personal development. In turn, I surrounded him in a harbor of unconditional love and family support. Together we worked to build a life dedicated to serving others in the world that we had dared to create.

POLICY ACTIVIST

*The strongest bond of human sympathy outside the family relation
should be one uniting working people of all
nations and tongues and kindreds.*
—ABRAHAM LINCOLN

I WORKED FOR METROPOLITAN HOSPITAL for twenty-three
years, starting at the bottom as an emergency room receptionist—a
union position—and ultimately rising to become the director for
patient relations. I loved working at the hospital. People were approachable, even the administrators. In all, there were one thousand employees who worked across the system's two hospitals and
eight community health centers. We were like family. We watched
out for one another, and we mostly knew one another by name.
Most of the employees were black, and I observed varying degrees
of comfort exhibited by whites who worked there. I was grateful for
my transcultural experiences and felt well integrated into the hospital community. I believed our family's experiences would also serve
our children well as they grew into the global community.

During this period, I was aware that my mother now found
herself in a similar racially mixed situation, but she experienced
a totally different outcome. Mother worked at Hudson's Department Store in the Northland Mall, a changing neighborhood. As
the racial makeup of Hudson's workforce transitioned, Mother

was unable to overcome her lack of experience with people of color. My sister explained that she became timid and fearful, withdrawing socially and finally quitting her job. I gladly would have shared all that I had learned with my mother and would have been eager to support her, but we were estranged by her choice, and I didn't know how to help her.

Metropolitan's ER sat on the corner of 12th Street and Webb on Detroit's Near West Side. Although it was small, it was second only to Detroit Receiving in the number of patients seen. It was that kind of neighborhood. The midnight shift was often a parade of gunshots, stabbings, drunks, and out-of-control mental patients. When I worked third shift, I experienced my neighborhood in new ways. As I drove the ten blocks from my home to the hospital around eleven p.m., I would pass folks hanging out on corners and handing around small brown paper bags or smaller clear plastic ones. Some faces were familiar; others sat in the shadows of dingy apartment building porches. I wonder, I would think as I drove by, how many of you I will see tonight.

All of Metropolitan Hospital's clerical employees were organized into Office and Professional Employees International Union, Local 42. Because of my active interest in working-class history, I was soon elected educational chairperson. My role was to remain in touch with other hospital union activists and keep Metropolitan up-to-date on how others were dealing with the issues we had in common. I was growing more assertive and sure of myself in developing well-educated union employees. But then, I almost got fired.

There were clear problems with patient services, especially in the emergency room. The first was in the registration process, which was designed to have patients present their insurance cards and pay up front, even before they had a chance to explain their reason for coming in for care. Folks in pain were often left to stand in line at the cashier's window. We pleaded for a change in the process, but no one in management would listen to us. My old activist habits surfaced, and I decided to use my camera to document what was happening to patients.

The second problem was a backlog in the medical records room. When a patient appeared for acute care for a chronic condition, it was the receptionist's job to call for the patient's chart, which detailed his medical history. Delays in access to a patient's chart could, in turn, delay patient treatment. Precious time was being wasted in the search for patient treatment histories.

Short-staffing of the medical records clerks was the root of this problem. Overwhelmed, the clerks had begun to stack charts in piles on the floor because they were so busy with requests for more charts that they didn't have time to file the returned charts to their rightful places. Well, my camera came in handy here, too. Since I was working midnights, it was easy to visit the medical records room, where staff let me in to document their dismay. Employees in both departments conspired with me. We all wanted to improve service for patients.

With the support of union leadership and the help of other staff members, we prepared a patient newsletter, complete with stories and photos, letting patients know that we were trying our best to support their needs, but the administration was not listening to our pleas. We asked our patients, who were primarily members of the United Auto Workers, to help pressure management into changing the emergency room registration procedures and hiring additional staff for the medical records room.

The guards were not in the union but were sympathetic. They let me into the nursing administration office, where I clandestinely used the copy machines. There, in the early-morning hours before I left my shift, I cranked out newsletters and placed them at the entrances, where patients could pick them up before management arrived around nine a.m.

The initial run of newsletters went fast. We were encouraged, so I created a second batch in the hopes of reaching even more patients. Shortly after, I received a written notice that I was to report to the hospital's lawyer, the administrator over legal affairs. He knew me; we had talked before, on occasion, and I felt that he respected me. I asked permission to leave my post in the ER, took a deep breath, and headed upstairs.

Mr. T., as we fondly called him, was an imposing hulk of a guy with dark hair and a countenance as Sicilian as his name, Alfonso. I was a little nervous as I entered his office in the inner sanctum of the hospital's administrative suite, but because he had always been pleasant when we'd exchanged greetings in the past, I expected no more than a simple reprimand. However, the starkness of the conversation caught me by surprise.

"Sit down, Joann," he said stiffly, without looking at me.

The newsletter was on his desk. I was getting a queasy feeling in my stomach. He leafed through the pages and stopped at a cartoon of a stick-figure administrator ignoring pleas of employees to improve care. The cartoon had been drawn by a fellow union member.

"Should I assume," he said slowly, with emphasis, "that, as the hospital lawyer, this cartoon is intended to look like me?"

At this point he looked up and met my eyes. The question was ludicrous. It was a stick figure, and Mr. T was quite round. I smiled, misreading his intent. He was not in a joking mood.

His words were sharp and unfriendly: "You've been a good employee, Joann, but I hope you realize that we won't tolerate this type of behavior. This is a formal reprimand. If your activities come to my attention again over any similar matters, you'll be dismissed." He handed me a written disciplinary action sheet outlining what he had just explained.

"You may go back to work if you agree to these terms. If not, you can be released now."

"I agree," I answered quickly, and soberly signed the disciplinary sheet.

Of course I agreed! In the future, I would have to find other ways to lobby for improving care.

Despite my "transgression," however, we succeeded. Hospital administrators soon set up a triage area in the ER to obtain information from patients in distress before they paid for the visit. The hospital also hired more staff to clean up the mess in the medical records room. Our strategy had worked. And I still had a job.

AS THE ECONOMY LAGGED in the mid-1970s, watching bottom lines came suddenly into vogue across the hospital spectrum. A period of nationwide economic stagnation occurred from 1973 to 1975 and it brought an end to America's post–World War II economic boom. For an auto-driven economy like the Motor City, there could have been few worse economic blows than the 1973 oil embargo launched by the Organization of the Petroleum Exporting Countries (OPEC) cartel, which sent prices soaring. It was against this painful backdrop that an influx of new graduates with degrees in management and business administration swarmed into the health-care industry. These young people were dazzling the marketplace by signaling to administrators that they had the skills required to balance budgets. Our institution was no exception. And as was—and is—almost universally the case, the first target they took aim at was union salaries.

It was not our intent to strike. We were pushed by management to do so. Over the years, our clerical workers enjoyed a sweetheart relationship with management, primarily because Walter Reuther, the hospital's founder, encouraged union affiliation for all employees as a matter of principle. It set an example that good employers supported unions. While we had the usual petty grievances between supervision and staff, there had been no particular broad issues that seriously threatened our management-employee relationship. So when it came time to renegotiate our contract, we were caught by surprise by management's offer to open negotiations with a cut in pay and to stand firmly by it.

As negotiations began to bog down, we gathered in the evenings in the hospital cafeteria for updates from Val, our union leader, and the negotiating team. As the situation grew tense, so did we. Everyone was thinking of their families. It felt like the administration was pushing us to strike. Our coworkers, the hospital technical staff—lab techs, X-ray technicians, and the like—knew that they would be next, and they moved to support us, sometimes joining us at our union meetings.

Talks were stalled, and I noticed that the materials management stockroom was overflowing, and items were spilling out into the hallway. Things looked bleak.

Our clerical staff was largely made up of women with dependent children. This was going to hurt them. Strike pay came only under certain conditions, and it could take weeks to kick in. But in the long run, we decided we couldn't give this up without a fight. We walked out.

At best, our only weapon was to interrupt the hospital's ability to carry out the clerical aspects of care, perhaps disrupt supplies, and generally create an inconvenience. This would give us a small, though far from crippling, edge. Someone suggested that our best option would be to make a lot of noise. As most of our patients were union autoworkers, it was unclear if they would cross our picket lines. We needed them to support us.

I trusted Val. She had experience in community organizing and was level-headed. The energy was high as we prepared for a picket line the following morning. I went home, wondering how this was going to affect us.

"It's going to be tough," I told Mike, who was working part-time on a rehab project at St. Benedict's Church. "It'll be hard to pay a babysitter for Alex." I realized I was worrying out loud.

"Don't worry, I'll work it out," he replied. "I'll keep him at home when I can."

I soon learned that walking a picket line for eight hours a day—in all kinds of weather—is tedious and exhausting work. It was intense, and days off just disappeared. I was assigned to a group tasked with blocking the emergency room driveway, a patient care entrance, and the dock where deliveries were made. It was only a short while before I saw a picketer turn away a patient who I knew came for daily shots in the ER. These shots were critical to her survival.

"No," I shouted, "she needs her shots!" I ran to the car to assure the patient that she would be taken care of. "Open the line," I called, and the group parted to let this patient through.

That simple reaction on my part gave me a role that I would continue to play throughout the strike. I talked with patients at the entrance to the drive. Of those who were not in distress, I asked if they would mind going to another hospital to honor our picket line. If they had urgent needs, we let them through.

The week dragged on, and police routinely stood by. One day, Mike had a dentist appointment and no one to watch Alex, who was almost one-year-old. So I carried him on the picket line as we chanted our slogans: "We need fair pay to feed our families!" "A fair day's pay for a fair day's work!"

"If you think that baby's going to protect you, you've got another think coming," one cop growled as I walked by. He was holding his baton. A paddy wagon was parked nearby. A wave of fear passed over me, and I clutched my child tighter. The cop had no right to intimidate me, to threaten harm to my child.

As the days progressed, we made an attempt to halt buses carrying scab labor and delivery trucks with supplies. Some of the trucks would nudge through, at first just touching us lightly and then gunning their engines and making us scatter. The cops did nothing to stop them. Standing all day in the hot sun was getting harder, and my emotions were escalating.

I saw two older EKG technicians begin to pass out small boxes of tacks. I knew these docile ladies, who worked just around the corner from the emergency room, and I was surprised that they would initiate such a risky action. As the boxes left one hand and were passed to the next, tacks were being scattered on the driveway where trucks were blasting their way through our line. When the boxes reached me, I, like the others, scattered a handful.

Suddenly, there was a ruckus, and the police were moving in. First, they grabbed Val by the back of her clothing, tearing her jacket. I was next and was dragged into the police wagon. My mind was racing. When would I get home? How would I let Mike know what had happened? Would anyone be hurt?

Three more women were shoved in behind me. It became obvious that the police knew the union leadership, as one by one we were shoved into the wagon. One of our ladies was six months pregnant, which was apparent, but did not exempt her from the police action. We were taken to the 13th Precinct station house, booked, fingerprinted, and placed in lockup. Our mother-to-be was very verbal, and the police roughly removed her from our cell and took her to an area where we couldn't see her. We spent a long afternoon, calling out, "Yvette, are you all right," then hearing her reply, "Yes . . ." followed by a bunch of expletives. We cooled our heels and waited impatiently, wondering if anyone was going to rescue us. Finally, a union lawyer showed up. The process seemed to take forever, but we were eventually released.

As the strike droned on, the union set up a food co-op for strikers, at which three bags of fresh fruits and vegetables could be purchased for $3. It wasn't a lot, but it helped.

The strike lasted for two weeks until the UAW put enough pressure on management to settle. We went back to work, grateful to maintain the pay and benefits we had enjoyed under our previous contract, but I couldn't help thinking that it had been a staged battle. We fought mightily, but we had only won the right to keep what we'd had before.

It became clear that the hospital had lost nothing in the strike, except perhaps a small demerit on their image as a UAW pillar of support for workers. Their bottom line advanced despite our success in renewing our previous contract, in that they are paid in advance for all the patients assigned to them by the health plan. Since they saw fewer patients during the strike period, their expenses dropped significantly. This was the first of many victories for the business management whiz kids.

At one point, a supervisory position opened up in the emergency room. The nursing director approached me apologetically. While I was his first choice, "certain information" about me had been shared that made me an untenable candidate. In the general day-to-day chaos of my work area, there was no opportunity for questions.

A young man who worked in the Medical Records Department was chosen to fill the position. He lasted about six months and then was fired. Again, the nursing director appeared. This time, the job was mine if I wanted it.

I was torn. I loved my work in the union. I felt as if I would be a traitor to my union buddies. The activist side of me wasn't ever going to disappear, but I had to balance that mission with other critical concerns. Ultimately, I took the job for my family. It was a stable position with higher pay. I moved on to become supervisor over my coworkers, a position which allowed me to exert some control over our working environment. I was determined to stay humble and fair. I listened to their concerns and implemented their suggestions whenever possible. And in fact, things proceeded smoothly, and we continued to work well together, assuring that patients came first.

Working in the ER was an experience in understanding life that I will always be grateful for. Being in a supervisory position, however, gave me responsibility for decisions that affected a lot of other people. It allowed me to play a larger role in meeting people's needs in our prepaid health-care plan. It also taught me how to be a team player and to progressively plan for improvements in a system that was essential to meeting life and death needs of patients. It became a great venue for me to apply the lessons learned from years as a movement activist and, more recently, as a community activist advocating for union and patient rights. My activist commitment, far from fading, was being redirected and I was up for the challenge.

OVER MY NINE YEARS IN THE ER, I worked my way up in this hotbed of activity from receptionist, where I met so many neighborhood folks, to unit manager. Women played a central role in our health system. In the ER, the physician director, the nurse manager, and the administrative director were all women, as was the member services division head at the health-plan headquarters.

In my role as unit manager, I was responsible for everything in the unit that wasn't medical: I communicated with other departments, supervised the clerical staff, and ordered the ER's medical supplies. My desk was inside the treatment area, where the phones were located and doctors shouted orders for special needs. "Contact the surgeon!" or "Get an ambulance for transfer to Children's." These were usual days.

A small sliding-glass window was positioned between the communications center and the reception desk, where patients registered for treatment. Due to the number of incidents that had occurred in the waiting room, the receptionists worked behind bulletproof glass. On the other side of the waiting area was the guard's office. They kept the door open so they could monitor what was going on.

One day, I was sitting at my desk near the sliding-glass window. The phone rang and I answered: "ER, Castle speaking."

"There's a man at the registration window now. Afro . . . brown leather jacket. Check him out," the guard relayed to me. I leaned closer to the window so I could see. "He matches the description of a 'Wanted' poster we have here. Police are on the way. Detain him."

My stomach turned; my heart pounded. I stepped out into the waiting area. The receptionist was completing his paperwork. He signed his name and sat down. I had no idea what I was going to say. I called his name. He looked at me tentatively, as I beckoned him to a quiet area in a corner with his back toward the door.

"Sir, may I speak with you a moment?" My mouth was dry. "Have you come here for treatment before?" I asked, looking directly into his eyes.

"Yeah, I've been here before."

"How long ago? Can you be more explicit? And your symptoms, how long have you been experiencing—"

"What the . . ." he said, raising his voice.

I realized his paperwork, which I was holding, was shaking in my hands, and I put it all behind my back. He seemed to grow taller, seemed to tower over me as he realized something funny was going on.

I saw the police car pull up at the door. Two cops rushed through the entrance and startled him, grabbing his arms and handcuffing him. As they roughly shoved him out the door, he looked over his shoulder at me.

A short time later I went to lunch, had a cup of hot tea, and tried to calm down. Talking with my peers seemed to help. It was over, I told myself. In a couple of hours, I would be out of there.

Back on the job, I quickly became involved in other activities, my mind again engaged in my tasks. But just before shift change, the little glass window slid open once again.

"Castle, he's back!"

I shot a glance toward the door and saw him entering. I grabbed the phone and dialed the guard.

"He's back, what should I do?" I squeaked.

"Hold on." A moment later the guard was back on the line. "Police station said he was cleared of charges. Someone else confessed to the crime. He's okay. Have him seen."

Just another day in the ER.

BECAUSE I WORKED AT A HOSPITAL, the children always knew where they could find me. Sometimes when I returned to my station, I would unexpectedly see one of them sitting in the treatment area, waiting for me amid the hubbub. They became comfortable there and knew my teammates; the staff in the pediatrics area, where they could find their doctor; and the medical director, who became our friend.

One day, I heard Alex tell a buddy that I was a doctor. I corrected him.

"You mean you've worked in a hospital that long and you're not a doctor yet?" he responded, succinct in his eight-year-old innocence.

As I look back, those were happy years for us. They centered on work and family. We laughed and cried together at our ups and downs. As the children grew, they became more independent and sought to make sense out of their own lives.

In 1978, Mike graduated with a master's degree in social work and was hired as an administrative assistant and fund-raiser in a program for geriatric mental health. Finally, our lives were stable, but Mike had something else on his mind.

"Now it's your turn," he said. I ignored him. "We need to talk about it," he pressed.

"Later—not now" was my answer. I was a definite no. Or maybe . . .

I have a friend who introduced me to the maxim "Leap, and the net will appear." I felt a kinship with the refrain somewhere deep inside, but I always kept it under wraps—under a blanket of fear that someone would be hurt or I would fail. I never aspired to higher learning and was afraid that, more than twenty years out of high school, I would be unable to meet the demands. Homework! How could I? When would I?

One evening a few weeks later, after the dishes were done and the kids had gone up to bed, Mike asked me to sit down. "We need to talk," he pestered.

"Okay, okay." I dropped my tired body into a chair at the kitchen table. "What's wrong?" I wanted to bask in the fact that the dishes were finally done but instead I braced myself, wary of a formal request to talk.

"I want you to go to school."

"You've got to be kidding! You can't be serious about this. All these kids, plus a full-time job. How can I go to school with a life like this?"

"The kids are more and more independent. I'll take care of things. I'm already taking care of Alex. It'll be okay. *I want you to go to school*," he said with emphasis.

"But I wouldn't know the first thing to do. I couldn't even pass an entrance exam at a university. You're stressing me out."

"There's a Labor School on Wayne's campus. You're interested in labor history. Just try it. You could get used to the idea. In September, take a class. For me, please," he said softly, and he took my hand. "You go; I'll make it work."

And so I did. In 1979, I enrolled in Wayne State University's Labor School.

I loved the stimulation of being in a classroom and had great success in my studies. Finding my strength and in a position to create my own work schedule, the following year I transferred to Wayne's Weekend College and began to earn college credits. I sopped up the learning like a sponge, earning all A's in my first year. It's not that I was smart. I just loved learning and exploring new ideas. I worked hard. Once I got onto something, I just couldn't quit until I was satisfied that I had done my best. I had found a new passion, a love of learning. I leaped, and Mike provided a net.

Once I started school, I knew what I wanted to do when I "grew up." I wanted to bring together the threads of my life and weave them into the tapestry of a degree in anthropology. I wanted to study people and cultures that were unlike my own. I wanted to dance all over the ceiling and free my mind to look at the world in new ways. In that way, I could plant seeds of change. The activist in me continued to evolve.

My undergraduate thesis was titled "Dream Builders." It explored the concept and implementation of Metropolitan Hospital and eight neighborhood health centers as an all-encompassing prepaid group health-care plan. The first of its kind in the Midwest, my research documented the building of the preventive-care group health plan using the Canadian Health Plan and the United Mine Workers plan as models. I interviewed physicians and medical directors who had worked in the plan and tracked down some members of the initiating design team who were still living forty-five years later.

I loved doing those interviews. They gave me an inside look at the lives and motivations of men and women who had dedicated a good chunk of their lives to constructing a dream that would benefit others. In their eyes were reflections of good ideas hammered into being, the dogged day-to-day work required, and the challenges that had to be overcome to make a health plan a reality.

In the process I was able to refine my interview skills, which I would need as an anthropologist. The method allows us to look at cultural practices from outside the box, so to speak. I truly believe that it's important not only to study and analyze lessons from our past, but also to examine how other cultures solve problems.

Often best practices can be found in even the simplest of cultures, and reading or hearing living narratives with historical figures can be a stepping-stone to gaining a better understanding of ourselves. My thesis was well received and respected and was indeed used in the Community Health Department at the

University of Michigan, where one of our health center managers reported that it became a text in his classroom.

After finishing three years of undergrad work, I began taking graduate-level classes in the Anthropology Department and used the credits for my electives. I loved anthropology and its unfettered acceptance of multiple views of the world and its peoples. In my studies, I could see how similar the primary physical and psychological needs of human beings were across cultures and across time. The classical anthropologist Franz Boas set out his theory on the unity of the human species this way: "There can be no doubt that in the main the mental characteristics of man are the same all over the world. . . . Certain patterns of associated ideas may be recognized in all types of culture."

I was fascinated. Racism is a cruel hoax; we are all the same. We just come to each other on different paths, from different cultures. If we believe this, we can learn from each other.

I continued to be intrigued with anthropological methods for learning about others and the breadth of work available in the field. An anthropologist listens and does not judge, which suited me, then and now. My early love of the cultural aspects of life worked well with my job in a multicultural setting. While working in the ER, I wrote a major paper on language barriers between doctors from Middle Eastern and Asian cultures and their black patients. The case studies in my paper were taken from situations I witnessed on my job. The dean of the Anthropology Department submitted my paper to a conference at the University of Windsor. My confidence level grew.

My schooling changed my life and led me up the ladder to a successful career. But something weighed heavily on my mind. Overwhelmed with my career and my education, I feared that I was losing touch with my children. I often worked holidays and Saturday mornings to make up for the time I took from my schedule to attend classes. If you asked me what was on the mind of any specific child at a given time, I could only confirm the reports from the habitual broadcasters, like Greg and Michael, whose lives were an open book. I was distracted, but I thought, I hoped, I was setting the example that education was primary; maybe I was, but there were only so many hours in a day. I sometimes had to remind myself that I was making a sacrifice for the long term. While it was a rational choice, my decision to pursue my education affected the whole family. The children had no say, although they suffered through the sacrifice, too. It's a rule in life: one sacrifices for the greater good. No one says it will be easy.

Sometimes I felt as if I had married my academic obsession to my activist obsession. Two marriages and a family are a lot to handle. When I had assignments at school, I integrated them into my work life. I started an (authorized) patient newsletter to help them understand our array of services and how they could find help when they needed it. I developed a marketing slide show about our hospitals and health centers, then used it to orient new physicians to the hospital's culture. It was simply impossible for me to put on hold my compulsion to make a difference. I saw the need all around me. I received academic credit for these projects and was praised by my administrators for the service to patients.

This was my chance for a fulfilling career, an opportunity to affect policy in a health-care setting, a platform to do good in the community while putting to use my unique skill set. While I continued to deal with the difficult balance between my education, career, marriage, and children, I foresaw that I could have an academic discipline of my own, where I could work, study, learn, and grow after all my children had left home.

I was crazy-busy in those years. When I left work, I was on my way to class or to the language lab or to the library. I usually took three classes a semester, a very heavy load for a full-time employee, mother, and wife. I was also writing a thesis, which required interviewing subjects and analyzing data. Mike was covering at home—cooking, washing, feeding, and nursing hurts when he could. We were a rare example of how a true partnership can work. Had I been a man, I expect much of my worry and concern over balancing my passions—whether activism, work, or academic —with my first priority, my children, would have been different. Social expectations, even now, allow men to too often bypass these kinds of concerns when deciding on careers and pursuits. My relationship with Mike was a stark contrast to the gendered choices so many women face, and my success was in large part due to that true partnership of shared responsibilities.

Still, I'm certain every mother looks back with regret at those moments when we chose our careers over time with our children. Usually, it's the long-term view that propels us. But those who stay home may also one day regret that they didn't demonstrate for their children the importance of getting an education and acquiring marketable skills. My schooling and career put me on the path to a deeper understanding of the world around me. My later life and contributions would have been tragically limited without those experiences.

The reality of taking on such a huge challenge came at a cost, though. As my stress mounted, one day while at work I began to experience chest pains. I was totally exhausted. It was late spring during my final semester as an undergrad. I was slated to graduate at the end of the month. But now the EKG indicated that I was in trouble, and I was hospitalized.

I objected, but the doctor wasn't listening. As specialists stopped by my hospital bed, I began to realize that it was possible I wouldn't be able to finish my studies and thus wouldn't graduate. That broke me, and I sobbed for almost two days straight. I couldn't stop. Now, behavioral professionals were stopping by my bed.

My response was to sign myself out against medical advice. I was back in control for the moment. Once at home, I began to reconstruct what I had to do to make up for the time I lost and I finished my thesis. Then I got out of bed and took my exams, completed the last step in earning my bachelor's degree. It was 1982.

Some years later when we were preparing to move, I discovered several handmade cards featuring drawings and a child's labored writing.

"Mommy, I am so sorry you are sick and can't spend any time with me. I love you." It was signed by my youngest girl, Christine. Tears welled up in my eyes as I fingered the fragile pages. During the years when Christine was growing up, my life was overflowing with radical movement work, my job, and then my educational endeavors. All those efforts came with a steep price, and I've had to accept that my decisions were not always popular with or desired by my children. Every working mother knows that her children don't get as much of her as they would like. Every child of divorce longs for more time with both parents. I can only imagine how helpless and worried Christine must have been when I was in the hospital. To this day—every day—I continue to make an effort to "refresh" my focus on being available to my family.

MY YEARS AT METROPOLITAN HOSPITAL were rewarding. Employees appreciated the active role I played in the union, and it seemed I was able to gain the respect of management as well. The emergency room was a hub that touched all areas of the hospital, both outpatient and inpatient. From my early days as a receptionist interacting with staff in other areas, I made it a point to speak with everyone and recognize their contributions to our mission of quality care—care that recognized the unique value and needs of every patient.

It was my hope that establishing relationships would not only make the work flow smoothly but also would offer opportunities to improve how care was delivered in ways that didn't trigger reprimands. As unit manager, my contacts broadened in many ways, including the handling of patient transfers to the inpatient floors, where I worked with staff on all three shifts. It exposed me to the reality of what puts real "quality" in health care.

Still, I was surprised when the hospital's director of patient services, a relatively high-profile position two steps up from mine, recommended me as her successor. Actually, I was overwhelmed. This was probably the most coveted job in our hospital system, once held by Anna Roosevelt Halsted, the daughter of President Franklin Roosevelt and wife of a surgeon hired when the hospital first opened. In this position, I would report directly to the hospital lawyer, Mr. T., with an indirect report to the medical director.

Employees seemed to trust me in my role as a watchdog, one who monitored how well the system was serving patients. They often approached me to point out barriers to service they recognized in their areas. I listened to them and did what I could to resolve issues. I also listened to patients. The most distressed and the most difficult usually ended up in my office. Administrators listened to me and provided the support I needed to do meaningful work. For me, director of patient services was a dream job. The daily challenges encouraged and inspired me to find creative solutions to problems.

My position had both community-relations and risk-management functions. Because of my training, I focused on cultural issues as well as quality issues that acted as obstacles to patient satisfaction. I had eleven patient representatives who listened to patients and solved problems before they blew out of proportion and resulted in litigation.

After my promotion to director of patient services, I was asked to prepare a training program for our doctors in patient relations skills. In the training program's exercises, I referenced examples straight from my linguistics paper. For instance, I conveyed to our doctors that addressing mature black patients by their first name makes them feel inferior; that when a Muslim woman requests that her husband be in the exam room with her, he has the right to be there; that doctors should not talk to a patient with their hand on the doorknob, but should listen for the patient's deep concerns, which he or she may have trouble expressing.

Since my department handled patient complaints, I worked directly with those doctors named in complaints, and we collaborated on solutions. These interactions were not always graciously accepted. An Iranian doctor once told me, "In my culture, we believe in killing the messengers." I treated the remark as if he was kidding, even though I wasn't certain what he was really thinking. I worked hard on repairing relationships and being gentle in these situations. Each case was a challenge.

In 1985, I completed my master's thesis on the increasing practice of corporate medicine, or, in other words, medical care designed by corporations. My thesis was an effort to document the fundamental changes to the traditional doctor-patient relationship that would result once third parties with conflicting motives intervened in patient care plans by determining what services would be paid for.

At the time, hearings were under way in the Michigan legislature, where a House Committee on Insurance was working with employers and insurers to fashion a package of benefits that would best meet their desire to reduce costs and be acceptable to the state of Michigan. I was permitted by our hospital administration to attend these hearings, speeding back and forth the ninety-three miles to the state capital on a moment's notice when a session was convened.

I was bearing witness to the fundamental changes occurring to our health-care system, both locally and nationally. These changes were the genesis of the crisis in care we confront as a society today. Metropolitan Hospital was a prepaid plan compensated by monthly capitation, a fixed price per person, from our insurance plan. We didn't do billing; we provided care, whatever the doctor ordered. Financially, it was unsustainable once Medicare diagnosis-related-group guidelines were implemented, which called for copious record keeping and paid providers by diagnosis.

I worked for the hospital for twenty-three years until it closed in 1995, after methods for hospital reimbursement under Medicare were overhauled. Henry Ford Hospital assumed our operations, and I was transferred to the Henry Ford administrative offices at One Ford Place in Detroit. I spent five years there as a project manager working under a research grant from the Hartford Foundation to design clinical services for frail elderly. But it was Metropolitan Hospital that stole my heart and my imagination in the service of my fellow human beings.

I AM GRATEFUL THAT I HAD THE OPPORTUNITY to bloom in the context of my years in health care, that I found a way to be of service to others in need. In a busy hospital, employees don't always have time to focus on each patient's specific situation. At times, it was up to my staff and me to interact with patients who needed personal attention. We were communicators, detectives, advocates, counselors, negotiators—whatever was called for. Sometimes, we were just friends who held a hand during a stressful or frightening time. It was activist's work, and we loved the fact that our intervention often made a difference in a patient's quality of life.

My "on the street" activist years turned out to be a great training ground for my later career as a policy activist: I learned to embrace change as opportunity and to contemplate the broader picture in my search for ways to improve humanity. I perceived the importance of understanding history and broadening my outlook in order to grasp how everything was interconnected. I was motivated by the belief that even though the world consists of myriad people with different cultures and experiences, in essence we are all the same. I also learned that my weakness is putting too many bricks on my board, sometimes pushing myself to a breaking point before it occurs to me to stop.

FAMILY RECONCILIATION

But we can't go back. We can only go forward.
—**LIBBA BRAY**

IN MY OWN HOME AS A CHILD, I didn't feel particularly loved. As an adult, I have no doubt that my parents loved me, but the scope of their worldview and their upbringing held them back. They passed their legacy on to me, and it threatened to restrict my development as well. I learned to accept this challenge. Becoming conscious of this has been a first step in attaining balance in the autumn of my years. Looking back has allowed me to realize how full and fruitful my life has been.

IN THE SUMMER OF 1985, I prepared for my master's-level comprehensive exams at a friend's rented cottage on Lake Superior, where she was already hard at work with her books. As I settled in my seat on a Greyhound bus bound for Michigan's Upper Peninsula, I marveled at how far I had ventured from the life for which I was originally prepared, and how grateful I was for each precious moment along that path.

While I spent several days out of town studying, the older children were either away at school or off on their own. Mike was home with Alex, who was now ten years old, and those two were like two peas in a pod.

After a punishing twelve-hour ride that rumbled through every small town and passed by every state prison up through the middle of the state, I disembarked in a small hamlet near a Native American reservation where my friend, Marie, was waiting. A plunge into the lake's icy waters cleared my mind of all my previous responsibilities and opened it to four days of focused study. Later, we drove back to Detroit in Marie's car, still discussing the classic theories and potential application of the practice of medical anthropology. I had hope but not a lot of confidence that it would all remain in my brain until I got it on paper during my exam.

When I arrived home, I found a message from my mother. She and my dad wanted to attend my graduation. It was awkward but exciting to have them there and gratifying to realize that they were proud of my accomplishment and wanted to share the occasion with me. Mother, of course, still would not speak to Mike.

Being on the raw end of prejudice was not unusual in our lives, and we took it in stride—sometimes confronting it, other times not. A couple like us must understand the reality of what we were and who we are. Mike and I have dealt with prejudice from both blacks and whites. Over the years, Mike received criticism, published and otherwise, from black intellectuals as well as black women who were angry and disillusioned over their seeming abandonment by black men. Black leaders with white wives are an easy target.

During his social work career, some of Mike's coworkers were awkward or avoided me. Sometimes blacks cannot find common ground to start a conversation with me. Sometimes they just don't want to. One time when Mike momentarily left a client in his office, he returned to find his picture of Alex and me had been turned facedown on his desk. I learned to step out of the way to give him room to interact with others. Racism is a reality, and I never wanted our relationship to detract from his important work.

IN THE FINAL YEARS OF HER LIFE, my mother became engulfed in bitterness. My dad retired early, without discussing it with her in advance, and bought himself a big Lincoln automobile with his retirement savings. He didn't cook, so each morning Mother fixed him breakfast then watched him close himself in his study to spend his time writing, mostly on religious themes, his lines sprinkled with the words *thee* and *thou*. He would emerge to take his meals. I thought he was slipping into dementia. Dad, like many men of his era, took what he needed or wanted and didn't look back. Mother, who had looked forward to companionship and travel during their retirement, was profoundly disappointed.

A few years after Dad retired, Mother became ill with cancer. I arranged to work half-days so I could help to care for her. Sometimes it was so painful to watch her decline that I would stop after work at a florist's nursery near her home. Watching things grow helped to offset the pain and helplessness I felt when I was with her. Her life, certainly not lived to its fullest potential, was steadily slipping away.

Occasionally, I purchased a plant for my yard in an effort to surround myself with sweet living things. Other times I purchased a small token that I knew Mother would appreciate. On one of these forays, I saw a small statue of a mother and child that stole my heart. The figures were featured in such a way that they could have been modeled on the two of us.

I was excited as I presented my gift to her, and she accepted it tenderly. As she thanked me, she said, "I wish now that I had lived my life like you have."

I understood her words in the depths of my being. She had never fulfilled her potential. I was filled with a surge of emotion, tears welling my eyes, and I hugged her small, frail body as she lay in a hospital bed near a large window in her dining room. After all those years, Mother and I were finally reconciled, and I was grateful we were able to complete the circle. Today, the statue is in my living room, and whenever my gaze lands on it, I am reminded of where I came from.

As Mother's condition reached the final stages and she was assigned to hospice care, she allowed Mike, a social worker, to search out resources for her, such as meal delivery and light housework services. These little inroads brought me great satisfaction.

I continued to leave work at noon to care for Mother so she could remain in her home. One very cold day in early March, I opened her drapes to let the sun shine in. New white snow covered the ground. The sky had cleared and small puffy white clouds dotted its blue palette. It looked warm, but the air was frigid.

"I want to go outside," Mother quietly announced.

"Mother, it's freezing out there!"

"I want to go outside," she insisted.

I looked around, helpless. We both loved the outdoors, but what could I do? I couldn't carry her alone, and it would take two people to get her into some warm clothes. She couldn't even sit up by herself. I looked and saw tears in her eyes. I couldn't seem to find the appropriate words to comfort her. I wanted to console her, but I remained speechless, lost in the pain of her impending death.

Within the week, Mother slipped into a coma. We lost her a few days later. It haunted me that I did not find a way to fulfill her request. Besides being with my kids when I'm ready to leave this world, my final wish, much like hers, will be to contemplate the wonders of the shining sun, a brilliant blue sky, and, for me, a generous portion of clear blue Great Lakes sailing water. In the end, we contemplate our mistakes and weaknesses and hopefully learn from them. But life moves on in its endless cycle, with or without us.

My mother's sisters and their families all came to her funeral. Mike and I arrived together. On our way out, I noticed that Mike's mother and sister were sitting at the back of the church. I reached out to them as I passed. As we prepared to move from the church to the cemetery, Mike disappeared from my side. I rode a limousine with my two aunts and my sister, Karen, wondering where Mike had gone. That evening, Mike told me that my sister had asked him not to join the family at the graveside. I was reminded of this, years later, when Mike's family placed a chair for me next to his mother's casket and I sat next to him holding his hand. Sadness overcomes me and I grieve at the acquiescence of whites in continuing to let ingrained racism rule.

After my mother passed, my father, who was quickly advancing in age, carried on alone. I visited him often and savored my relationship with him in the last ten years of his life as he struggled to maintain himself after my mother's death. In his last years, Dad remained fiercely independent. Returning to his faith for comfort, he became more and more religious. One night, consumed by the idea that God had sent him a message, he set out in his car to find St. Aloysius Church. Confused, he headed west and drove his car into a ditch; the police found him the next morning. After treatment for his injuries, he was sent to a facility for skilled nursing care.

At the end, as Dad lay pale and immobile, his mind often drifted into his past. I sat with him each day after work. "What was the name"—he slowly began one day— "of that woman with the wrinkled face, who beat me up and told me I had to marry your mother?"

The pieces fell together like a family quilt. I guess I always knew the truth: my birth was not planned by my parents and not desired by my father. But in the end, he stayed—for Mother and for me.

"I'm not proud of my early life," I heard him say.

"But I'm proud of you," I said. "Look how far you've come."

Slowly, sadly, Dad declined until he, too, succumbed to the ravages of cancer. I remain grateful to this day that my severed relationship with my parents was restored before I lost them.

Losing one's parents is a shocking milestone in anyone's journey through life. As an oldest child, I suddenly realized that I stood at the head of the family, in historical continuity with all those generations that preceded me. I was determined to be a rock that the family could depend on, and I had Mike at my side. Our relationship was sealed, our work meaningful, our lives more stable, and our future more certain. And through it all, our house—our amazing house—continued to shelter us, keeping us safe and together. What more could one ask of life?

THE END OF AN ERA

Security is mostly a superstition.
It does not exist in nature, nor do the children of men
as a whole experience it. Avoiding danger is no safer in the long run
than outright exposure. Life is either a daring adventure, or nothing.
—HELEN KELLER

ON A SATURDAY MORNING, September 11, 2010, Mike and I celebrated our thirty-fifth wedding anniversary. We renewed our vows in a small ceremony on Detroit's beautiful International Riverwalk. Over the past year, Mike's health had been deteriorating, and we very much wanted to renew our commitment.

Mike wore his version of a tuxedo, a black suit with a cummerbund and bow tie, which made everyone smile because Mike was never a "dresser." I chose the burgundy linen suit that I had worn for Alex's wedding some years earlier, plus a beaded necklace Mike had bought me ages before that I had yet to wear. I'm just not a jewelry person. Moved by melancholy earlier in the day, I had rushed to the farmer's market, where I purchased a perfect bouquet of fall wildflowers to carry.

Our small party consisted of three special friends, three of our children, and our youngest grandchild, Ashton, surrounded by the cascades of colorful fall flowers at the river's edge. Rain was predicted and the sky was gray, but thankfully the showers held off for the brief period that we needed to repeat our time-tested vows.

The ceremony was conducted by Ed Ramey, a layperson and close friend of Mike's who is actively engaged in a youth program called Brothers on the Porch, where he mentors young boys of single mothers in the city. The program operates out of Sacred Heart Church in the Eastern Market area. Although Ed is a devout Catholic, that day he wore an elegant African ceremonial robe. We hadn't done much planning. Things just seemed to fall together in a unique and satisfying way. To me, it reflected the simple way we had chosen to live.

We recited our vows at the site of our family's commemorative brick, which we hope will remain intact for many years. Our brick, engraved with "The Castle-Hamlin Family," is embedded next to the children's carousel. I can't think of a happier place for it to be.

It happened that this day was the ninth anniversary of the terrorist attacks on New York City and Washington, D.C., and Ed began by reflecting on that somber day in our country's history.

"Today is a day when we search for meaning in the way we conduct ourselves in our world community and strive to discover ways to achieve a shared humanity that cares for one another," he said. "Mike and Joann met forty years ago amid the struggle for civil rights and the quest for sanity in our country's war against Vietnam. They recognized at once their shared values in the search for a better world, and they continue to work today to achieve that goal."

Ed lifted his eyes to include our small group of well-wishers.

"They are proud, today, to share this moment with others who feel the same," he said. "Joann, do you have anything you would like to say before you renew your vows?"

I had labored for days over what I would say, reaching deep into my heart to offer just the right words to express my commitment to Mike.

I began to speak, "Today, we reaffirm our friendship and shared values at the heart of our romance. To be loved by you is a gift . . ." My emotion ran over, and tears of joy streamed down my face at the open expression of our years together. "I am what I have become with you."

My voice began to crack, and suddenly, I had to laugh at my disabling emotion over my good fortune to have shared a love so deep, so giving. Now Mike's hand was on my shoulder, and he was chuckling, too. I felt his warmth. I still had one more thing to say.

"I thank you for indulging my sense of freedom. You encouraged me to pursue an education and have learned to tolerate my sense of adventure. After all, without all that, how could I have chosen you?"

Yes, we were an unlikely pair. We all laughed. I was giddy, like a young bride.

Mike effortlessly, eloquently ad-libbed his continuing commitment with the same grace and power that he always added to life as it unfolded around him. I don't remember precisely what he said, but I inherently understood his meaning. I was committed to caring for him as he had cared for me and my family.

After the ceremony, we proceeded to the Golden Fleece restaurant on Monroe Street, the same Greektown restaurant where Mike and I had lunch after our wedding thirty-five years earlier. Once again, we joyously shouted "Opa!" as the flaming cheeses were served.

Mike was a good and gentle husband. He afforded me every opportunity to develop my potential, and my personal and professional skills, albeit some more comfortable for him than others, like my captaining a sailboat in foreign waters. We had a good life, and the vows that I wrote for our recommitment ceremony remain a tribute to my love and gratitude for his years-long devotion.

WE LIVED in the West Boston Boulevard house for twenty-three years, from 1967 to 1990. Those were passionate years in the movement, and I associate the house with the very best of those experiences. During those years, I truly believed that I could make a difference and leave this world better than I found it, not just for my children but for all children who will inherit this planet from us.

By 1990, the older children had moved on to their own lives, and the big house felt hollow. While it still held a measure of love found in the lingering scent of memories and echoes of laughter past, the rooms were empty and the place needed repair. The neighborhood was also declining. Summer nights were occasionally punctuated by gunshots and fire bombings. Our house lay quiet during the day, and we had been lucky. But it was clear that serious drug problems had overtaken the community.

By the early 1980s, the apartment house that overlooked our backyard, once filled with professionals who worked in the city, gave way to drug trade. From the upper floors of those apartments, one could see our comings and goings. There had been robberies in the homes on either side of us. The elderly people next door to us had been locked in a closet by intruders on three occasions while their house was systematically emptied of its treasures. They hired security guards, and I once witnessed a shoot-out between the intruders and the guards on our front lawn. Whether by skill or by design, the bad guys got away.

Mr. Siegel, in the house to the east of us, fled after druggies repeatedly broke in and took his family's antiques. One night an off-duty policeman, hired to protect the Siegel homestead, shot a burglar who didn't realize the officer was inside.

Each afternoon when I arrived home from work, I would park the car in the driveway to avoid opening the garage door to any surprises. Then, before I entered, I circled the house on foot, looking for any signs of a break-in. We got a bigger dog, a Bouvier, who probably forestalled some trouble, but when we had a break-in one night as we lay in our beds, our "vicious" dog, too used to strangers in the house, didn't even bark.

It seemed that every night about four a.m., some kind of adverse activity awakened us from our sleep. We still hadn't had a conversation about leaving our home, but we knew we needed to protect and sustain ourselves with some downtime, away from center-city Detroit.

OUR LIFE WOULD CHANGE when one week the "Life" section of the Sunday newspaper included an article on driving destinations within easy reach of the city. We decided on impulse to visit Pointe Pelee, a provincial park in Ontario that's less than an hour's drive past the Ambassador Bridge spanning the border between the United States and Canada. Once there, we were so captivated by the beauty and tranquility of the area that we began discussing how sublime it would be to own a cottage on the beach as a place to get away from it all.

We began to search until we found a small, postwar cottage not far from the park. Perched on the beach of Lake Erie, the cottage was so close to the water that, from the inside, we had the feeling we were on a house boat. It was not expensive, and we were easily able to finance the purchase with a home equity loan. A new way of life was upon us, offering an escape and our very own water world.

My life was in transition. I had graduated. My grandmother, my mother, my father, and my mother's sisters had all passed from this world. All my children except Alex had left home. The weight of changing generations was on me. I was still working at the hospital, but I had a feeling of emptiness that I wanted to fill with activity.

In Leamington, Canada, people's lives and livelihoods were tied to the water rather than to the land. One weekend as we were arriving at the lake, I noticed a small sailboat that was for sale. The sign read $150. It was my fiftieth birthday, and the urge was irresistible. I would buy myself a birthday gift that would get me on the water. I walked to the cottage where the boat was parked, feeling both excitement and apprehension. I had never been on a sailboat, but they looked so graceful skimming across the water.

The owner dragged the boat to the beach, and we boarded, one on either side of the centerboard of this sit-on-top wet boat. The wind, the expanse of sky, and the comforting sounds of the water around the boat's hull took my breath away. I kept my head and negotiated a reduced price of $90. I didn't know what sailboats usually cost, or I would have anticipated a problem.

I didn't have a clue how to sail. We had a neighbor, well into his eighties, who offered his advice: "Just push it into the water, let the sail out until the wind catches it, then pull it in and off you go." Now any sailor knows that this is a recipe for disaster, but, of course, I was not a sailor and remained blissfully unaware. Once on the water for the first time, I had no knowledge of how to get this perilously dangerous, unstable, waterlogged boat back to shore. It took three people to drag the seemingly multiton watercraft back onto the beach and drain the intruding lake water from the bilge.

By the next summer, I knew I needed a more floatable boat that I could manage by myself. I was so driven to be on the water that I shopped for an upgraded boat while I was on crutches nursing a broken foot. Mike couldn't swim and had no desire even to get his feet wet, but he helpfully scoured newspaper ads looking for a boat. He drove me all over the tri-county area as I hobbled up and down driveways, until I finally found a pretty little Puffer, complete with a hookup for a spinnaker.

All summer I tried with little success to get the boat to behave, blithely jibing back and forth as I tried to come about, and nearly knocking my sister out of the boat after she bravely agreed to go out with me. On many occasions, out of control, I was washed ashore by the wind and waves; sometimes I just lay down on the bow and paddled the boat to shore with my hands. I usually landed within a quarter mile of my launching spot and I was either towed or walked back home by one of my patient neighbors.

I remember the gorgeous deep blue of the sky and the warmth of the late September sun on that fateful fall day. Mike pushed me off in his usual manner, getting wet to the waist only to make me happy and then returning to the cottage to watch television or read the newspaper. I set out thinking that I had wonderfully calm water. It was late in the season, and most of the cottages were boarded up for winter. As I expected, the water near the shore was flat, but the farther I moved onto the lake, the more the wind began ripping at the sails, and I realized that I was quickly moving away on an off-shore wind. The noise of the flapping sails was frightening, and I couldn't manage to turn the boat back toward shore. I had no idea what to do. It occurred to me that I hadn't seen any other boats on the lake all day.

I watched as the silhouette of the cottage grew increasingly smaller. My options were dwindling as well. Then I realized that the water itself was moving away from shore, and as I drifted out, I saw the waves were getting bigger. Now, I am not a great swimmer, but I had a life jacket on. All I knew was that I had to make it back to shore. I grabbed the painter—the towline at the bow of the boat—held my breath, and jumped overboard. It was my intent to swim to shore, pulling the boat behind me. Now that I was in the water, nearly invisible bobbing next to my boat, I tried to swim and pull the boat, but the force of the wind and water made it impossible. My decision to enter the water had been a mistake, and now I realized that I could not get back in without capsizing the small skiff.

The boat and I began to drift farther off-shore toward Ohio, thirty-five miles away. I had been in the water for some time by then, and I was getting cold. I remember looking at the incredible deep blue sky and thinking for the first time that I could die on this beautiful day. Then I saw someone on the beach, and I screamed for help at the top of my lungs. The feeble little sound was lost across the expanse of water. I waved my arms to no avail. I was a small speck in the vast lake.

I was getting colder, and my body was shivering uncontrollably. I began flopping around in the water, trying to increase my circulation. Still holding on to the painter for dear life, I heard the sirens. Help was on the way! But no, the fire trucks streamed past on the road, heading toward the park. Someone must have been drowning in the park; every year people drowned in the park. No one knew I was in peril. It was so unreal. I felt so alone. Time seemed endless. I must have been in the water nearly an hour.

Then I saw that the man on the beach had an inflatable. He was trying to get his engine started, and it kept stalling. He launched the little boat and kept trying, but the engine wouldn't catch. Now, he, too, was drifting. Then seemingly from nowhere, a brown-and-white fishing boat appeared between me and the shore. The man in the inflatable was standing up waving his arms in a distress signal. As the boat approached him, he pointed to my drifting boat, and they turned my way.

A short gray-haired woman, well past seventy, piloted her boat toward mine. When she pulled up alongside me, I could see she was accompanied by a younger man and woman, her son and his wife, I surmised. At her direction, the younger couple lowered a tarp and lifted me out of the water. I was still clutching the painter of my little boat. The older woman gently took the line from me and tied my boat to the back of her fishing vessel. The younger couple wrapped me in the tarp.

As we got under way, the woman quietly told me that she herself had once had a boat like my own. "I want you to promise me one thing," she said, and I waited, listening intently. "Promise me that you won't be afraid to go out in your boat again."

"Yes, I promise," I replied, and saw a Coast Guard boat pull alongside us.

When we reached shore, I noticed that the fire trucks with the flashing lights sat just beyond the cottage. Yes, in fact, they had been looking for me. The fishing boat headed back out onto the lake, and Mike took me inside and wrapped me in blankets. My fingers were blue where I had been clutching the painter. Later we went down the beach to find the man with the inflatable to thank him. He lived in his place all year round. When we asked him about the rescuers in the brown-and-white fishing boat, he told us he wasn't familiar with them.

The identity of those in the fishing boat remained a mystery. We checked with the local marinas and our boat-owning friends, but that boat seemed unknown in these waters. It occurred to me that the fishing boat captain bore a strong resemblance to the short gray-haired woman I last saw as a twelve-year-old and so adored: my grandmother. Could she have been looking out for me that September afternoon?

We soon closed the cottage for the winter, and our attention was once again drawn to our vocations in health care. But as the earth moved toward the following summer, Mike began to panic. He knew that his activist wife would soon be back on the water, and he insisted she learn how to sail for real.

"Activists must be trained," he soundly cautioned as he scoured the newspapers for information on boating. By spring, having been reminded that education and experience are the essentials for reaching your destination, I had joined a sailing club that offered a broad training program and had begun my lessons.

WE STAYED A LONG TIME in that house on West Boston Boulevard because . . . well, because it was our home and because one adapts to change—even change for the worse—when it happens incrementally. I understand why people are reluctant to leave a family home. One's everyday life becomes so interwoven with habit and memories that the idea of abandoning what's known is unthinkable. Memories are in the very air you breathe and buried in the gut of who you are. But by 1995, my job was getting unpredictable in terms of time demands, and I was beginning to travel. We knew it was time to go, but we lingered into summer.

Ultimately, our decision to leave was only partly related to the increasingly unsafe neighborhood surrounding us. When the plumbing failed under the 1940s glass-brick shower adjacent to our bedroom, water leaked through the floor and damaged the library below. The extent of the damage was more than our limited home repair skills could manage. Our children's educational expenses didn't leave us money for these types of repairs. It was time to move on.

Another concern we had was for Alex. Our Detroit neighborhood no longer had other children for him to play with. Since his sisters and brothers had launched into their own lives, he was very solitary and often fearful of venturing outside our doors. In addition, Alex was attending the Burton International Academy, a multicultural educational endeavor in the Cass Corridor. There were forty-three children in his class, many of them from new immigrant families who did not speak English. Funding for schools had been cut, and his teacher had lost her assistant. As wonderful as the cultural atmosphere was at Burton International, Alex had attention span issues and was not testing at his grade level.

I learned from a professor friend at Wayne State that Cranbrook Middle School, a boy's private school north of the city, was offering scholarships to urban kids in an effort to diversify their student body. We applied, and Alex, who in fifth grade tested deficient in English and writing skills, soared with a tenth-grade score in mathematics. He was accepted. We took a deep breath and began driving fifty miles round trip, twice a day, to get him to and from the campus.

After weighing the house's maintenance needs, Alex's safety when home alone and his educational needs, we were finally convinced that it was time to go. Our plan was to move to Bloomfield Township, where Alex could ride his bike to school until he was safely grown and graduated. Then we would return to the city, where the soles of my shoes would continue to walk the path of my ancestors. At this point in our lives, our activist work was intricately intertwined with our urban-based careers and Detroit will always be my home.

OUR BIG, OLD HOUSE on the boulevard created a unique setting for us to give what we could to the movement and to become who we are today. It played a major role in sheltering our extended family and offering a base for the work that so consumed us. Without it, none of the experiences that we today remember so dearly could have happened.

Our house of memories, shaped like a big hug, had been the beating heart of our family and our activist life for years. We sold it within twenty-four hours of putting the sign up on the front lawn. We had the shower damage fixed and the house was a bargain, solidly built, and in good condition despite its extraordinary use.

On the final day of our mortgage agreement, after the last of our things had been put into storage until we found a new home, I heaved a sigh of resignation as I got ready to walk out the door for the last time. My hand was already on the latch when I paused. It was so hard to let go. I needed one more deep breath of the familiar scent of our home. Turning, I released the latch and walked deep into the house for one more communion with our past.

Despite its use by the movement, the house had always remained a family home. Life for us had been, in Helen Keller's words, a daring adventure, with our family and our souls deep at the heart of it. I wandered through the first floor.

The dining room was where we shared meals with foster kids, neighborhood kids, movement friends, and visitors. Early on, we removed the dining room chairs and built picnic benches in order to fit more people on either side of the table. Our dining room was a joyous spot where our extended family slid in next to us, to nourish our bodies and nurture our family bonds.

The dining room also doubled as a work space for several movement activities. Hourglass and the CCC Book Club were headquartered here. The Black Workers Congress held their executive meetings here. Over the years, many deep conversations took place here, connected by a common cause—to be our brothers' and sisters' keepers. By 1973, I began to have occasional hospital union leadership meetings here, too.

When I combined my university studies with hospital activist work, our sideboard became my homework table, where I developed service projects that helped patients and, at the same time, enhanced my experiences as a budding medical anthropologist. Though on a slightly different road, my activism continued to be the driving force in my life.

Wandering through the rooms, my attention was captured by our kitchen's casement window, which opened just above the lilac bush in our yard and allowed the lovely scents of early fragrant springs to waft inside. My gaze swept across the backyard, past the rock garden covered with wildflowers that Nancy had brought from her home in Colorado, on to the tire swing forsaken by our leaving, across the vegetable garden and the back gate, and then to the garage. The garage roof, reached by climbing our crab-apple tree, was often a child's reading perch or just a place for solitude.

Next, I moved toward the front of the house and stopped at the door of our study, which also served as a library. The room had originally been built as a soundproof music room, the heavy oak pocket doors slid into the side walls, creating an impenetrable sound barrier. Over the years, the library had held emotional family scenes of diligence and change. It was here that Don and I agreed to part ways, and where we had talks about poor decision-making when the kids were in their teens. It was also here, in that ugly brown chair, where years ago I had struggled to determine which bills to pay and which would have to wait. During the movement activity in the house, this room was the site of intense analysis and debates about strategies and tactics. This was also the room where I had my breach with Jim Forman over his intruders.

As I made my way back to the living room, I was struck by its size. This was where we had gathered around the fireplace for holidays and graduations. We had looked out this window for twenty-seven years—from 1967, when the Michigan National Guard was stationed on our neighbor's lawn, to more recent days, when evidence of the failed "war on drugs" was apparent to the people who lived nearby—all the while watching our interesting neighborhood conduct its vibrant life.

During the CCC Book Club years, the "family" using our living room expanded. At our monthly training meetings, we often exceeded our seating capacity, the spillover sitting cross-legged on the floor. My children were often among us as we discussed material and prepared for the monthly book club sessions, defying the members of law enforcement in unmarked cars outside who wished to silence us. This room held the warmth of activists coping with what life had dealt them, seeking a wider community, and making sacrifices on behalf of humanity.

A large part of our contribution was giving up our privilege and opening our house to the community. Our life was rich, not with money but with depth and adventure. This was the experience I gave my children.

Finally, it was time for me to halt my tour through the house. My emotions were running over, and I didn't dare go upstairs. I shut my eyes, took a deep breath, and stepped outside, closing the door on my life as a mother who had brought her family into the movement.

One gut-wrenching wail escaped me as I drove away from all the precious memories of my children running on the stairs and playing ball in the backyard, of the rainbows reflected on the faces of all the people around our dining room table as the setting sun beamed through the beveled glass windows. Leaving the house was like tearing out my heart but expecting me to continue living. Yet that's the natural progression when children grow up and leave home. You give up your empty nest and move on.

The last time I saw our house—or what was left of it—was after a fire had destroyed it. Little more than a hole in the ground, its footprint was much smaller than seemed possible for the huge part it had played in our lives. As I stood at the edge of the gaping space and wrapped myself in its memories, I noted that in the pile of scorched bricks, where our library had once been, were the charred remains of a few books we'd left behind. Our life there had been rich; my experiences in the house, unforgettable.

As I look back, two things played large in our lives: our uniqueness as a family and the opportunities that flowed from our unusual home. Over the years, my children were exposed to many cultures and many perspectives. The character of each child was shaped by these experiences in a multitude of ways. In the long run, each one would decide how he or she felt about what they had been exposed to, and they responded in a variety of ways. Sometimes they were comfortable and joined us in step; sometimes they pretended not to know us so they could avoid a long explanation to their friends of how they came to have a black stepfather.

"Some folks just don't get it. And they never will," Jeff told me once, with a shrug of his shoulders.

I respect the strong and sensitive people my children have become. It is to their credit that they have thrived, despite their nontraditional upbringing. Each one of them, in his or her own way, is making a contribution toward a better world. If they are happy and adjusted, I feel I've reached my goal.

I AM FORTUNATE in that I have always been inherently an optimist. I envision a brighter future, and I meet each new day with enthusiasm for what could be. Over the years, in a rudimentary way, I think I grasped the value of flexibility and creative thinking in the face of adversity. Today, my best advice to pass along to young activists are words from the late Grace Lee Boggs, who so wisely advised young people in struggle in this way: "You must learn to take the negative and turn it into a positive."

Life asks much of us. Following Boggs's philosophy, you will go far in accomplishing your goals. I stand as proof of that.

Generation Next Activists

Nothing that we did mattered . . .
No, everything *that we did mattered!*

"Guess who I ran into today?"

Mike was animated. He'd bumped into an old friend from our days in the movement. Running into activists we once worked with is always a cause for joy. Mike said he'd invited our old friend to lunch so we could catch up. I looked forward to sharing old memories over a meal and was eager to learn about his life in the intervening years. We hadn't talked since the 1970s.

When we arrived at The Grill, I encountered the vaguely familiar, yet worry-worn face from the past. I had to make my usual internal adjustments, as though I was waiting for a slow computer to process a software update. We are all older now, and time has not been kind. We worked hard, and it shows in the creases on our brows. We are so different than we were, and yet so much the same.

"It's so great to see you," I ventured cordially as I slid into my chair. Looking at the pale man seated across from me, I felt as if I was seeing an empty shell left in the wake of his heroic history, but I understood. We gave the social justice movement of our era everything we had.

As our conversation rattled on, about people and places, about events through which we all lived, we got lost in our memories. We laughed, sometimes almost being brought to tears as we recalled our antics. Suddenly, Mike turned to our companion and said with great enthusiasm, "I'm having a party, and I want you to come."

It was to be a great get-together for Mike's eightieth birthday, and all the good people from the past who stood together fighting against American racism, capitalism, and imperialist wars were invited. We were a subculture.

"It will be like an extended family reunion of folks who cared about each other," Mike said. He wanted it to be an opportunity for those gathered to talk about what we had accomplished and what we were doing now.

Mike and I were both a bit startled by our old comrade's response.

"Accomplished?" he blurted out. "You don't mean that. Are you kidding? We lost! Nothing that we did mattered. Look around you. It's the same old shit."

"I guess you don't understand where I came from," Mike retorted. "I'm from Mississippi. Blacks emerged from semi-slavery in Mississippi in my lifetime. We destroyed so many of the barriers, in so many areas where people were oppressed, and exploited, and forgotten. Sure, we didn't achieve 'a revolution'—we were young and angry and unsophisticated. But we made enormous changes."

"Nothing that we did mattered," our friend continued mournfully.

"No," I countered, an old fervor rising in me, "*everything* that we did mattered!"

I scrutinized our friend's face. I'd heard about his losses. He was a man of stature who'd made enormous contributions, one of the most successful attorneys in his field. He was known for serving the working class, people both black and white, often pro bono. He won his first case for $7 million against a cop for beating a black man in a wheelchair.

Burying himself in the all-consuming intensity of his movement work in those passionate days had had irreversible consequences. His wife left him and took his young daughter. Devastated and rootless, he sought his escape in drugs and lost his job. His passion morphed into pain. It's rumored that he now lives in his law office above a bar in downtown Detroit. He's an embittered casualty of the movement—the phoenix that could not rise.

As to the party, our friend RSVP'd on his legal stationery and confirmed that he would join us on the appointed day. He never showed.

I BELIEVE THAT MY STORY IS RELEVANT for upcoming generations because I have witnessed both the rise of the civil rights and black self-determination movements in the 1960s and their dissolution in the early 1970s. Our efforts were thwarted by the stunning effectiveness of infiltration by the state and a lack of understanding of the pressure cooker of human behavior in our activist ranks. Some of us survived—even thrived—after the destruction of our activist infrastructures. Others became embittered. We made irreversible strides in our communities through activism. But how one emerges out of one's time deep in the fight for social justice is critical, as the fight began before us and goes on long after we're gone.

The civil rights movement is over. The antiwar movement—from the Vietnam War to the "war on terror"—is on pause. The middle class is an endangered species, in large part through the sabotage of the once powerful labor movement by corporations and the expansion of the new "gig" economy, which has rendered so many workers as independent contractors. The environmental movement has been taken hostage by our new president, who has reversed critical environmental regulations, withdrawn from the Paris Accords, and severely cut funding to all things science-related.

The specific issues that are driving a new wave of social movements today are born directly out of the world around us. But lessons from those who have been in similar positions in the past can offer vital perspectives on the human pitfalls that every activist must face. Being right is never enough. Even as movements go on, we must never give up—not on ourselves, and not on the fight.

There is a raft of literature on social movements, but in my experience, social movements can be defined by two general patterns. Here's my hard-won cheat sheet for movement survival:

First, you must always understand what kind of movement you find yourself in. Some movements are "spontaneous," others are what I will label "strategic." When you're swept up in the passions and power plays of the moment, you may know only that you're angry, even enraged, and that you just won't take it anymore. You feel disenfranchised, hurt, and perhaps even hopeless. This kind of pain needs an outlet, and that is how spontaneous movements are born.

Erupting unexpectedly, spontaneous movements can spread quickly, like wildfire. They can catch fire on the political right or on the left—consider the Tea Party and Black Lives Matter. The injustices each movement targets may have been brewing for a time; then a trigger incident, like a hate crime or a presidential election, ignites the fuse.

Spontaneous movements often evolve following an identifiable pattern. They generally begin with the fervor of a few. People watch and then take sides. Sympathy for the cause grows, and more people decide to take the risk; they join the fervent core. As the movement grows and gains support, the risk is diminished and more and more join the cause, incorporating it into the social consciousness of a culture. Spontaneous movements generally have a loose leadership structure that cannot sustain itself for the long haul.

The antiwar movement of the Vietnam era was one such spontaneous movement. It burst on the scene with marches on Washington, anti-draft protests, and the burning of draft records to cripple the selective service system. The women's liberation movement is another example. It was accelerated by the publication of Betty Friedan's *The Feminine Mystique* in 1963. It was an on-the-streets movement. Women poured out of their homes and onto the streets in protest. The women's liberation movement did not have centralized leadership, long-term goals, or an overarching strategic plan. The energy of this spontaneous movement culminated in the U.S. Supreme Court's *Roe v. Wade* decision in 1973.

In the early twenty-first century, we have watched Black Lives Matter—a network founded by Patrisse Cullors, Opal Tometi, and Alicia Garza—utilize technology to organize against police brutality. Black people and their multiracial allies in cities and towns all over the country have harnessed social media to express outrage at repeated police killings of unarmed black men. Tweets turned out people to protest in the streets, and this spontaneous opposition raised an unprecedented level of national consciousness about police misconduct.

Even more recently, we saw the outpouring of women around the country demonstrating against the election of Donald Trump, as well as crowds carrying "Welcome" signs and clogging airports to protest President Trump's travel ban against immigrants. These spontaneous expressions are indicative of something having gone terribly wrong.

Social media, however, is an activist's tool that comes with both rewards and risks. These new fast-paced, large-scale responses driven by technology ignite inevitable, equally fast pushback and divisiveness, such as the All Lives Matter response to Black Lives Matter, which ignores the reality that not all lives are under attack. Likewise, mass media is a communication platform that invites mass surveillance underwritten by the global war on terror. Increasing one's presence on social media can also increase one's risk of hackers, who can use your information for their own purposes. We live in complicated times.

By contrast, strategic movements are slow to form and may take generations to mature. They are deliberate and have specific goals and a broad constituency. Although they may appear to happen naturally, they are actually thoughtfully planned and guided over time. They have a sustainable foundation, specific objectives, and usually strong leadership with concrete plans and tactics, including communication and education programs. They are committed to creating broad and sustainable societal change.

The labor movement, the women's suffrage movement, the civil rights movement, the black power movement, the successful gay rights movement, as well as many movements from the Third World that culminated in revolution, are examples of these long-term efforts. These are often supported by, and grow alongside, determined community efforts, sometimes over decades, which provide resources or defend the vulnerable, like the National Association for the Advancement of Colored People or the American Civil Liberties Union.

Spontaneous movements can become strategic, but that takes strong leadership, hard work, the development of goals and tactics, and the painstaking process of analysis and reassessment. All this must occur in conjunction with enhanced communication methods, a plan for how decisions will be made, and avenues for input by those on the ground.

TODAY'S ACTIVISTS face unique, difficult challenges. The world has changed so much since the end of the civil rights movement in the early 1970s. Some of that change is the result of the successes stemming from our efforts. The last vestiges of outright, state-sanctioned Jim Crow–style racism were banished from all but the most backward parts of the country. The black labor movement under Detroit's black power leadership won significant gains in black labor practices. In fact, there were many Revolutionary Union Movements (RUMs), all around the country, like the DRUM and ELRUM. Changes were made in how black labor was used in the production of goods, in hiring and firing practices, and in access to supervisory positions. Judicial reforms were also made to court systems and jury selection. Women's rights were expanded and recognized rapidly, shifting the foundations of our social understanding of what gender allows one to do and be. The ecological ravaging of late-stage capitalism was finally confronted with new awareness and new environmental protections. The recognition and wide-scale acceptance and support for LGBTQ communities has grown rapidly, allowing people to live openly as their true selves now more than ever before.

But even as we've witnessed a tremendous evolution in society over the last fifty years, the issues that have bedeviled us socially have evolved as well. Today's young activists are the vanguard in addressing these issues. The context for the movement work that must happen today is different than when I was an activist. Even as things have changed, a core understanding of what has driven these social issues in the first place, the history of how we got here, and the interconnection with the activists that came before is vital in order to avoid repeating mistakes that can be avoided. We are experiencing changes in technology, economics, social values, and mass media that have radically altered the playing field, and adapting to these changes—evolving how activism operates in the environment we now live in—is the first and biggest challenge facing activists today.

Confronting this challenge means being nimble on your feet and flexible in your ability to adjust organizational efforts to be responsive to the moment. Here's an example of what I mean: Black Lives Matter and the NAACP are working toward a shared vision of a more just society with regard to the treatment of diverse communities, particular those in the black community. But they are at opposite ends of the organizational spectrum. Black Lives Matter has been, arguably, the most effective spontaneous movement in recent memory, sustaining street activity with vibrancy for nearly four years now. But in the Age of Trump, the group has reportedly understood that its tactics need to change; they must evolve to meet the times and the conditions. Conversations about, in the words of a recent *Washington Post* article, "a new phase—one more focused on policy than protest" have started. In other words, they've begun the transition from spontaneous to strategic.

Now take the storied NAACP. The group has been operating in a strategic capacity for decades. In the past, it has been one of the nation's most effective organizations in raising awareness and combating racism. Yet in recent years it has been dealing with what so many long-term strategic organizations must face: the fight to remain relevant to conditions on the ground. This issue recently came to a head when the NAACP president was ousted by a fired-up base looking to shake up the group. *The New York Times* wrote about his departure: "The mood among the members is one of direct action and confrontation." The members want the NAACP to recover some of its spontaneous roots.

This mood—of action, of building, of organizing—is being felt everywhere. It's helping to propel activists forward, to think about what kind of strategy makes the most sense for their aims. After a period of painful adjustment to the new conditions in which we find ourselves, we are seeing a rise of new perspectives and voices that refuse to ask for permission from the status quo. I applaud the work being spearheaded by young people across our country to revitalize the never-ending call for social justice, equality, and accountability—the things that a movement must be made of.

SOME POWERFUL, SMALL-SCALE STRATEGIC movement work toward these ends has sprung up in our country as activists work to change the way we think about ourselves and offer ways to sustain ourselves on the ground, in our communities. It is notable that many of them, such as Black Lives Matter, are led by women.

An influential strategic movement on Detroit's East Side has been going on at the Boggs Center. The late Detroit activist Grace Lee Boggs was a Chinese philosopher who married James Boggs, a black activist factory worker. For the duration of Grace's life, she was a Chinese woman in a black world. Grace spent her life studying change, ultimately concluding that revolution is not a one-time event but an evolution, coming about through a series of small steps; this she graphically displayed as (r)evolution.

"A revolution is not just for the purpose of correcting past injustices," Grace and Jimmie wrote. "The only justification for a revolution is that it advances the evolution of man/woman."

After Jimmie's death, Grace turned her attention to neighborhood-based youth programs and community-based work in urban agriculture, grassroots media, and place-based education for the community's children as well as training for young activists, many of whom stay on to work in Detroit. This work continues under the James and Grace Lee Boggs Center to Nurture Community Leadership.

Charlene Carruthers, national director of the Black Youth Project (BYP-100), is another person to watch. Her organization rose out of Chicago, but its local strategic mission has been recognized as serving a need beyond its home community. It now has a presence in cities around the country, including Detroit. The organization trains young black activists in direct-action grassroots organizing skills, which they apply in their home communities. Charlene extols another call for unity: "Until all of us are included, none of us will be free."

Elsewhere, activists are taking up national issues, using cross-cultural and intergenerational coalitions to bring more people into movement work. A couple of years ago, I had the pleasure of meeting Linda Sarsour, executive director of the Arab American Association of New York. Sarsour, the mother of three, is a Palestinian American who embraces coalition work. I heard her speak to the Michigan Coalition on Human Rights echoing the idea that all oppressed people should support the black struggle, because "when blacks are free, all of us will be free." Linda was one of the primary organizers of the January 2017 Women's March on Washington. She is an outstanding example of a mother who has found her place in transforming society through social activism.

What is unique about today's social movement organizations is the vision that citizenship in this country is not enough. Allowing blacks to integrate into the old system of injustice that we fought for during the civil rights movement did not bring full citizenship, equality, or freedom. Young folks realized that having a black president and many black mayors, police chiefs, and attorneys general hasn't solved our problems. We still live in a violent and repressive country. Now is the time to move on, to move forward, to create a new system that we can all be part of as we struggle for human rights.

One of the biggest lessons of the civil rights movement was that we underestimated the power of the government to infiltrate. Movements have patterns, and we know that when we rise up again, there will be resistance. Six months before the 2016 presidential election, my husband and I talked with a seasoned leader who was in the black power struggle fifty years ago and was still active on the East Coast. We had a delightful conversation about our work in the past, and I asked him, "Do you sense that a resurgence is under way?"

"The movement has never stopped," he said. "It's like a river running underground. Yes, there are outward manifestations of change with Black Lives Matter, but we know it's already been infiltrated."

I thought about this a few weeks later, when my husband and I were invited to participate in a discussion group. The leader had been persistent in calling to confirm that we would attend, taking our history for an introduction to the group. The meeting was short—not many people attended—but we spent some time chatting. Something didn't feel right to me. As we walked out the door, Mike and I looked at each other and said in unison: "Police." They're still here, still watching and listening.

Another lesson that's critical is the need for coalition building across all strata of society, but maybe none is more crucial than between different racial and ethnic communities. Despite the gains of the civil rights movement, America is more segregated than it was in the 1960s. We've grown estranged from one another, making it all the easier for the things that divide us—race, religion, sexual orientation, gender, place of birth—to settle into the gaps between us. The old saying "The people, united, will never be defeated" takes on a new resonance today when so many of us are easily divided.

Building coalitions requires a lot of patience and trust. White activists have a special role to play in this regard. As we learned in the 1960s and '70s, it's critical for disempowered people, both individually and organizationally, to be supported by white allies.

Black leadership in the city of Detroit in the 1960s and '70s made extraordinary gains that were felt across the country. This history offers a model of fearless work on the people's behalf. Black activists' coalitions with the white left aided their ability to educate whites of conscience and increase their sphere of influence. Such coalitions also helped to protect blacks' vulnerable position in the dominant culture.

I firmly believe that the most oppressed should lead us. It's the first step toward unraveling the racial coding that ensnares us all and ensuring that the community's voice and concerns remain heard and fought for. But doing this requires recognition of white privilege—a concept that even well-meaning white liberals can struggle to recognize and own. This is absolutely critical if the kind of cross-cultural, interracial coalition building is going to occur. Acknowledging the reality of white privilege and committing to listening more than speaking are good first steps toward overcoming this social disability.

Finally, as we learned through our experience with the CCC Book Club, we can effectively work together to raise consciousness about the critical issues faced by society. As a reveler in the joys of lifelong learning, I've spent my own life trying to continue to expand my understanding of the world around me. Activists are uniquely positioned to take their burning passions and turn them into opportunities to enlighten others. Expanding awareness to issues in our midst is vital to achieving change. If we are to succeed in raising consciousness, we must embrace all communities in our efforts. Incorporating educational components into a strategic activism plan is a must for any organization or group truly committed to fighting for a more just future.

We live in the midst of a great struggle between those who control our resources and those who have essential needs but lack the power to attain them. From the ground up, we need to assure that people have adequate access to food, clean water, clean air, health care, shelter, and clothing. We need to be an army at work, demanding and participating in efforts to improve life in our neighborhoods, to participate in real work on the community's behalf, to reform law enforcement and the court systems, to reestablish basic services in poor communities, and to protect our most vulnerable citizens. We need to experiment with plans for neighborhood cooperatives and mentoring programs for young people, and we must create networks to share our results so others can learn from our experiences. We cannot be isolated from our communities. It is urgent that we undertake this important work.

PART FIVE

Past Forward

THE ACTIVIST'S SURVIVAL GUIDE

It's the action, not the fruit of the action, that's important.
You have to do the right thing. It may not be in your power,
may not be in your time, that there'll be any fruit.
But that doesn't mean you stop doing the right thing.
You may never know what results come from your action.
But if you do nothing, there will be no result.
—MAHATMA GANDHI

FORESIGHT ALWAYS TRUMPS HINDSIGHT when you're considering a commitment to an activist lifestyle. Being a good foot soldier demands reflection and clarity. These are two things that you swear you will not have time for but must attend to. As a witness to the process of creation and disintegration in many types of movements, I offer to the next generation of activists the following lessons learned, what I call my Activist's Survival Guide.

— THE ACTIVIST'S SURVIVAL GUIDE —

1. BECOME A STUDENT OF SOCIAL ACTIVIST HISTORY
Failure to know our own history dooms us to repeat avoidable, sometimes fatal, mistakes. Study the history of social justice and freedom struggles, both in the United States and

around the world. These long and courageous histories will inspire you and guide you in your own movement involvement. Group study (in the tradition of the CCC Book Club) is an effective way to learn movement history. Encourage your organization to put together an educational program if one is not already in place. Yearn to learn.

2. Know Your Organization

Research any organization you're considering joining. Go slowly as you integrate yourself into the work. Be cautious about the cult of personality and clear about the motivations and ethics of group members. Commitment to a structured, respectful communication process should be built into your organization's DNA. Learn how your organization is financed and how such funding may influence its decision-making.

3. Be Willing to Pay the Price

As JFK said, "The cost of freedom is always high." Your passion for change can consume all of your time, your energy, your relationships, and your mental and physical well-being. You will be tested, and at times you will fail yourself . . . and others. But in failing you will learn to rebuild and begin again. Your commitment may require sacrificing your piece of the capitalist dream. Yet by embracing a compassionate, altruistic concern for the welfare of others, you'll find a spiritual depth that gives greater meaning and purpose to life.

4. Save Yourself

While sacrifice is an unavoidable part of being an activist, you're no good to your cause if you're irritable or ill. Eat right. Sleep enough. Stay positive. Recognize your abilities and limitations, and choose your role accordingly. Remain physically and emotionally refreshed with periodic downtime. Avoid time-wasting conflict. Write down short-term and long-term personal goals for your involvement. Be honest with yourself. Periodically review your personal goals against those of your organization, in order to ensure that you're both still traveling in the same direction.

5. BE THE CHANGE YOU WOULD LIKE TO SEE

Pursue and define your own moral code; don't let anyone else do it for you. Trust your instincts and intuition. Things that don't feel or look right probably aren't. Maintain your integrity and principles—something easier said than done. Cultivate and nurture meaningful relationships with friends and significant others who will provide support while still allowing you to honor your commitments. Be trustworthy. It's not wise to share secrets, even in a world where there seemingly are no secrets. Loose lips sink ships and destroy lives.

6. LOOK, LISTEN, AND JOURNAL

Listen before you speak. Listen after you speak. Listen *more* than you speak. Keep track of what you hear, what you see, and what you say. Journal notes will help you evaluate your progress and reflect on your observations. These notes are for you alone. Be sensitive to recurring patterns—both your own and those of others. Strive to understand relationships and contradictions. Remember: When there are movements, there are often countermovements. Keep yourself attuned to the opposition.

7. ASSUME YOU ARE BEING WATCHED

Surveillance and infiltration broke the back of the civil rights and black power movements. Those abilities pale in comparison to the post-9/11 surveillance state. If you use a cell phone or a computer, if you log on to social media or use a credit or debit card, you are already being surveilled. The stakes rise rapidly in the movement. Be aware of your potential risk exposure. Recognize the power of the

government and the police. Think before you post to social
media. Handle information wisely. It's subject to collection
by authorities and can easily be distorted and repackaged
to misrepresent you and your organization.

8. LAWYER UP

Movement work can involve enormous risks. You need to
protect yourself legally, even if it seems unlikely that you'll
ever need an attorney. Ask trusted friends and explore your
options. Don't wait until it's too late. Look for represen-
tation that has experience helping people in your similar
situation. Lawyers with social justice sensibilities can also
be proactive. They may offer sound advice as you develop
your organizational structure and plan your strategies and
tactics.

9. LET'S TALK ABOUT SEX

Sexual relationships in the movement are not often discussed, but when handled poorly, such relationships can
be hazardous to individuals as well as to the organization.
Personal and sexual relationships can alter allegiances and
affect outcomes, and young activists need to be aware of
the pitfalls. Sexual liaisons—whether they last for a night
or a decade—can significantly affect your work. Individuals
often make contradictory calculations when sexual feelings
are involved. Have a frank discussion about how intimate
relationships can impact your organization and put together
a procedure for addressing the conduct of those who exploit
others.

10. FOSTER INTERGENERATIONAL DIALOGUE

The strongest defense against the rollback of social justice
gains is to foster an active conversation between generations of activists. This continuity is critical. Gray-haired
activists have a raft of experience and lessons learned from
their work in movements that can enhance and inspire the

journey of our young people. Young activists understand the realities on the ground and are able to translate that context to their elders. When both sides come together in a spirit of humility, trust, and openness, the sharing that results will promote an evolution of understanding and an unfolding of solutions that will pave the way to better results.

11. PLANT YOUR FEET ON THE GROUND

Get involved in your community. You live there—take an active interest. Attend meetings of community groups to understand the issues your neighbors are facing. Contribute to social interactions and stand up for those who are in need of support. Find ways to facilitate interracial and intercultural discussions with community members. Without the understanding generated by the free exchange of ideas and experiences, we will never overcome white privilege or black and brown disenfranchisement. It's critical that we all learn to walk in someone else's shoes.

THE STRUGGLE CONTINUES

MIKE AND I WERE GOOD FOR EACH OTHER. Our life together was not governed by gender roles or race but by shared
values and uncompromising commitment. I was blessed to find a
partner who always supported my desire to self-actualize, to live
life to the fullest. We raised our seven children, who—despite my
concerns, my misgivings, and my missteps—have done exception-
ally well. We loved each other, we loved people, and we found
inextinguishable hope in our shared vision of a better world.

We—pretty gracefully, I would say—grew old together. We began each day over the morning newspaper, discussing issues and
opinions, loving the process of agreeing and disagreeing that en-
gendered long discussions. As I reflect on the passage of time, I
see in this ritual a mirror image of our younger selves and the
common ground we experienced that day in 1969, when we met
at Sheila's house and read the newspaper together, unaware of
our grand journey that was to come.

With the morning edition of *The New York Times* spread to
the left of our breakfast plates, I'd start with the front section.
Mike would take the back, and then we'd switch, chatting
our way through the news. One recent morning I discovered
an Op-Ed piece that suggested social media reinforces
our individualism, leading to isolation and polarization and a
breakdown of the social fabric.

"Perhaps it's time for our society to hit the refresh key," I commented. "I'm worried that communication is being reduced to
liking, tweeting, and posting emoticons. Young people isolated by

technology may miss the full picture. The social movements of our era were not generated in isolation. They were created on the ground, in communities."

Mike stopped reading the sports page and looked at me. I listened to the clink of his spoon against his coffee cup, feeling cozy with my tea.

"It's clear that, in our politics, we're losing our ability to engage with others who don't agree with us," Mike said. "A bedrock principle of movement work is that consensus needs to be built from many different perspectives."

I knew Mike believed that social media can jump-start the deeper conversation required to provide the history and depth of knowledge necessary for young people to lead. But it can't be a substitute.

"Our activist heirs have a struggle on their hands and they know it," I added. "Even young whites recognize that their future has been compromised. When fires are raging all around you, it's a precipitous moment. The smoke makes it hard to think clearly or to strategize about how to make changes or decide who should lead."

Mike responded with an axiom: "If young people want to change the world, they need to study and be prepared to take risks."

I found myself thinking of Mike's niece, Alena, who had stopped over a few weeks earlier while we were engaged in our morning ritual. Behold a beautiful young black woman, smart as they come. She's thirty, strapped for time, raising a sibling, working a job, and, at the same time, getting her master's degree in social work. Alena smiled when she saw us reading a printed newspaper. "My generation doesn't have time for that," she said. "We just go to our devices and look up what we need to know. The whole world is at our fingertips."

Mike looked at her. "Social media is simply a tool, an autonomous reference point that can speak falsehood or truth," he said.

"We can't turn back the clock," I countered. "Technology has already changed the fabric of our social relations and our economy.

Social media is a fine tactical tool, but organizing a movement has to be based in something deeper. Social justice requires knowledge, compassion, and commitment."

Then I glanced at Alena and added, "I know it's hard to live daringly when your very survival is at risk. Young people have a huge task ahead of them."

Alena considered our points before responding: "Young people have grown up with information bombarding them from every direction, all the time, every day." She noted that many of her generation have developed rigorous filters and become highly discerning. That information fluency has also led to a generation more diverse in its viewpoints than any other in history, able to pull from a wide range of sources to formulate new ways to deal with old problems reemerging in new forms.

"Fifty years ago, there was no Internet, but look what we accomplished," Mike said. "We struck a blow against the crippling legacy of oppressed blacks and against white supremacy. We understood the struggle between the workers in society and the wealthy was the world's primary contradiction. Racism is a by-product of that contradiction."

"We worked from the ground up," I added, "educating through newspapers and newsletters, classes and training forums—look what we did with the CCC Book Club—with no social media."

I thought back to the groundwork that was laid long before the wave of technological change in society. It took bold action and organization, and we learned directly from one another. We collaborated and built coalitions. We discussed contradictions and where to direct our blows. We gathered in demonstrations large and small but all were community-based, where people lived their commitments. We took action, developed strategies and tactics. We studied successful revolutions, acted boldly, challenged one another, and took risks.

"Yes, these gains were super-critical—we owe so much to what you guys did," Alena said. "I think it's more that we see that history as *an* example of moving forward—not *the* example. Technology allows young people to reimagine a way forward through a wide world of experiences and perspectives, but technology can never be a substitute for action." Then she thoughtfully acknowledged that the more mature her generation of activists becomes, the more they will understand this.

As she gathered her things together to leave, Alena said, "We're lucky to have all this information and history to pull from. Believe me: We're ready get out there and change the world."

THERE HAS BEEN A FLURRY OF ACTIVITY IN DETROIT relative to the fiftieth anniversary of the rebellion. Both Mike and I were interviewed for the Detroit 1967 Project, sponsored by the Detroit Historical Society, and we each have pieces in the Museum Exhibition Hall. A new documentary titled *12th and Clairmount,* produced by the *Detroit Free Press,* premiered at the Detroit Institute of Arts Film Theater in the spring of 2017. The film is based upon home movies from the era. It shows a very segregated city with severe economic disparity, and highlights how this division erupted into the largest civil uprising in the history of our country. A small segment from the narrative was taken from my interview, and I was humbled to see my name in the film credits. *Hour Detroit Magazine* even featured a segment from Mike on why the civil uprising was a rebellion as opposed to a riot.

When our grandchildren ask what we did in the civil rights movement, we know that they see us as we are now, not as we were then. The steps that we took in our lives mirror the crossroads they will soon face as they make decisions about the direction of their future lives. We try to explain that we were focused on improving life for others and that we believed in giving selflessly of everything we had. Of course, we remind them, we worried: Did we give enough? Could we have done more? Did our mistakes hurt others? Did we ignore our families?

Yet our children and our grandchildren seem to have inherited an essential respect for people and their rights, an ethic of caring with no fear or resentment of hard work. They stand strong for one another and a better future.

Ken, my firstborn, is an engineer. He paid his own way and followed his own path and ultimately earned a master's degree in mechanical engineering from the University of Michigan. Today, he is a partner in a company that develops prototype engines and parts for automobiles and space travel. Ken lives in Ypsilanti, Michigan, with his wife, Gail, a massage therapist.

Greg, my second son, is gifted in social skills. After earning a two-year degree at a state college, he became an outstanding salesman and was on the brink of establishing his own business when he developed progressive multiple sclerosis. The disease ravaged his future. Greg had a special T-shirt made to profess his philosophy on life: "Don't ever give up . . . Ever!" Greg has a daughter, Nikki, who has given us three beautiful great-grandchildren.

Jeff, my third son, has a degree from Eastern Michigan University. He had to be alert in his first career as an animal keeper at the Detroit Zoo. After too many cold winter days chopping ice, struggling to free water for the animals, Jeff got in his car and drove to sunny California. There, he added a teaching degree and became a devoted middle school teacher. Jeff lives in Fresno, California, with his wife, Jeanine, who is a social worker, and his college-age son, Joshua.

Carolyn, our oldest daughter, is sweet as honey and tough as nails. Throughout her life, she has struggled to hold her own in a world of challenges framed by her limited vision. Carolyn earned a degree in education from Central Michigan University and taught special education until her declining vision made it impossible for her to continue. Carolyn assists her husband, Joe, a professional golfer, with his program to teach underprivileged kids how to enjoy and excel in the sport.

We call Michael, my fourth son, the "die-hard" because he never quits. Michael earned scholarships to the University of Michigan, where he graduated with undergraduate degrees in engineering and mathematics *(magna cum laude)* and a master's degree in computer engineering. Michael is a marathon runner and has participated in the International Paralympic Games and competitions around the world as a member of Team USA in the visually impaired category. Michael lives in Paris with his wife, Valerie, and their two children, Ella and Leo.

Christine, my youngest daughter, is a joyful, strong-willed, and capable woman. Today, Christine excels in a responsible position at a real estate title company in Ann Arbor, Michigan. She has raised and nurtured two beautiful daughters, Lisa and Julie, who are studying in the fields of veterinary medicine and education, respectively.

Alexander, my child with Mike, is a technical geek. Coming into adulthood on the cusp of the computer age and indulging his love of technology, Alex turned his attention to earning a long string of certifications from Microsoft, which propelled him into a position at a software company. Alex and his wife, Christina, a graphic artist, have two young sons, Wesley and Ashton. Earlier in 2017, Alex found himself displaced following a reorganization of his company. He and his family have moved to Seattle, Washington, a city of technical growth and expansion, to restart their careers.

SADLY, ON APRIL 17, 2017, I LOST MY HUSBAND, MIKE, to the ravages of heart failure. He gave himself to others until he had nothing left to give. It is hard to write about my loss because my grief is so fresh and painful. I am still struggling to accept this new reality. Mike was my inner strength and my greatest cheerleader with regard to this book project. So I challenged myself to complete this work in his honor. I know that I must continue to be the strength he saw in me.

Mike believed that there were lessons in my story that could support young people's journey into the activism that is so sorely needed in our times. That belief drives me forward. It has been inspiring to see young people in our family step forward after Mike's passing and pledge their futures to carrying on his activist legacy. A nephew and niece of his are deeply involved in union work and attribute their commitments and their dedication to Mike's example. And there's Alena, who smiled at our reading of a print newspaper. She has now graduated with her master's in social work.

She has high hopes to do organizing in Southwest Detroit, the area where she grew up. I salute her resolve and her youthful drive to do everything that she can to change her old neighborhood into a better place where young people can grow and thrive.

Everywhere, the deeds of earlier generations of activists are serving as examples to the latest generation ready to take their place in the long, interconnected procession of change. *Now* is a critical time for organizing. With the new administration in Washington and the quick rollback of so many human rights gains, our hopes lie with the younger generation. Fertile ground for organizing lies in communities desperate for help rebuilding community infrastructure from the ground up.

I see the paths now being mapped out by my younger brothers and sisters, and I have great faith in them. Controlling our own destiny requires consistent struggle. I hope my Activist's Survival Guide will offer insights into preparing for a lifelong and successful activist journey. Each activist's trek begins with taking the first step, joined by another, and then another—until millions of feet are marching together for a common cause. I'm confident that today's young people will reach the destination toward which they are headed. In fact, they must—they must keep on marching, keep on organizing, and keep on fighting so the gains of the past can be retained and the promises of the future can be realized.

Acknowledgments

I AM GRATEFUL for the life bestowed upon me by my parents, Esther and Barry Reschke. I know they loved me. My parents gave me my sister, Karen, who has loved and supported me throughout these years without making judgments about the decisions I have made.

I lost my maternal grandmother when I was still a child. Yet, somehow during our brief encounters, I absorbed a piece of her inner self that helped me shape an image of who I wanted to become.

In my adult life, there were many who were pivotal in my growth and political development. Father William Cunningham was the catalyst responsible for changing my life and introducing me to the idea of commitment to the cause of humanity. There were others whom I met along the way: Jim Francek, Patrick Mason and Rosemarie Mason, Dennie Moloney, Tony Locricchio, Sheila Murphy Cockrel, James Forman and Dinky Romily, all of whom influenced my development and contributed to my growth.

Indeed, I owe a debt of gratitude to my first husband, who fathered my first six children and who has continued to be a part of our lives to this day.

I am grateful to those who supported my efforts to get an education and develop a successful career. Among those were the dedicated employees of Metropolitan Hospital, one thousand strong, who were like family to me.

I was encouraged by my professors at Wayne State University, particularly Sue Taylor, Ph.D., and Gloria House, Ph.D. At Henry Ford Health System, Nancy Whitelaw, Ph.D., and Marybeth Tupper, M.D., challenged me to be all I could be. We were a great team and continue to be friends.

Among those who contributed to making this book a reality, I am grateful to Gloria Aneb House for making insightful suggestions. Sylvia Hubbard, single mother of three and founder of the Motown Writers Network, was an inspiration and showed me the way, step by step, to finishing and publishing a book.

I want to thank Gabriel Turner and others in his writing circle for patiently listening and critiquing my early efforts. I also want to thank Donna MacDonald and Cheryl Deep from Wayne State's Institute of Gerontology who encouraged me to persevere.

Among those who agreed to read my early drafts was my friend Donna Ridella from the Theatre Arts Club of Detroit, an all-women theater group that adds dimension to my life. There I also found support from Monica Quinn, Kristine Pierce, and Sandy Novacek. Sandy, who has experience in publishing, has devoted many hours to mentoring me.

I am grateful to others who have been so kind as to read the manuscript and comment, including Kae Halonen, Nancy Whitelaw, Sandy Stevenson, Tom Krell, Elaine Crawford, and Beverly Schneider, and to Michelle Moton for assistance in selecting aphorisms for my chapters. Also to Susan Dicosmo, Linda Westervelt, and Cheryl Deep, who gracefully volunteered their assistance to push my efforts over the finish line. Thank you all for your time, your suggestions, and your encouragement.

I am especially grateful to Elza Dinwiddie-Boyd, who connected me with my distinguished editor, Cheryl Woodruff, President of BookMavericks. Cheryl has inspired and driven me to complete a work much broader than I ever believed I was capable of. Any credit is hers; any errors are mine. As my writing came to a close, Cheryl connected me to Colby Hamilton, a talented and creative journalist who deftly reorganized my bloated manuscript, gave it direction and a coherent theme, and reduced it to a length my readers will appreciate. Thank you, Colby.

Not to be forgotten are my stalwart BookMavericks team: Nora Reichard, my extraordinary copy editor, Kristine Mills, who created a cover design that captures the spirit of the times, and Cindy Shaw, who produced a beautiful interior design and photo insert. I also owe a heartfelt thank-you to Louis Jones and Deborah Rice at the Walter P. Reuther Library, Archives of Labor and Urban Affairs, Wayne State University, for their steadfast assistance.

High on my list of those to whom I owe thanks are my children. They took the time to share their memories—fond and otherwise—to give this work depth and meaning. I have relentlessly pushed to finish this book in order to leave them something tangible that expresses my love. They have never let me down.

Above all and in all ways, I thank my late husband, Mike Hamlin. To be loved by Mike was a gift. Over these last forty-five years, we built our lives together, established a home for our children, and extended ourselves to help others in need of support. I am who I have become with Mike. He was my strength, my comfort, and my joy.

Notes

PROLOGUE: FOOT SOLDIERS

1 **These were the years of:** COINTELPRO was the FBI's
massive counterintelligence program, which involved political
surveillance, infiltration, and dirty tricks operations aimed at
radicals in the 1950s and '60s. The program was conceived
and personally overseen by J. Edgar Hoover, the FBI director.
Counterintelligence was conducted against Americans such as
Dr. Martin Luther King Jr., John Kerry, and other dissenters in
the anti-Vietnam War movement as well as against those in the
civil rights movement, including Viola Liuzzo. The program was
allegedly terminated on the day of J. Edgar Hoover's death in
May 1972.

2 **Some years earlier, Dr. Ossian Sweet:** The story of Dr.
Ossian Sweet, a Detroit physician who fought back when a mob
of whites attacked his home, can be found in Kevin Boyle, *Arc of
Justice: A Saga of Race, Civil Rights, and Murder in the Jazz Age* (New
York: Picador Books, 2004).

11 **By 1950 . . . Detroit's urban renewal plan:** Rochelle Riley,
*Detroit Mayor Offers a Lesson on Race, Says Detroit's History Cannot Be
Its Future.* "Urban Renewal Destroyed Black Bottom, Paradise
Valley and 400 Black-Owned Businesses." *Detroit Free Press,* June
1, 2017.

CHAPTER 2: MOTHERLY EVER AFTER

41 **Vatican II was a timely message:** The Second Vatican
Ecumenical Council (Vatican II) was opened under Pope John
XXIII in 1962 then closed after his death in 1965. Pope John
wished the Council "to increase the fervor and energy of
Catholics, to serve the needs of Christian people." In Italian,
John was able to express his desire in one word—*aggiornamento*—
the Church must be brought up to date, must adapt itself to
meet the challenged conditions of modern times.
www.christusrex.org/www1/CDHN/v1.html.

42 **"Rather than support the poor":** I have reconstructed
Father Cunningham's eloquent sermon from memory.

47 **Viola Liuzzo, another white woman and mother from Detroit:** Viola's story can be found in Mary Stanton, *From Selma to Sorrow: The Life and Death of Viola Liuzzo* (Athens: University of Georgia Press, 1998).

51 **Viola would not have died in vain:** Viola Liuzzo was assassinated on March 25, 1965. The Voting Rights Act was passed by Congress and signed by President Johnson on August 6, 1965.

CHAPTER 3: IN SEARCH OF A MOVEMENT

53 **I did not know at the time:** Death threats against Father Cunningham are noted in Jack Kresnak, *Hope for the City* (Detroit: Cass Community Publishing House, Detroit, 2015).

CHAPTER 4: THE 1967 DETROIT REBELLION

77 **when police raided an after-hours club:** Details about the raid on the Blind Pig can be found in Thomas J. Sugrue, *Detroit 1967: Origins, Impacts, Legacies* (Detroit: Wayne State University Press, 2017).

80 **Don and I invited Dennie inside. . .** The diary entries of Deacon Dennie Moloney were instrumental in allowing me to reconstruct the conversations we had on the first night of the Detroit Rebellion.

85 **the paranoid mood back in Taylor:** From the interview with Eleanor Josaitis found in Robert H. Mast, *Detroit Lives* (Philadelphia: Temple University Press, 1994).

88 **In the coming days:** Statistics from the rebellion—deaths, arrests, incarcerations—are from Sugrue, *Detroit 1967*.

91 **"Out of the violence, tumult, madness":** Father Cunningham on the response to the rebellion found in Msgr. Anthony Tocco, review of *Hope for the City*, by Jack Kresnak, *Michigan Catholic*, December 22, 2015.

CHAPTER 5: HOURGLASS

104 **To start, I wrote several letters:** In the Walter Reuther Archives at Wayne State University, I have been able to access many communications between Bishop Gumbleton, Archbishop Dearden, and myself.

106 **"primarily white" . . . "to fight for liberty at home":** Statement of Black Catholic Clergy Caucus, April 18, 1968.

106 **"The hour is late":** National Conference of Catholic Bishops, Washington, D.C., April 25, 1968.

108 **"one of the most realistic"** . . . **"funded with money from ADF":** Bishop Gumbleton to Archbishop Dearden, May 16, 1968.

Chapter 6: Unfaithful Clergy

115 **no one was thinking about the poverty program . . . Martin Luther King was speaking about "curtains of doom":** King at Grosse Point in 1968: "The question now, is whether America is prepared to do something massively, affirmatively and forthrightly about the great problem we face in the area of race and the problem which can bring the curtain of doom down on American civilization if it is not solved." http://www.gphistorical.org/mlk/mlkspeech/

116 **Mayor Cavanagh appointed a fact-finding committee:** "AOP Review scheduled by U.S. Aides," *Detroit Free Press,* October 15, 1968.

116 **The program's administrators had been aware:** A full report of the mayor's committee's findings is on file in the Papers of Mike Hamlin and Joann Castle, Walter P. Reuther Library, Wayne State University

117 **we delivered an open letter to the offices of Mayor Cavanagh and Archbishop Dearden:** The letter is on file in the Papers of Mike Hamlin and Joann Castle, Walter P. Reuther Library, Wayne State University

117 **I encountered His Holiness in the elevator:** "Dearden Confronted by AOP Pickets," *Detroit Free Press,* October 15, 1968.

123 **A special police task force called STRESS (Stop the Robberies Enjoy Safe Streets):** After the 1967 riot, city officials created a special police task force called STRESS (Stop the Robberies; Enjoy Safe Streets). Detroit Historical Society and Dan Georgakas and Marvin Surkin, *Detroit: I Do Mind Dying* (Cambridge, MA: South End Press, 1998).

Ken Cockrel's successful fight against the brutal STRESS unit is depicted in the forthcoming documentary Dare to Struggle, Dare to Win, developed by the group The Work and produced by Erin Henneghan. Kate Cockrel, Ken Cockrel's daughter, was one of the executive producers.

124 **Believers . . . in nonviolence . . . decided they would proceed with Dr. King's plan for a Poor People's Campaign.** Gerald McKnight, *The Last Crusade: Martin Luther King, Jr., the FBI, and the Poor People's Campaign* (New York: Basic Books, 1998).

CHAPTER 8: REVOLUTIONARY DETROIT

147 **James Forman was the author:** The "Black Manifesto" was written by James Forman, with the assistance of the League of Revolutionary Black Workers, at the Black Economic Development Conference (BEDC) in Detroit, on April 25–27, 1969. The manifesto called on white churches and synagogues to pay $500 million in reparations to black people for their role in black enslavement and continuing oppression. Church services were first interrupted on May 4, 1969, at Riverside Church in New York City with a demand for payment. A complete copy of the document can be found in Mike Hamlin and Michele Gibbs, *A Black Revolutionary's Life in Labor: Black Workers Power in Detroit* (Detroit: Against the Tide Books, 2013).

147 **"compensation is necessary to combat":** That reparations need to be paid was the conclusion of a study by the UN's Working Group of Experts on People of African Descent, a body that reports to the international organization's high commissioner on human rights. According to the panel's report, the reparations could come in a variety of forms, including "a formal apology, health initiatives, educational opportunities . . . psychological rehabilitation, technology transfer and financial support, and debt reduction."

148 **the League of Revolutionary Black Workers, which was a magnet for black labor activism at the time:** Finally Got the News is a documentary film that reveals the activities of the League of Revolutionary Black Workers inside and outside the auto factories of Detroit. It is available for viewing at https://www.youtube.com/watch?v=gw2Wr-odBJg.

156 **People in the League were well known in Detroit for . . . organizing the Dodge Revolutionary Union Management (DRUM):** "Nine months and 5 days after the Great Rebellion, the work of General Baker, Mike Hamlin and Ron March bore fruit when on May 2, 1968, 4,000 workers shut down Dodge Main in the first wildcat strike to hit that factory in 14 years. The immediate

cause of the strike was speed-up and both black and white workers took part, but the driving force was the Inner-City Voice group . . . The activities and ideas of DRUM were to inspire black workers in factories throughout the United States." Quote taken from Georgakas and Surkin, Detroit: *I Do Mind Dying.*

149 **growing up in a Catholic Worker house:** Catholic Worker houses were founded in the 1930s by Dorothy Day and Peter Maurin. The Catholic Worker movement is grounded in a firm belief in the God-given dignity of every human person. It offered hospitality for the homeless, hungry, and forsaken.

152 **I was reading an article:** "Detroit Churches Promised Time to Meet Manifesto," *Detroit Free Press,* August 30, 1970.

153 **that the reparations demand amounted to extortion.** "Manifesto Witnesses Move to Kill U.S. Jury Subpoenas," *Detroit Free Press,* July 1, 1969.

153 **the group called the move by law enforcement a witch hunt.** "Manifesto Probe Is Branded a 'Witch Hunt,'" *Detroit Free Press,* July 8, 1969.

154 **"death-dealing exploitation of people":** From the statement of the D.C. Nine against Dow Chemical: "An Open Letter to the Corporations of America," March 22, 1969.

160 **Taylor called Detroit the "American Petrograd":** Petrograd, the capital of Russia, was originally called Saint Petersburg. The name was changed to Petrograd at the onset of World War 1. When the Russian Civil War broke out in 1918, the soldiers and workers of Petrograd became the core of the Red Guard, which later turned into the Red Army. The city was renamed Leningrad in 1924. In 1991, the name was changed back to Saint Petersburg.

CHAPTER 9: THE CONTROL, CONFLICT, AND CHANGE BOOK CLUB

170 **established counterintelligence "Red Squads":** Red Squads were police intelligence units set up in city police departments. They specialized in infiltrating and gathering intelligence on political and social groups. They were common in large cities and were used as a weapon against labor unions, communists and other dissidents.

172 **VISTA, the domestic Peace Corps:** Originated by President
Kennedy, VISTA (Volunteers in Service to America) was a national
service program whose mission was to fight poverty. Volunteers were
recruited from all over the country to work in poverty-stricken areas.

CHAPTER 16: GENERATION NEXT ACTIVISTS

286 **"A revolution is not just."** Grace and Jimmie Boggs, *Revolution and
Evolution in the 20th Century,* (New York: Monthly Review Press, 1974).

294 **The cost of freedom:** from John F. Kennedy's Address on the
Cuban Missile Crisis, October 22, 1962.

Sources and Bibliography

Boggs, Grace Lee. *The Next American Revolution*. Berkeley and Los Angeles: University of California Press, 2011.

Boggs, Grace and Jimmie. *Revolution and Evolution in the 20th Century* (New York: Monthly Review Press, 1974).

Boyd, Herb. *Black Detroit: A People's History of Self-Determination*. New York: HarperCollins, 2017.

Boyd, Herb. *We Shall Overcome*. Naperville, IL: Sourcebooks Inc., 2004.

Boyle, Kevin. *Arc of Justice: A Saga of Race, Civil Rights, and Murder in the Jazz Age*. New York: Picador Books, 2004.

Carson, Clayborne, Ph.D. *Civil Rights Chronicle: The African-American Struggle for Freedom*. Lincolnwood, IL: Legacy Publishing, Publications International Ltd., 2003.

Curry, Constance, *et al. Deep in Our Hearts: Nine White Women in the Freedom Movement*. Athens, GA: University of Georgia Press, 2002.

Georgakas, Dan, and Marvin Surkin. *Detroit: I Do Mind Dying*. Cambridge, MA: South End Press, 1998.

Glaude, Eddie S., Jr. *Democracy in Black: How Race Still Enslaves the American Soul*. New York: Crown Publishers, 2016.

Hamlin, Michael, and Michele Gibbs. *A Black Revolutionary's Life in Labor: Black Workers Power in Detroit*. Detroit: Against the Tide Books, 2013.

Hedin, Benjamin. *In Search of the Movement: The Struggle for Civil Rights Then and Now*. San Francisco: City Lights Books, 2015.

Hitchcock, Jeff, and Charley Flint. "Decentering Whiteness," Center for the Study of White American Culture Inc: Roselle, NJ, 2015. Available online at www.euroamerican.org/public/DecenteringWhiteness.

Holsaert, Faith S., *et. al. Hands on the Freedom Plow: Personal Accounts by Women in SNCC*. Champaign: University of Illinois Press, 2010.

Katz, Marilyn. "Detroit's Downfall: Beyond the Myth of Black Misleadership," in *Portside*, August 13, 2013. http://portside.org.

Kresnak, Jack. *Hope for the City: A Catholic Priest, A Suburban Housewife and Their Desperate Effort to Save Detroit.* Detroit: Cass Community Publishing House, 2015.

Manning Thomas, June. *Redevelopment and Race: Planning a Finer City in Postwar Detroit,* 2nd Edition. Detroit: Wayne State University Press, 2013.

Mast, Robert H. *Detroit Lives.* Philadelphia: Temple University Press, 1994.

McKnight, Gerald. *The Last Crusade: Martin Luther King, Jr., the FBI, and the Poor People's Campaign* (New York: Basic Books, 1998).

Medsgar, Betty. *The Burglary: The Discovery of J. Edgar Hoover's Secret FBI.* New York: Alfred A. Knopf, 2014.

Rowan, John. "Dialectical Thinking and Humanistic Psychology," *Practical Philosophy,* July 2000.

Stanton, Mary, *From Selma to Sorrow: The Life and Death of Viola Liuzzo.* Athens: University of Georgia Press, 1998.

Stone, Joel, editor. *Detroit 1967: Origins, Impacts, Legacies.* Detroit: Wayne State University Press, 2017.

Sugrue, Thomas J. *The Origins of the Urban Crisis: Race and Inequality in Postwar Detroit.* Princeton: Princeton University Press, 1998.

Taylor, Kieran. "American Petrograd: Detroit and the League of Revolutionary Black Workers." In *Rebel Rank and File: Labor Militancy and Revolt from Below During the Long 1970s.* Edited by Aaron Brenner, Robert Brenner, and Cal Winslow. London and Brooklyn: Verso Books, 2010.

Wilkerson, Isabel. *The Warmth of Other Suns.* New York: Random House, 2010.

Photo Insert
Illustration Credits

Page 175
All photos from the author's private collection

Page 176
Frank Ditto, courtesy of Ken Castle; U.S. Army, courtesy of Dr. Carol Chadwick Burleson, Detroit Historical Society Collection; Joann, author's private collection; cops on 12th Street, public domain; Castle children, author's private collection; West Boston Boulevard house, author's private collection; Father William Cunningham, from Detroit News Collection, courtesy of the Walter P. Reuther Library, Archives of Labor and Urban Affairs, Wayne State University

Page 177
Ad Hoc protest, courtesy of Ken Castle; Anti-STRESS, courtesy of Ken Castle; news clipping of Joann, *The Detroit News*, courtesy of Hamlin and Castle Papers, the Walter P. Reuther Library, Archives of Labor and Urban Affairs, Wayne State University; Mike Hamlin still, courtesy of *Finally Got the News*, a Blackstar Production; news clipping of Dow Chemical protest, *The Detroit News*, courtesy of Hamlin and Castle Papers, the Walter P. Reuther Library, Archives of Labor and Urban Affairs, Wayne State University; Ad-Hoc activists, courtesy of Ken Castle

Page 178
All photos courtesy of Ken Castle

Page 179
All photos courtesy of Ken Castle

Page 180
All photos from the author's private collection

Page 181
All photos from the author's private collection

Page 182
Joann and Mike, author's private collection; Joann and Karen, author's private collection; Mike, Joann, and Alex, author's private collection; Ella, author's private collection; Viola Liuzzo banner, Women's March 2017 © John Causland

About the Author

JOANN CASTLE is a lifelong Detroiter and political activist. Castle was the mother of six young children when she became involved in the radical Catholic crusade for racial equality during the civil rights movement in the mid-1960s. Already a working mother, Joann enrolled in Wayne State University in 1978, earned an M.A. in medical anthropology, and embarked on a twenty-seven-year career in health care services.

Castle married Michael Hamlin in 1975, at the height of his work in the black power movement. Alexander, their son together, rounded out their blended family. Castle and Hamlin dedicated their lives to the service of others.

Castle's writing is drawn from her recollections of her personal experiences and corroborated by materials that she and Hamlin donated to the Walter P. Reuther Library Archives, which are housed on the campus of Wayne State University.

In 2012, Castle founded Against the Tide Books, under whose auspices she edited and published Hamlin's book, *A Black Revolutionary's Life in Labor: Black Workers Power in Detroit.*

What My Left Hand Was Doing: Lessons from a Grassroots Activist is her first endeavor as an author. Her work focuses on lessons she learned during her activist years that today's young people can apply to their own lives when they themselves take up the banner of activism.

Castle lives in downtown Detroit.